Reading to Write

A Practical Rhetoric

Reading to Write

A Practical Rhetoric

Kathleen Ann Kelly

Northeastern University

ST. MARTIN'S PRESS
New York

Senior Editor: Mark Gallaher
Development Editor: Bob Weber
Project Management: Caliber Design Planning, Inc.
Cover Design: Doug Steel

Library of Congress Catalog Card Number: 88-063042

Manufactured in the United States of America.
43210
fedcba

For information, write:
St. Martin's Press, Inc.
175 Fifth Avenue
New York, NY 10010

ISBN: 0-312-01143-1
Instructor's Edition ISBN: 0-312-03153-X

Acknowledgments

Judith M.Bardwick, excerpts from *Psychology of Women: A Study of Bio-Cultural Conflicts* by Judith M. Bardwick. Copyright © 1971 by Harper & Row, Publishers, Inc. Reprinted by permission of the publisher.

Better Hearing Institute, Washington, D.C. Advertisement reproduced with permission.

Geraldine Brooks, "Australians Have a Devil of a Time Tracking (Extinct) Tasmanian Tiger." Reprinted by permission of *The Wall Street Journal*, April 22, 1987. Copyright © Dow Jones & Company, Inc. 1987. All Rights Reserved Worldwide.

Jan Harold Brunvand, excerpt from *The Study of American Folklore*, 2nd ed., chap. 14. Copyright © 1978 by W. W. Norton & Company, Inc. Reprinted by permission of the publisher.

Sarah D'Eloia, "The Uses—and Limits—of Grammar," *Journal of Basic Writing*, Spring–Summer 1977, pp. 15–16. Copyright © 1977, *Journal of Basic Writing*, Instructional Resource Center, Office of Academic Affairs, The City University of New York, 535 East 80 Street, New York, NY 10021. Reprinted by permission.

Acknowledgments and copyrights are continued at the back of the book on page 339, which constitutes an extension of the copyright page.

For my families: the Kellys,
the Murphys,
and the Hobermans

preface ■

I suppose I've been thinking seriously about the process of writing since 1978, when I started teaching basic writers under the guidance of David Lauerman at Canisius College in Buffalo. The following year, when I was studying and teaching at Georgetown, James Slevin invited me to look critically at theories of composition and challenged me to develop my own. During my years at the University of North Carolina at Chapel Hill, Erika Lindemann, mentor and friend, further shaped my ideas about teaching writing and about teaching others to teach writing. Now that I direct the Introductory Writing Program at Northeastern University, I find that at least once a week I ask myself, "How would Erika do this?" I cannot imagine a more helpful mantra.

Reading to Write is a kind of grand palimpsest of every teaching handout that I have ever borrowed and every conversation about the teaching of writing that I have had with colleagues and friends. The following individuals deserve special mention: La Vinia Jennings, a dear friend who always adds a refreshing and wise perspective on things academic and things far more important than academics; Buffalonians Walter Winkler and Barbara and Joe Kilbridge, three people who are almost family to me; Dick Garth, for whom the art of argument is an abiding passion; Maureen Shannon Salzer, a true pal and constant source of original ideas about the teaching of writing; Jo Koster Tarvers, a sympathetic sister medievalist and rhetorician; Susan V. Wall, who has gently nudged me in the right theoretical direction over the last few years; Lolly Ockerstrom, a model of good common sense and commitment to teaching; Vince LoRusso, who was a close friend long before he became my favorite student; Sally Riggsbee Humble and Tom Humble, who always knew just when to offer their encouragement and easy hospitality; and Mary Titus Bashor, Jackie Gray, Lisa Salem Manganaro, Marc Manganaro, Lisa Nanney, Karen Olander, Michael Schaefer, Tram Turner, and Eric Walker, all of whom shared those invigorating years with me in Chapel Hill. Above all, I'd like to thank my husband, Barry Hoberman, who has taught me more about writing than I can ever properly acknowledge—and more about sports than I normally would care to admit.

Ann Berthoff presents this argument:

The centrally important question in all teaching is, "What comes next?" We must learn continually how to build on what has gone on before. . . . Of course, we follow something with something like it, but we can't do that authentically unless we can identify the first something: what is really going on? Theory can help us see what act we're trying to follow.   (32)

I would like, then, to acknowledge some of the many acts that I am trying to follow, especially those of David Bartholomae, Ann Berthoff, Lil Brannon, James Britton, Sarah D'Eloia, George Dillon, William Irmscher, Wolfgang Iser, James Kinneavy, Cy Knoblauch, Martha Kolln, Andrea Lunsford, Elaine Maimon, Anthony Petrosky, Mike Rose, Mimi Schwartz, Mina Shaughnessy, Frank Smith, Nancy Sommers, Lynn Quitman Troyka, and Richard Van De Weghe.

I hope that those who reviewed the manuscript of *Reading to Write* will see the extent to which their comments and suggestions shaped the book. My thanks go to reviewers Rance Conley, University of Illinois at Chicago; Jan Delasara, Metropolitan State College; Betty Dixon, Rancho Santiago College; Margo Eden-Camann, DeKalb Community College; Sallyanne Fitzgerald, University of Missouri, St. Louis; James Garmhousen, College of San Mateo; Elsie Galbreath Haley, Metropolitan State College; Muriel Harris, Purdue University; Margaret Pyle Hassert, University of Delaware; Eric Hibbison, J. Sargeant Reynolds Community College; Joseph LaBriola, Sinclair Community College; Martin McKoski, Univesity of Akron; Josephine Koster Tarvers, Rutgers University; and Barbara Weaver, Ball State University.

My original editor at St. Martin's Press, Susan Anker, skillfully shepherded me through the first overhaul of the text. I am deeply grateful to Susan for the confidence she showed in a novice textbook author, and for her continuing friendship and encouragement. Mark Gallaher, Susan's successor, picked up where she left off without missing a beat. But no one did more to improve the text of the book than Bob Weber, whose remarkable flair for clear, concise prose is matched by his thoughtfulness, his capacity for hard work, and his gentle wit. He was assigned to this project as development editor, but for many months I regarded him as a wholehearted collaborator.

In the end, my greatest debt is to my students, who have constantly challenged me to teach them, and to make it new. I especially want to thank the following students who gave me permission to use their work from Canisius College, Clarkson University, Elon College, Northeastern University, and the University of North Carolina at Chapel Hill.

Maria Calvado
Kim Collins
Tom Costanzo
Larry Crowley
Daniel Fabbri
Anthony Ryan Fairchild
Elizabeth Fischi
Dawn Gibson
Nikki Hall
Burt Hallisey
Peter Hanson
Walter Healy
Mike Herrity
John Hoyle
Melinda Hunt
Connor Jennings
Cathy Johnson

Demeatrice Johnson
Paula Lesack
Barbara Lesane
Teresa Mackie
Vanessa Manuel
Mehegan O'Connor
Kari Packer
Cheryl Parent
Tracy Rose
Greg Sobczak
Karen Stone
P. J. Tucker
Mary Warry
Sharon Washington
Cynthia Wong
Jill Zweig

Work Cited

Berthoff, Ann. "The Teacher as Researcher." *Reclaiming the Classroom: Teacher Research as an Agency for Change*. Ed. Dixie Goswami and Peter Stillman. Portsmouth, NH: Boynton/Cook Heinemann, 1987. 22–39.

contents

part **two**   ■

Your Audience and Your Message   25

---

part **three**

Your Purposes for Writing   75

chapter **6**   Writing to Express Yourself   79

chapter **7**   Writing to Inform   117

chapter **8**   Writing to Persuade   161

part **four**

Editing Your Writing   191

chapter **9**   Keeping Track of Your Errors   195

chapter **10**   Recognizing Parts of Sentences   199

chapter **11**   Recognizing Types of Sentences   219

Reading to Write

A Practical Rhetoric

part **one**

The Reading and Writing Process

Keeping a Journal
Strategies for Reading and Writing

Introduction

Reading and writing reinforce one another. By learning to read in a more thoughtful, sophisticated way, you also will learn to write essays that are more thoughtful and more sophisticated—and more detailed. And by keeping a journal in which you record your experiences and ideas, along with your responses to whatever you are reading, you will discover that writing strengthens reading, and reading strengthens writing.

Like writing, reading involves hard work and commitment; it even involves writing itself. As you progress through this book, you will find that reading well—like writing well—has its rewards. Mike Rose, Director of the Writing Program at the University of California at Los Angeles, describes how he discovered the rewards of reading well:

> We worked with *The Metaphysical Foundations of Modern Science* for some time, and I made my way slowly through it. Mr. Johnson was helping me develop an ability to read difficult texts—I was learning how to reread critically, how to tease out definitions and basic arguments. And I was also gaining confidence that if I stayed with material long enough and kept asking questions, I would get it. That assurance proved more valuable than any particular body of knowledge I learned that year.
>
> *Lives on the Boundary*

You, too, are likely to find that if you stay with material long enough and keep asking questions, you will "get it." The following two chapters will

1

give you that opportunity—first, by showing you how to keep a journal and, second, by helping you connect your reading to your writing. Student Jill Zweig puts it this way:

> Trying to understand what you're reading is important, and what helps your understanding is trying to relate what you're reading to your experience or what you already know. That's a good idea.

chapter 1

■

Keeping a Journal

The humorist James Thurber said, "It is better to know some of the questions than all of the answers." In other words, answers aren't always important; sometimes, simply asking questions can be a valuable learning experience. But how often do we get an opportunity simply to ask questions or to explore ideas for their own sake? That is the value of keeping a journal. It allows us to ask questions without worrying about answers. It is a way to get ideas down on paper without having to think about writing for others. Your first reader is always yourself, and a journal is your opportunity to record and explore ideas that interest *you*.

A journal can be much more than a list of the things you do on a particular day: "I woke up at 7 AM. I ate a bran muffin. I missed the bus and was late for my first class. Only two more days until my birthday!" Instead, you can use your journal in the following, more creative ways:

— To record your thoughts and experiences
— To record ideas for essays
— To record your responses to the assignments throughout this book
— To record your responses to classroom assignments
— To record your questions about the reading and writing you do, so that you can discuss them with your teacher. (Your teacher may want to look at your journal from time to time. Circle or put a star near your questions so that your teacher can find them easily.)

However you use your journal, it will help you become a better reader and writer by giving you an opportunity to record and explore your ideas.

How to Keep a Journal

Choose any loose-leaf binder (so that you won't lose pages), and open up the notebook so that you are looking at two side-by-side pages. Label the right-hand side of the notebook "Notes," and label the left-hand side "Responses." In this way, you create a **double-entry journal**, which is both a personal journal and a place to record notes about your reading and writing.

Use the left-hand side of your journal (under the label "Responses") for your personal entries, for some of your writing assignments, and for your responses to reading assignments. Use the right-hand side (under the label "Notes") to record factual information about your reading, such as summaries and outlines. Also use the right-hand side to comment about the personal entries and writing you do on the left-hand side. In this way the left-hand pages will become a record of what you learn about reading and writing.

Left Pages: Your Personal Responses

Write on the left side of your journal whenever you get the urge—in the middle of the night, or while you're waiting for your next class to start. Record your personal responses—your ideas and reactions to what you read, see, feel, and hear. During class, make notes about things you agree or disagree with—and why. On the left side of your journal you can write about anything, even about things that seem to have nothing to do with the subject at hand. If something comes to mind as you read or listen, write it down. You also might write about a topic of your choosing (or a topic assigned by your teacher) for five minutes at the beginning of class as a kind of warm-up. After class, record your reactions to the discussion, and list any questions you have. You also should use the left-hand side of your journal to write drafts of your essays.

Figure 1 is an example of a personal entry that a student made in response to an open writing assignment. Notice how exploratory the entry is; the student is using his journal to test his ideas on paper, to see where the topic will lead him. As we'll soon see, it takes him in a number of directions.

Writing Assignments   ■

On the left-hand side of your journal, make a personal entry about one of the following topics.

1.   What kinds of experiences have you had with writing? How would you describe your attitudes toward writing? For about ten or fifteen minutes, record whatever ideas come to mind. Write at least one page about your experiences and attitudes regarding writing.

Responses

Computers are now being taught to understand voice commands, etc. I have almost no trust in society when it comes to new technologies. When these new technologies arise, they are welcome by society. But give the human race a couple of years to work with it and we will find a way to abuse it. I know this might sound far fetched, but think about it. Look at automobiles . . . they do us more harm than good. Look at nuclear power. Look at aerosol sprays. I could just see the world in the future, when we have mastered the ways to teach a computer to understand commands as well as a human does. I can just see some politician suggesting that we use robots as a police force instead of using humans. Sound far fetched? I don't agree. Who would have thought a hundred years ago that one could put a plastic card in a machine and in turn receive money? Who would have thought a hundred years ago that machines would "talk"? The point is, I'd hate to see these robots walking around policing the state. It would be dangerous, to say the least. It seems to me that the more progress we make as humans the worst our world looks for our children. In my opinion, progress is regression.

Figure 1   A personal response written on a left-hand page in the journal of Peter Hanson, student

2.   Write a personal entry about something you learned to do recently. It might be anything—practicing a foreign language, finding your way around campus, choosing courses, riding a motorcycle, improving a basketball shot, preparing an income-tax form, dealing with a depressed friend. Describe what you did as you were learning. Did things go smoothly, or did you make a lot of mistakes at first? What kinds of mistakes did you make? Based on your experiences and mistakes, how would you go about teaching someone else how to do what you learned?

3.   Look again at the first paragraph of this chapter, at the quotation by James Thurber: "It is better to know some of the questions than all of the answers." On the left side of your journal, explain in detail what you think Thurber means. Can you think of examples from your own life that illustrate this quotation?

Right Pages: Your Notes about Assignments

Studies have suggested that readers do not gain understanding just by underlining passages in a text. But when readers have to take notes and then summarize their reading *in writing*, they are far more likely to recall and understand the

Notes

After writing this, I realized that I could use this for an essay—tell people about my fears about technology, and so on. But I know I like technology, too—CD players, movies, and stuff. Maybe I don't really mean it? It was easy to write, but now as I think about it, it's pretty complicated. I mean, how did I get from computers to robot police forces? Now what?

Figure 2   The right-hand page of Peter Hanson's journal, commenting on the entry he wrote in Figure 1

material. (Chapter 2 will describe some strategies to make you a more effective reader.)

Use the right-hand side of your journal to take objective notes about your reading and about class discussion. Record direct quotations that you want to remember or to use in your own writing. List important terms and ideas, and write a summary of the information. In other words, record the *content* of the material. After each class, summarize what you learned that day, using the right-hand side of your journal.

You also can use the right-hand pages to write about your writing, directly opposite your personal responses on the left-hand pages. For example, you might want to explain why you wrote about a particular topic, or what happened as you wrote, or what else you would like to learn about the topic. By writing about your writing, you can gain insights into how you go about writing in the first place. By examining your personal writing process, you can learn what works for you and what doesn't. In other words, you can begin to look at your writing from the outside. This will make you a better reader of your own writing, which is an important first step toward revising and improving your writing.

Figure 2 shows Peter's notes about the personal response he wrote in Figure 1. These notes appear on the right-hand page, directly opposite his response. In the notes, Peter raises questions that show he is thinking about his topic in a serious way. He realizes that he has both positive and negative feelings about modern technology, but in his notes he is not yet concerned about answering his questions. He also sees that his drafted response has an organizational problem: "I mean, how did I get from computers to robot police forces?" Peter's question, "Now what?" is not a cry of desperation but a jumping-off point for talking about his topic with his classmates and his teacher. (In fact, Peter's topic

Responses   *Notes*

Reading this was like taking a course in a foreign language. Before, I had thought of Black English as an off-the-cuff dialect which had no real importance—speakers of it should learn "real grammar"—I guess I meant "White English." It made me think of my confusions between learning Italian and Spanish in my family. I always confuse Italian "Ti amo" with Spanish "Te llamo"—I guess this kind of confusion can happen in Black English.

Geneva Smitherman, in "It Bees Dat Way Sometime," addresses in an interesting way the controversy of labeling Black English a dialect of nonstandard English through switching from "standard" English to BE throughout. The purpose of this brief course in Black English is to enable her readers to bridge the gap created by linguistic and cultural differences between whites and blacks. Smitherman describes the distinctive features in Black English in the same way that a foreign-language textbook does.

Figure 3   Responses and notes from the double-entry journal of Elizabeth Fischi, student

evolved into an entertaining paper about his love/hate relationship with technology.)

Figure 3 is another example of double-entry notes. In this example, Elizabeth was asked to read "It Bees Dat Way Sometime," an essay about the features and rules of Black English by the linguist Geneva Smitherman. First, Elizabeth briefly summarized the entire essay in the "Notes" section on the right-hand side of her journal. Then, she used the left-hand side—directly opposite her summary—to record her personal responses to the article.

Writing Assignments ■

1.   Look over any part of the textbook that you have read so far, and make notes on or summarize its content, using the right-hand side of your journal. Then, on the left-hand side, respond to what you read.

2.   Read over what you wrote about learning how to do something for the first time (in the previous group of writing assignments). Directly opposite your essay, on the right-hand side of your journal, comment on your writing. Describe the experience of writing: How did you decide what your subject would be? Did

you have a few ideas at first and then reject all but one? Did you have trouble finding a topic? Did you work out in your mind what you wanted to say first, or did you discover what you wanted to say as you wrote? Was it hard to describe your topic? Why? Did the writing go smoothly, or did you start and stop many times?

3.   On the right-hand side of your journal, jot down what you think are your strengths and your weaknesses as a writer.

As you can see, a journal is a place to jot down your ideas and reactions to the world, as well as a place to raise questions about the work in your writing class. Don't be concerned about writing on the "wrong" side of your journal; it's not so important that you follow these suggestions exactly. You may want to invent your own method for keeping a journal, a method that suits your needs. The main point is for you to start writing as soon as you can. And what better audience to begin with than yourself?

chapter 2 ■

Strategies for Reading and Writing

Reading Strategies

Some readers view the process of reading as a haphazard activity in which the "right" meaning of a text will light up the brain's circuits like the lights of a video game. ("Text" here means anything written—a poem, a novel, an essay, a letter, a newspaper article, a diary, and so on.) This view is based on the notion that reading is a passive activity—that the meaning of a text is magically revealed just by looking at the page.

In reality, however, when readers try to determine what a piece of writing means, they not only rely on the text itself but also actively put words, sentences, and paragraphs together. Readers must struggle to grasp connections, and they must pay attention to the structure and meaning of a text. Rereading, studying, taking notes, annotating, attending to cues, outlining, summarizing, and talking with others are all *active* ways to read. Like writing, reading is hard work.

The way we read is influenced by the kind of text involved. We read a movie review differently than a job application; we study a chemistry textbook differently than a novel. We also approach texts differently, depending on our purpose: Are we reading to pass the time? To amuse ourselves? To learn something new?

Throughout this book you will learn to pay more attention to how reading works in general—and to how *you* read in particular. As you become a better reader, you also will become a better writer. By learning what readers do, you will anticipate their needs when you write. You will learn to ask, "Exactly how do my readers read, and what must I do to help them read better?"

Although each individual has a personal way of reading, we can make the following general observations about reading as a process.

Reading Begins *Before* Reading

When we say that we "psych" ourselves to do something, we mean that we "put ourselves in the right *psych*ological frame of mind in order to succeed." Athletes may psych themselves before a major competition, and actors may do it before going on stage.

Readers also psych themselves, or prepare themselves, before reading—often without realizing it. Before we even start to read the words on the page, we have ways of getting ready to read. If we know that we are about to read a poem, we begin to plan for "poem." Many readers are conscious of changing their frame of mind when switching from one kind of reading to another. Most of us are aware that we read a technical report differently than we read a newspaper, and we get ready before we even begin to read.

Reading Depends on Interpreting *Cues*

Readers expect a writer to provide **cues** (clues, hints, signals) to guide our memory, attention, and imagination while reading. But readers also must be prepared to search for cues and recognize them. Particular words act as signals to guide us from sentence to sentence, from paragraph to paragraph, in an essay. For example, such words as *next, therefore,* and *but* indicate relationships between one idea and another. Later, in the book, we will come back to this idea of cues.

Reading Requires Active Participation

Although we can point to specific words and phrases that cue readers to a text's content and structure, it is difficult to point to specific meanings that result from the interaction between a reader and a text. Often, recognizing cues is not enough, because words alone do not make a text. Rather, the meaning of a text is greater than the sum of its parts.

Reading words, then, is only the first step in reading. Lawrence Sterne, an eighteenth-century British writer, made the point that a text is like "a two-way conversation" in which the writer must give readers "something to imagine." In other words, texts take on meanings—they come *alive*—only when readers actively engage in this "conversation" with the writer.

Reading Depends on Prior Knowledge

A text's meaning results when readers associate the ideas on the page with the ideas they already know. Thus, new knowledge is added to the old. Of course, not all readers have prior knowledge about every subject they encounter when reading. Through *learning* we assimilate (absorb) new knowledge, adding it to and making it part of what we already know. The less prior knowledge we have, the more we must concentrate on the reading—and on learning.

Memory helps readers in two ways. First, it helps us retain what we have just read so that we can connect it to what we are about to read. Second, memory aids our reading by calling up prior knowledge so that we can apply it to the reading at hand. Our own experiences and memories thus shape how we read and interpret a text—how we "converse" with the author to give a text meaning.

Reading Depends on Prior Reading

Two kinds of knowledge are important when we talk about reading. The first kind concerns content, or *what the text is about,* as discussed above; the second kind of knowledge concerns *how texts are made.*

People learn to read by reading, and by developing plans and strategies based on past reading experiences. For example, if you read mystery novels often, you might compare (without thinking about it) each new one with others you have read before. In this way, you learn what the main features of a mystery story are, and you begin to have certain expectations in mind; when you read a new mystery, you look for those features.

Reading Isn't Done Word by Word

Depending on the type of reading and on one's reading ability, we read in chunks, not word by word. Prior knowledge allows us to predict what is coming next, so that we don't have to read word by word. Such knowledge may be about content. For example, a reader who has already studied precalculus will be more open to reading and learning from a calculus textbook. But readers also have prior knowledge about how texts are made. When we come across a cue like "There are three good reasons to vote," we search for the three reasons, because we have seen similar cues before.

If reading were done word by word, we would read very slowly indeed. Even those of us who think they are poor readers read in chunks most of the time. When a text is particularly difficult—which depends partly on how much prior knowledge we have—we may slow down on purpose to read word by word.

Reading and Writing Assignment   ■

Try this experiment: Using a small piece of paper, cover up part of a text so that you can only read one word at a time. As you read, also cover up what you have just read. Do this until you have read several sentences. What do you remember about the passage? Can you express its meaning in your own words?

Now, remove the paper and reread the passage. Pay attention to how your eyes move. Do they move back and forth and jump over a section of text as you read? Now can you sum up the passage?

In your journal, jot down some notes about what you discovered in this experiment.

*Re*reading Leads to Understanding

A text is full of surprises the first time we read it. We have no idea where the writer is headed. In fact, the first time through a text, we may spend so much time trying to guess what comes next that we miss most of the meaning.

Because memory doesn't always work as well as we would like, it is important to reread a text. Did you ever get to the end of a chapter in a book and not remember what the beginning of the chapter was about? By quickly skimming and rereading important sections of a text, you will increase your understanding and remember it better.

Reading and Writing Assignments   ■

1. Choose at least ten pages from a text—anything that you are reading at the moment, whether for pleasure or because it was assigned in a course. After you read the ten pages, stop and take notes about what you did as you read. Then reread the passage. How is the second reading different from the first? Record your observations in your journal.

2. Stop for a moment and quickly skim this entire book. Look over the table of contents, including the section headings (that is, the headings within each chapter). Also skim the index. On the left-hand side of your journal, write a short description of what you expect to learn and do as you progress through this book.

Writing Strategies: Invention

"Only amateurs believe in inspiration," wrote novelist Frank Yerby. Your own experience as a writer has probably shown you that inspiration rarely comes when you need it. Like reading, writing is hard work.

If inspiration comes—wonderful! Sometimes your best ideas for writing might come as you sit on the bus, or drift off to sleep, or do some mindless task like sorting socks. Don't underestimate your subconscious; it works out ideas even when you make an effort to stop thinking about something. In fact, many writers purposely take a break from their work in order to let ideas "simmer" or settle down. For the most part, however, don't rely on inspiration. You can't depend on it, especially when you're trying to meet a deadline.

Finding a topic or a subject to write about often raises some basic questions:

— What do you know about?
— What do you know that others don't know?
— What do you want to find out about?
— What do you think is important for others to know about you?
— What do you think is important for others to know about subject X?

Answering basic questions like these will help you get over the feeling that you have nothing to say. You will discover ways that you can develop a vague idea into a solid, interesting topic. In the following sections we will explore more ways to ask questions that will lead you to subjects to write about.

Freewriting

A good way to discover a writing topic is to turn writer's block into writer's cramp: Just put your pen to paper and write without stopping for five minutes or ten minutes or fifteen minutes. **Freewriting**—writing without worrying about correctness or subject matter—may lead you to subjects for essays. When freewriting, don't stop and stare into space—just keep going until the time limit is up. Write even if you simply repeat yourself, even if you write, over and over, "I can't think of anything to write; I can't think of anything to write; I can't think. . . ."

Following is an example of one student's freewriting:

what am I going to do all I can think about is lunch—a rough draft is due thursday Thursday and i am braking out in a sweat oh no i spelled breaking wrong oh yeah how about a paper on stressful situations in my life—sort of humorous accounts of how I have gotten out of hot water—like the time I skipped school. . . .

Tom Costanzo, student

Through freewriting, this student wrote his way into a subject—he discovered what he wanted to write about. This approach to writing frees you from getting anxious. You don't have to keep looking at what you wrote to see if it's OK. You can even begin freewriting by listing some of the worries that are blocking your creative thinking. Then, write your worries away and keep on writing.

Another way to use freewriting is to start out with a specific subject that interests you. Just write about it for ten or fifteen minutes without worrying about what you're saying or how you're saying it. This will help you discover how to break your subject into manageable pieces.

Writing Assignments   ■

1.   Try freewriting, either in class or on your own. Begin by writing for five minutes, and then increase the time to ten or fifteen minutes. Remember that you are not to lift your pen from the paper for the whole time. When the time is up, look over your freewriting and circle any ideas that appeal to you, that you might want to write about.

2.   Try freewriting by finishing one of the following sentences on a left-hand page in your journal:

a.   Ten years from now, I. . . .
b.   I really like. . . .
c.   I really don't like. . . .
d.   I always. . . .

3.   Try freewriting about one of the following subjects (use a left-hand page in your journal):

a.   A fad that you once enjoyed but now find silly
b.   A rule or law that you broke and whether or not you regret it
c.   A belief or opinion that you once held which was different from what most people thought

In your journal, make notes about what you discovered about freewriting.

Brainstorming

Sometimes, listening to other people will give you ideas for writing. When a group of people with a common problem to solve get together and call out their ideas—no matter how far-fetched or unrelated they seem—it's called **brainstorming**. Following is a record of how one short brainstorming session went. Notice how wide-ranging the ideas are—and how a few of the participants focus those ideas:

> *Kim:* This *writing* assignment! I . . . really don't know where to start.
> *Ralph:* How about writing something about school?
> *Kim:* Boring!
> *Eleni:* I want to write about . . . feeling homesick.
> *Ralph:* Are you really homesick?

Eleni: Well-ll, all I can think of is going home this weekend. And I just got here.
Ralph: You could compare being at school—uh—with being home.
Kim: How about writing about how freshmen get . . . get *lost* here?
Geoff: How do you think *I* feel? I'm twenty-six, and I'm surrounded by home-sick freshmen.
Kim: So how is being twenty-six and lost different from being eighteen and lost?
Ralph: Geoff, how about writing about how being older than most people affects your—um—social life?
Kim: I think I'd like to write a . . . survival guide for freshmen from a fresh-man's point of view. I could interview other freshmen for tips. . . .
Eleni: I don't *want* to write about being homesick. Maybe I could just find some-thing to read about events on campus so I can keep busy.

Even without a group of people, you can brainstorm on your own. Just ask yourself questions, and then try to answer them as well. But *listen* to your answers. Simply listening to or watching the world around you is another kind of brainstorming, as long as you pay attention to your thoughts. Read a maga-zine or newspaper. Listen to people passing you on campus, or sitting near you on the bus. Look at photographs and paintings. Eat fortune cookies and ponder their advice. Really look at the natural world. Whatever approach you take, use your journal to keep track of your "brainstorms."

Writing Assignment   ■

Brainstorm as a class activity, or with a small group of friends who have the same writing assignment. Simply call out whatever comes to mind, and listen to what others call out. It's like freewriting out loud. Don't judge the ideas or comment on them—simply jot them down in your journal so that you may use them later.

Also in your journal, make notes about what you discovered about brain-storming.

Listing

Another good way to find a writing topic is to list all the subjects that come to mind. In a way, listing is like freewriting, except that you record one-word items or short phrases. For a set period of time, list your ideas without judging them. Following are some ways you can organize a list:

1. List your ideas the same way you freewrite—with no overall plan; list whatever comes to mind.

2. List your ideas by starting with a specific subject (like school, family, dating, and so on).

3. List the questions that a journalist would ask about a subject: Who? What? When? How? Where? Why?

4. Choose a general subject, and pair it with some sort of strategy to explore it. For example, if you want to write about why people gain weight, list as many *causes* as you can think of.

5. Choose a general subject, and divide your list into sections like "Problems" and "Solutions," or "Causes" and "Effects."

6. Choose a general subject, and then narrow it down by listing:

a. A specific example
b. A specific time
c. A specific place
d. A specific number
e. A specific person
f. A specific type
g. A specific result
h. A specific feeling
i. A specific experience

You might think of listing as a very informal way of outlining. Outlines can take many forms—from formal, numbered outlines to rough summaries of projected sections. If you usually outline a paper before writing, and you find an outline helpful, by all means use one. Following is a student's formal outline for an essay about the special language used by restaurant workers:

I. *Introduction:* Working in a restaurant taught me a new language
II. Why restaurant workers use a specialized language on the job
    A. Convenience
    B. Speed
    C. For the fun of it
III. Examples of special terms
    A. Used by waiters
    B. Used by chefs
    C. Used by dishwashers
IV. The effects of this specialized language on outsiders
    A. What happened when I began working
    B. What happened when I used restaurant terms with my family and friends
V. *Conclusion:* Language must fit the audience

Writing Assignment ■

On the left-hand side of your journal, try out two of the suggestions given for listing. On the right-hand page, make notes about the two methods you selected. Which approach worked better for you, and why?

If you prefer to use a formal outline, on the left-hand page prepare an outline for a paper. On the right-hand page, make notes about how you created the outline. Did you have each point in mind before you wrote, or did ideas come to you as you outlined?

When You Are Assigned a Topic

Much of the writing that you will do in college and on your job will be in response to a specific assignment. In college, you may be asked to write an analysis of a poem in an English class, or a lab report in a biology class, or a book review in a history class. On the job, you may be asked to write a memo about how a task could be done more efficiently, or a report on the activities of your department.

When you write for yourself, it is usually a pressure-free activity. You have no obligations, no instructions—and no deadline. But when you accept an assigned subject, you have committed yourself to your teacher or employer; you must follow instructions; and you must meet a deadline.

The poet T. S. Eliot noted that, when one is forced to write within a predetermined framework, the imagination is disciplined and taxed to the utmost, yielding the richest ideas. In other words, the limitations of a given assignment require you to be creative. The instructions and the deadline are like the rules and the time limit of a tennis match; within them, anything can happen.

When you are given a writing assignment, first look it over to make sure you understand it. Look for cues that tell what you are supposed to do. Words like *evaluate, discuss, research, list,* and *summarize* will guide you in structuring your writing.

Next, try to restate the assignment in your own words. Doing this will make you feel comfortable with the assignment. It also will remind you to use freewriting, brainstorming, and listing. After you explore the assignment in your journal or with classmates, look again at the instructions to be sure you have stayed within them.

Some teachers give detailed written instructions for assignments, and some give only verbal directions. If you do not get detailed instructions, it is up to you to discover what you need to do. Discuss the assignment with your instructor to make sure you understand it and know how to proceed.

Here are some examples of history assignments that illustrate different approaches to giving directions. Which set of instructions would be most helpful to you?

1.   Verbal directions: "Write a book report on some aspect of the Constitution that interests you—due February 16."

2.   Your assignment is to write a clear and insightful review of a recent book on American-Russian relations. Good models may be found in the Sunday *New York Times* book review section, *The Atlantic, Time, The Smithsonian,* and in other well-written publications aimed at the educated, nonspecialist public.

3.   Find a descriptive eyewitness account, written between 1870 and 1910, of an American city, state, territory, or region. The account may be in a book or periodical, but it may not be from a work of fiction. The author can be a journalist, foreign traveler, soldier, scout, essayist, keeper of a personal diary— just about anyone. But the account should be descriptive, not simply a history of events.

Read the account or a section from it. You ought to read 30 to 70 book pages; if the account is in a periodical with fine print, you may read a shorter section. Use your judgment.

Develop an essay concerning the author's viewpoint, assumptions, biases, goals, and intended audience. You might keep questions like the following in mind as you read and write: Does the account appear to be reasonably objective? How does the author feel about the events, customs, and people in the account? Does the author romanticize or condemn particular aspects of American life? What sorts of information is the author most concerned with reporting? Are there other kinds of data that he or she seems to have omitted intentionally? What aspects of the account will seem most dated to readers today? What aspects still seem pertinent?

As these assignments show, teachers have different attitudes toward their role as makers of assignments and toward a student's role as the writer of an assignment. Perhaps the first teacher, who gave verbal directions for an essay about the Constitution, assumes that students know enough about historical writing that they do not need detailed instructions. The teacher who wrote the second assignment may expect students to read a book review and figure out how to write one themselves. But the teacher who wrote the third assignment (which is perhaps the best assignment from the student's point of view) is willing to guide students.

Throughout this textbook and course, you sometimes will have to develop your own subject, and sometimes will have to respond to written instructions. Your teacher will let you know which kind of assignment you should do.

Reading and Writing Assignments   ■

1. Read any one of the assignments at the end of Chapter 6, Chapter 7, or Chapter 8. In your journal, make notes about the cues you find for responding to that assignment. Then describe how you would go about fulfilling the assignment.

2. In small groups, discuss the writing assignments you were given in other courses. How detailed are the instructions? How might you go about responding to them? In your journal, record what you discovered about instructions for writing assignments.

Writing Strategies: Planning

If you think that writing is supposed to follow some magical 1-2-3 formula, you may find it very difficult to begin. There is no such formula. You probably know this already, of course, but still you would like some magical rules for getting things right the first time. Most writers would.

Think of writing not as a series of 1-2-3 steps—as in marching forward—but as a movement back and forth, as in a dance. Figure 1 (page 20) shows how we might diagram the **writing process.** Notice that the arrows between *planning, drafting, revising,* and *editing* go in more than one direction. As we write, we may backtrack, leap ahead, move forward with an idea, and then back up again. This back-and-forth movement applies not only to the overall process of writing but also to each main task, from planning through editing. At any point in the process, it may be helpful to jump to or return to another point. How, then, should we begin?

Getting Started: Write Before Writing

Advice about planning the first draft can be summed up in one word: Write! Simply write. Do what you usually do to get something on paper—no matter how short or incomplete it is, no matter how you feel about it. Only then can you really begin to talk about writing. Use this prewriting stage as a way to talk to yourself on paper. In this **discovery draft**, don't worry about organization or style or whether you have things in the right order. Write quickly just to get your ideas flowing. Consider your discovery draft to be "writing before writing."

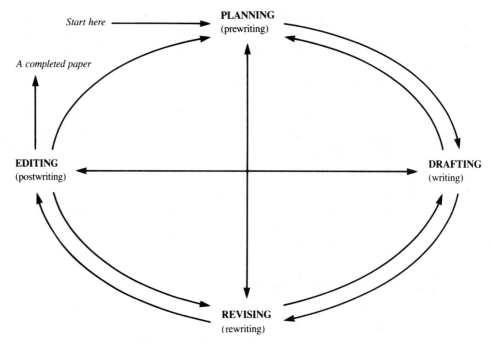

Figure 1   The writing process: A dance, not a march

After you have discovered some possible subject, you might want to explore it through freewriting and brainstorming. Another good approach is to make lists or to prepare an informal outline. Perhaps writing begins for you with a word or phrase or picture in your mind. Get it down on paper. List facts and ideas—both for and against the points you want to make. Think about points where you might have problems either in expressing your ideas or in carrying out your purpose for writing.

Many writers feel that they must follow little rituals before they can begin to write. One writer might need to clean the house, for example, while another can write only after midnight, and yet another must sharpen every pencil. Understand that such behavior is not unusual—but don't let your rituals keep you from actually starting.

When you do begin to write, set reasonable goals for yourself. Instead of planning to finish the entire first draft in one sitting, plan to do just one page or even one paragraph at a time. Take a short break if you feel stale. Don't expect everything to come all at once. Remember that writing is a process by which you explore many ideas in order to work out your best ideas.

If you still can't get started, write *any* sentence first. The introduction may not come to mind until you've worked out some of your ideas. So start in the middle, or with one short description, or one good example. Write the conclusion first, if that is already clear to you. Just start anywhere that you think is the easy part. You can draft the other parts later.

To make revision easier, write your discovery draft on one side of the paper only, and leave plenty of space for crossing things out and adding material. (By writing on one side of the paper, you won't have to worry about what's on the other side if you later decide to move parts around by cutting up your draft. Writers often need more than pen and paper to draft—scissors and tape are also very handy.) If you do your writing on a computer, print out the draft often so that you can get an idea of it as a whole. Don't throw away your discovery draft. You may find it useful later.

Get used to looking at an unfinished piece of writing. Nobody said that your discovery draft had to be perfect. Use it to find your ideas. For now, you are both writer and reader.

Talking to Yourself

Even before writing, you may have a good idea of what your paper will be like. Words and phrases may come to mind, and you may even know how you want your readers to respond. But as you sit staring at a blank sheet of paper or a blank computer screen, you, too, feel blank. This is the time to freewrite! Just as it helped you to discover a subject, freewriting will help you to develop the subject. Don't think of your readers yet; think of yourself. Ask yourself what you know about the subject. Talk to yourself. Imagine yourself reading your draft. How would you react to it? What do you like about it? What do you dislike? Which ideas are strong, and which need more work? When you find a weak part, keep freewriting to see if you can improve it.

Brainstorming with a friend or your teacher is also helpful at this point. Just blurt out ideas about your subject without worrying whether they are logical. Talking about your subject will help you to explain it, because another person's questions will make you clarify your thoughts.

If you used listing or an outline to get started, remember that you can add or cross out ideas. You made the plan, and you can change it as you discover new or better ideas. And don't forget to use your journal during drafting. You may already have ideas in your journal entries that fit your subject. Or maybe you recorded some personal experiences that you can use as examples. Develop any details or examples that you want to include. You can rearrange them with scissors and tape later.

Write First; Edit Later

Marion Zimmer Bradley, a science fantasy author, says this about drafting: "Since I wrote 20 books on the corner of a kitchen table using pen and paper and a second-hand Remington [typewriter], it took a lot of work to edit drafts. I learned to write the first draft in my head." You, unlike Bradley, are not being asked to write perfect essays the first time. You don't have to worry about creating a perfect draft. In this writing course, you will have second and third and fourth chances.

Don't worry about spelling and grammar when you write discovery drafts. Write quickly just to find out what you want to say. Expect that you will have to revise and edit your drafts later. That is part of the writing process, and we will study it in later chapters. For now, try writing without thinking that someone is going to look over your shoulder and point out all the mistakes. Your real concern at this point is to develop ideas. If you want to put a checkmark or a star in the margin of your draft to remind yourself to check something, fine. But save the editing for later. Part Four will help you to do that, but only after you have revised your draft into a strong statement of your best ideas.

The following discovery draft was written by a student who did make an effort to ignore the fear of making errors. See whether you can follow her ideas:

> The yellow cabs racing eachother inbetween buses and cars as the heat and smoke swelter off the streets and onto the sidewalks. Larege bushels of bodies keep up a fast stride, weaving in and out avoiding venders. The air is filled with the strong smells of fumes and exhaust. It is combined with the sweeter smell of warming pretzels and aromes of Chinese noodles, fast foods. The ears ring at street noises and voices, "hey man right here real Madonna jewlry, and hey bud get out of my way." Looking up the sky scrapers seem to be moving in from all directions, and the senses tingle from the whole ex-pierence.

> Over a solid mass of steel, its strong sides all interwound rushing by your window as the waters run far beneath. Passing the soke stack factorys, the sun sets on the cit's sky line behind. Onto the well paved roads with bright steet lights and neatly cleaned gutters. They are filled with gren grass, on which houses that all look alike sit, one after the other. Fast sport cars whiz by filled with good looking teenagers. The BMW's whisper by, its passenger, a yuppie off to a office building ona hill with a long winding driveway. Through the town the new sidewalks are dipersed with arow of fine shops. Thier windows catch the eye decorated with expensive sport and dress ware. The nose rise to smell of gormet delis and bagel shops. The doors open to Gucci bags and fake diamonds, all for a days shopping. Passing by the head turns to the gossip,

"oh, skippy is off to Harvard." "Oh, well I didnt know that, Buffy is in the Ivy League also, down south though.

The long vast highways that connect states from opposite ends. The open fields and straight roads seem never ending,with the monotonous scenery by its side. Even the exit seems like a trip in itself. In the country side the air smells fresh and still. The traffic moves slowly, all is mellow and it is a feeling of inert environment. Driving slowly allows for the absorption of the surroundings, small houses, a church and fast food places. The food here is served slowly with a whistle, no hurry. Walking around everything coincides with this attitude. The trees sway by, the clear sky shines down.All the faces smile with bright white tetth saying, "hi how ya all doin?" Becomming at ease with the situation the body relaxes with a deep breath. The bewilderment subsides as the corners of the mouth raise, "fine, thankyou how about yourself?" The transformation begins, drifting off in a new atmosphere.

Kim Collins, student

Note that this draft is crammed with ideas and pictures. It has no real focus, and the writer has not paid any attention to spelling and grammar. That's OK—now she has something solid to work with.

Writing Assignment ■

Look over the journal entries that you have written so far, and circle any ideas or passages that you would like to develop into an essay. Then, choose one idea and write a discovery draft, following the suggestions on the previous pages. Save the draft, and return to it when you are asked to write a paper. You may be able to use it then.

part **two**

Your Audience and Your Message

Understanding Your Audience
Revising Your First Draft
Developing Your Ideas

Introduction

In the following chapters you will concentrate on your audience; on developing your ideas (which sometimes involves bouncing your ideas off what you're reading); and on revising your drafts. The students who wrote the following advice did so after working through this part of *Reading to Write*:

> Be prepared to have your classmates read your paper. I have learned how to take suggestions and apply them to each draft. It really helps when you have to think about how readers might respond to your writing. Usually your final draft will look totally different from your first draft, because part of revision is asking yourself about what readers might say.
>
> Karen Stone, student

> Be prepared to write more than one draft. Usually, what you think is your final draft is really a rough draft.
>
> Burt Hallisey, student

> Do not get discouraged! You will rewrite, rewrite, and rewrite. You might get angry at times, but it all works out in the end. And don't forget to get help if you need it; no one is going to help you if you don't ask.
>
> Tracy Rose, student

> Some advice for writing better: DON'T PROCRASTINATE! In order to write well, you must take your time, think about your audience, and get help

from your classmates. Go to the Reading Lab; believe me, it can really help your writing.

Nikki Hall, student

These students learned to think about writing as *re*writing, and they learned to talk with others about their writing. It came as a pleasant surprise to them that their classmates could help so much just by saying, "I like this part, but I don't understand the ending."

There's little point in talking about ways to improve your writing until you have something on paper to share with others. That's what this part of the book is all about: how to talk about your draft with your audience—your class-mates—so that you can clarify and refine your ideas when you revise.

chapter 3

Understanding Your Audience

Every time a writer sits down to write, she or he has to make three related decisions: (1) What form will the writing be in? (2) What subject will it be about? (3) Who is the audience?

The **form** is the *type* of writing you decide to do—whether an essay, a report, a letter, a poem, and so on. In Chapter 1 you began to write one such form, the journal entry. (Soon you'll study another form, the essay.) In Chapter 2 you spent time on the **subject**—what you decide to write *about*. And here we will consider the **audience**—the readers whom you decide to write *for*.

Sometimes a writer starts with one of these concerns and then moves to the other two. For example, if you decide to write to a friend, you may not yet know your subject. But by deciding on the audience, you also decide quickly on the form—a letter or a card is likely. The subject then follows from your decisions about audience and form. But suppose you decide on your subject first—for example, springtime. You then probably would ask yourself, "What form should I use (essay, poem)?" and "Who might read it?"

As these examples show, the questions of form, subject, and audience are so intertwined that it is often difficult to tell where one begins and another ends. As shown in Figure 1 (page 28), form, subject, and audience are like three pieces of a puzzle. When the pieces fit, the writer's message is clear and effective. In this chapter we will focus on the audience for your writing. That will help you fit your form and subject to the readers' interests and needs.

A Sense of Audience

When a woman decides to wear a gray suit with a skirt rather than a pair of slacks to a job interview, she probably bases her decision on what she thinks is expected in that situation. In other words, she considers her audience—the peo-

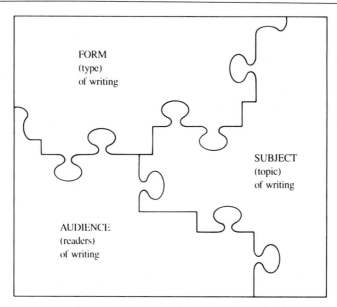

FORM
(type)
of writing

SUBJECT
(topic)
of writing

AUDIENCE
(readers)
of writing

Figure 1   The writer's puzzle: Fitting form, subject, and audience into a clear picture

ple whom she must meet and impress. In the same way, a man may decide not to wear a strong aftershave lotion to the office, because he wants to be taken seriously. Again, he thinks of his audience—the people who work with him.

Most people behave according to particular rules even when there is no specific audience. For example, have you ever noticed how people follow a certain pattern of behavior if they trip in public? Usually they frown, shake their head, and look behind them to see what they tripped over.

Situations—whether a job interview, meeting a date's family, or just going out in public—seem to invoke certain patterns of behavior. We base our behavior, in part, on the awareness that someone might be watching. We know there is an audience, and we adjust our appearance (form) and our behavior (subject) to fit it.

Writing Assignment ■

On the left-hand side of your journal, write a page about something you wrote or said recently with a particular audience in mind. Perhaps you had to persuade your parents to give you more responsibility; perhaps you had to tell someone that you did not want to do what he or she wanted. Discuss how you prepared your speech or your letter. What decisions did you make about what you were going to say and about how you were going to say it?

One way to look at writing is that you begin by talking to yourself and then you shape what you say with others in mind. As you draft your writing, you move outward from yourself toward others. In fact, **rhetoric** is the art of using and arranging language to influence others. If you judge your audience correctly, you may get the response you want. You can interest people in yourself, your situation, or your ideas. You can get action on the campus, in the community, or from a company. And you can earn praise for your accomplishments—including praise for a well-done piece of writing. For all these reasons, developing your sense of the audience is one of the most important lessons you can learn about writing.

Readers can help you to write even before you put your message on paper. By imagining your audience as well as you can, or even making up an audience, you can find ways to shape your message more effectively. To see how this may work, spend some time on the following writing assignments.

Writing Assignments ■

1. In your journal, answer the following questions, either about your real audience or about an imaginary audience.

a. What single thing about you is likely to be most important?

b. Is the audience part of your own community (however you define it)? Related in some way to your community? Or outside your community?

c. How old are your readers? How does age matter?

d. What is the gender of your readers? How does gender matter?

e. Describe the kind of education your readers have had. How does this matter?

f. What is the economic or social background of your readers? How do these factors matter?

g. Describe the political, religious, or philosophical beliefs of your readers. How do these factors matter?

h. If your audience is made up of people of different ages, genders, backgrounds, and beliefs, how will you fit your message to all of them?

2. In your journal, name a topic that you want to write about. Then answer these questions about your message.

a. What special or technical terms will you have to define for your audience? Will your audience respond to slang if you use it? Why or why not?

b.   How can you present your ideas without losing your audience? Make a plan to follow that will keep your readers reading. Are any of your ideas likely to upset readers or make them angry?

c.   What would work best—being logical, being emotional, or coming across as someone the readers can trust? Say why. Should you combine all three of these strategies? Why or why not?

d.   What kinds of facts and examples will your audience need to understand your point or to be persuaded that you have something important to say?

3.   Whether advertising is logical or not, it appeals to our *ideal* selves—the secret selves that we would like to present to the world. Advertising tells us that, by buying the "right" product, we can be smart, or sexy, or sophisticated, or rich.

Pick an advertisement from a magazine or newspaper. You yourself may be attracted to the product or the ad, and thus may be part of the intended audience; or you may recognize that you have nothing in common with the intended audience. On the left-hand side of your journal, write an analysis of the ad by describing its intended audience.

Beyond the Classroom Audience

Since you are in a writing class, your main audience is your teacher and your classmates. In most of your classes, the teacher is your main audience—whether you are writing an essay for an English course, making a lab report in a science class, researching a paper for sociology, or answering an essay exam in history. In fact, whenever you write as part of your course work, it is difficult to think of anyone else *but* your teacher. Oddly enough, however, your teachers in every course expect you to have a larger audience in mind—an audience that extends beyond the walls of the classroom.

In a writing class, for example, your "teacher" supervises the classroom, but she or he also responds to drafts of writing as a "reader." This part of the relationship between teacher and student can be confusing. One student, after discussing his writing with his teacher, revised a draft but left out important details. When asked why he didn't include them, he said to his teacher, "But I told you the details yesterday!" He forgot that the teacher is also a reader who needs the same information as other readers. No matter how well your teacher may know your ideas and writing, he or she is also a member of your audience.

After your teacher, your classmates are the next audience. If they are about your age and come from a similar background, they are likely to share some of your experiences, expectations, and hopes. And if your classmates are very different from you, then your first challenge is to find out about them. In either case, as you begin to get to know your classmates, your ideas about them may change. As a writer, you then are faced with juggling what you can predict about them as an audience and what you actually know about them.

Think of your teacher and classmates as *representatives* of your larger audience. If you are writing for a particular audience—such as the readers of the college newspaper or the owners of your apartment building—your class then stands in for these people. Even if you have imaginary readers in mind, and you invent characteristics, your class stands in for this imaginary audience.

Ideas about your audience may change as you draft and revise. Your writing itself may change as you get a better picture of your readers and include more and more people in your audience. As you move from draft to finished writing, your audience will keep expanding, like this:

— Yourself as reader
— Yourself as main reader, but other readers as well
— Readers who are just like you
— Readers who know some of the things you do
— Readers who don't know any of the things you do
— Readers who are very different from you
— Complete strangers

Writing with Your Audience in Mind

Readers want to know what a writer knows, and they want a writer to express ideas carefully. They look for correct information and clear definitions. They want to focus on what the writer says, without being distracted by errors.

We all appreciate writing that is well-organized and logical, and we enjoy a certain amount of style. When a writer makes a point, we expect it to be supported by facts, details, and examples. In short, as readers we expect a writer to think about us. And to be good writers, we have to think about our readers.

Reading Assignment

Let us examine how writers think about their audience. Read the following letter from a teenage girl to Miss Manners, who answers questions in a newspaper column about social customs and etiquette:

Dear Miss Manners,

The first time my boyfriend and I spent time in my bedroom, talking and nothing else, my mother said that I couldn't ever go into the bedroom with him again, simply saying it wasn't right.

Then she agreed that I could go into the bedroom with him, as long as the door was kept completely open, but when he came over, she said she'd never agreed to anything of the sort.

The next time, he and I were discussing a structural problem with a model helicopter in my bedroom. Everything was innocent. My mother came in and very rudely started telling us to leave.

She's always rude to him, but when he's gone, she says she likes him and denies she's been rude.

My question is: Haven't I got the right to be in my own bedroom? I'll agree to keep the door wide open, as long as she's not in there every five minutes checking up on us or asking me to wash the dishes when my friends are over.

My friends have complained, and I can't blame them. Shouldn't she keep her word? There have been times I haven't kept my word, but I've paid the price.

The young woman who wrote this letter understands that Miss Manners doesn't know her or her situation; therefore, she tells all the facts in the order they happened so that Miss Manners (and the newspaper's readers) can easily follow her story. Notice that she uses words and phrases like *the first time*, *then*, and *the next time* so that her audience can follow the order of events.

This writer's main purpose is to inform Miss Manners, but she also wants to present her side of the story in a way that will get a favorable response. Notice how she writes that she and her boyfriend were "talking and nothing else," to emphasize that they were not doing things her mother would disapprove of. Then she gives a specific example of what they were discussing—"a structural problem with a model helicopter." She offers the example to prove that she and her boyfriend do have serious matters to discuss; they are not just wasting time together.

At this point, however, the writer begins to get more emotional. She complains that her mother is "always" rude to her boyfriend; she says that her mother checks up on her and her friends "every five minutes." It is understandable that the writer switched to an emotional approach—after all, she wants Miss Manners to take her side. As a reader, do you think the writer lost control here? Or do you think that she helped her case by expressing her feelings?

Now, read Miss Manners' reply. (Don't be put off because she refers to herself as "Miss Manners" or because she addresses her reply to "Gentle Reader"; she always does that in her column.)

Gentle Reader,

Without defending your mother, who certainly should keep her word and not treat your friends rudely, Miss Manners feels sorry for her.

Your mother is behaving the way she is because she has not thought the problem through.

Like most grown-ups, she knows that appearances, as well as actual behavior, can be important. But instead of explaining that to you, she has tried to give in on the point of your entertaining in your bedroom. Then because she has conceded something she cannot really endorse, she cannot stick to it.

Miss Manners does not doubt that your behavior is innocent, but for a couple to go off alone to a bedroom in a family dwelling is suggestive of something else. If it were a bed-sitting room in a dormitory, commonly used for social as well as sleeping purposes, that would not be the case.

This is such a subtle argument that your mother doesn't attempt it because she is afraid she would lose to a youthful declaration of rights and wrongs, in which mere appearances are discounted, and issues of social custom dismissed as trivial if not hypocritical, compared to actual moral behavior.

Nevertheless, violation of customs is offensive. Your mother can't stand it, and, Miss Manners assures you, your boyfriend's parents would also be swift to condemn you.

You are, however, right in wanting a private place in which to entertain. Surely there is some place in the house—the living room, a recreation or sitting room—that can be set aside at certain times for you and your guests.

When conventionality is satisfied, you mother will be more ready to trust your moral behavior.

At first, you might say that the audience here is the young woman, but think about that for a second. If you were in the teenager's place, and Miss Manners answered you in the newspaper and seemed to be on your side, wouldn't you immediately show the reply to your mother? Miss Manners probably had this in mind when she wrote her reply. First of all, she agrees about two important points right away—one should keep one's word and not be rude. Indeed, it is difficult to argue otherwise. But then Miss Manners seems to go in two different directions. She sympathizes with the mother, who has different ideas about appearances than her daughter does. And she also sympathizes with the daughter, saying she should have "a private place in which to entertain." Miss Manners trusts the teenager ("does not doubt that your behavior is innocent")—a remark that also flatters the mother by saying that she did a good job in raising her daughter.

Writing Assignments

In your journal, respond to the following questions.

1. Do you think Miss Manners is being equally fair to both mother and daughter? Do you think she takes one side more than the other? Whose side is she on? How do you think this reply affected the mother and daughter? Why?

2. Toward the end of her reply, Miss Manners says that the parents of the young man would "also be swift to condemn" this behavior. In your journal, take the side of the boy's parents, and write a letter to the mother of the girl. But rather than criticizing the teenagers' behavior, support it. How would you write to the mother to convince her that the behavior is OK without offending her?

3. Imagine that you are the mother of the young woman. In your journal, write a letter to Miss Manners telling your side of the story. What points would you make to support the mother's position?

Ways to Approach Your Audience

The letters to and from Miss Manners show that a writer's idea of audience can influence the writing itself. Now we'll look at some of the ways that writers address their audience. This, too, can affect the writing.

Sometimes a writer may choose to address readers directly by simply saying "you." This can often create a sense of intimacy or togetherness, because *you* pulls people in. In the introduction to an essay, *you* invites the readers in; and in the conclusion of an essay, it urges readers to action.

Reading Assignment   ■

The following passage is from the book *Adult Children of Alcoholics*. "Adult children" of alcoholics were raised by at least one alcoholic parent; as adults, many of them are still working out the problems of their childhood.

> Adult children of alcoholics overreact to changes over which they have no control.
>
> This is very simple to understand. The young child of the alcoholic was not in control. The alcoholic's life was inflicted on him, as was his environment.
>
> In order to survive when growing up, he needed to turn that around. He needed to begin taking charge of his environment. This became very important, and remains so. The child of the alcoholic learns to trust himself more than anyone else when it's impossible to rely on somebody else's judgment.
>
> As a result, you are very often accused of being controlling, rigid, and lacking in spontaneity. This is probably true. It doesn't come from wanting to do everything your own way. It isn't because you are spoiled or unwilling to listen to other ideas. It comes from the fear that if you are not in charge, if a change is made, abruptly, quickly, without your being able to participate in it, you will lose control of your life.
>
> There is no question that this is overreaction. And when there is an overreaction, it generally means that it is caused by something in one's past experi-

ence. At the moment, the thing you overreacted to may seem foolish to others. But it is an automatic response. "You can't do that to me. No, I will not go to the movies when we decided we were going roller skating." It's almost an involuntary reflex.

When you look back on your reactions and your behavior later, you feel somewhat foolish, but at the time you were simply unable to shift gears.

Janet Geringer Woititz, Adult Children of Alcoholics

Beginning with the fourth paragraph, the writer switches from *he* to *you* in addressing the readers. Remember that this writer has a particular audience in mind: adult children of alcoholic parents. In discussing their tendency to over-react when they feel they have lost control of a situation, she refers to the adult child as *he*. This allows readers to think of an *imaginary* person. It makes readers more receptive to the writer's ideas by giving them some emotional distance. Then, by switching to *you*, she says: "OK, I am talking about you, not about some hypothetical case. You know what I mean."

In contrast, a writer might choose *not* to address readers directly—or not to address them at all. This approach makes writing more formal, because it separates the writer from readers. Academic writing often requires this kind of distance. When a writer uses *one* or *he* or *she*, readers are not invited into the discussion. They are kept at a distance so that they will consider the writer's case without emotion.

Following is an example of how a writer can keep readers at a distance by addressing them in the third person:

By now the reader should have a clear picture of. . . .

When you do choose to address readers directly, think about your audience carefully. There are times when *you* may cause problems. Consider these two examples:

The physical therapist must always be gentle with her or his patient. You should try to turn the patient slowly enough so that you don't cause any pain.

Belonging to a fraternity can be a rewarding experience. For example, you can build lifelong friendships.

Unless all readers of these passages are either physical therapists or young men interested in fraternities, some readers may resent being included in those groups. How did you feel when you read the passage about adult children of alcoholics? That writer was aware of a broader audience, but her main purpose was to address a very narrow group—the adult children themselves. In doing so, she also addressed readers who are not in that group.

When *you* doesn't include a broad enough audience, a writer will sometimes use *we*. This also draws readers in:

> The obstacles to discovery—the illusions of knowledge—are also part of our story. Only against the forgotten backdrop of the received common sense and myths of their time can we begin to sense the courage, the rashness, the heroic and imaginative thrusts of the great discoverers.
>
> Daniel Boorstin, *The Discoverers*

Because this passage is talking about a shared history, the writer includes all of us who have a part in it.

What about *I*? You may have been taught not to use *I* in a paper, because writing is more "formal" than speaking. It is true that some readers are bothered by *I*. In technical and scientific writing and in formal news reports, for example, writers rarely use *I* (or *you*). Instead, they avoid naming anyone in order to focus on the information. But some writing is meant to be personal, and some readers resent it when a writer is too distant. In these cases, avoiding *I* might weaken the writing style or its effect on readers. If a writer's purpose is to make contact with readers and to include them emotionally, words like *I*, *you*, and *we* can help. Before using them, however, you should check whether your teacher wants you to address readers directly. On the job, you also should learn whether your employer has any policy about this issue.

Sexist Language

Look again at these sentences from the passage you read earlier: "The young child of the alcoholic was not in control. The alcoholic's life was inflicted on him, as was his environment." The writer does not mean that only *male* children have alcoholic parents. She is using the masculine pronouns (*him* and *his*) to include *all* children of alcoholics—both sons and daughters. Until recently, masculine pronouns were considered **generic**; that is, they included all members of a group.

Today, people often disagree about the use of generic words. Some argue that words like *man*, *mankind*, *he*, *him*, and *his* include women when they are used generically. To them, a sentence like "Man cannot live by bread alone" means "Man and woman cannot live by bread alone." But a growing number of people today say that such language excludes women, even if the speaker or writer intends to include them. Many people consider generic masculine pronouns to be sexist, because they ignore the role of women in society.

However you feel about this issue, as a writer you should realize that a fair number of people today are uncomfortable with the use of generic masculine words. If you use them, you run the risk of offending some of your audience.

Perhaps you have noticed that people often stumble over masculine pronouns in speech. They may begin with *he*; then pause and add *she*; and finally give up, saying, "You know what I mean—everyone." This sort of confusion indicates that more and more people are trying to change old habits when it comes to using masculine words in certain situations.

Writers may choose to avoid sexist language and still write gracefully. For instance, rather than always using the masculine pronoun *he*, we can use *he and she*, or *she and he*. (Or, more simply, we can use *he* in some sentences and *she* in others.) Another approach is to use plural nouns, which require plural pronouns like *they* and *their*. And sometimes articles (*a*, *an*, and *the*) can replace generic pronouns.

Look again at the passage and how it can be revised to avoid sexist language:

Generic masculine pronouns
The young child of the alcoholic was not in control. The alcoholic's life was inflicted on *him*, as was *his* environment.

Both pronouns and an article
The young child of the alcoholic was not in control. The alcoholic's life was inflicted on *him or her*, as was *the* environment.

Plural nouns and pronouns
Children of alcoholics were not in control. The alcoholic's life was inflicted on *them*, as was *their* environment.

Using generic masculine pronouns is not the only way that you might unintentionally exclude half of your audience. Instead of writing *man* or *men* all the time, you can say *men and women*, or *people*. *Humanity* often has the same meaning as *mankind*, and it more clearly includes women. Words like *manpower* and *the man on the street* can be replaced by *work force* (or *personnel*) and the *average person*.

Keep in mind that no rule says that males must come first, as in *he or she* or *men and women*. You can just as easily reverse the order (*she or he, women and men*), which adds variety and fairness to your writing.

In the past, people tended to assume that maids, secretaries, nurses, and elementary teachers had to be women, and that waiters, office managers, doctors, and college professors were almost always men. As a result, phrases like *male nurse* and *lady doctor* were coined (invented). Today, they sound silly. We're used to writers using *businessperson* or *executive* (rather than *businessman* or *businesswoman*); *police officer* (rather than *police man* or *police woman*); *workers* (rather than *workmen*); *student* (rather than *coed*); and *homemaker* (rather than *housewife*). Some of the older words are even less accurate:

Is a "housewife" married to a house? And which word describes the job better—
fireman or *firefighter*? In the same way, *member of Congress* or *representative*
is more accurate than *Congressman*.

Words like *authoress* and *poetess* sound old-fashioned today; we're more
likely to say *author* and *poet* for both sexes. In the same way, a *waiter* or *server*
can be female or male.

When you are talking about a specific person in your writing, you well
may want to use words that *do* make his or her gender clear. But when you
make general (generic) statements, it is always better to include everyone, female and male. After all, when you address your readers, don't you want all of
them to listen?

Reading and Writing Assignment   ■

Find a piece of writing—in a textbook, a newspaper, a novel—that you think
uses sexist language. Or find a piece of writing that you think *does not* use
sexist language. In your journal, make notes about how the author handles or
mishandles questions involving gender and language. Report your findings in
class.

When to Ignore Your Audience

There is a time to ignore readers other than yourself. As noted in Chapter 2,
when you write your discovery drafts, it might be helpful *not* to think about
your final readers. Until you know what *you* want to write about, don't try to
please "your readers."

Read the following passage:

> The first amendment of the United States Constitution states that there is
> freedom of the press, religion, speech, petition, and assembly. The people in
> Washington, D.C., exercise that right to its fullest. In order to get their voices to
> be heard, they petition with demonstrations, painted signs, and letters. These
> actions let the government know how the public really feels about issues hap-
> pening all around the world in hopes that as a result, something will be done to
> improve certain situations.
>
> Dawn Gibson, student

Although this paragraph is "well-written," it lacks the personal touch. In
discussing her subject with her teacher, Dawn said that she had been very impressed by all the demonstrators she saw in front of the White House. But when
she was drafting her paper about this experience, she thought she had to write
"for the teacher." As a result, she began to write in an impersonal, formal way.
She wrote about the "facts," but she didn't add any of her own ideas or feelings

to them. Because she had a mistaken idea about what her teacher expected, she couldn't find her own voice to say what she really wanted to say. She wrote for her teacher, instead of for herself and a broader audience.

If you run into a similar problem, ask yourself if thinking about your readers helps or hinders your writing. Work on writing for *yourself* before writing for others. Remember that you are your first audience.

The Audience's Idea of You

Do you have any special ways of speaking that you save for particular occasions? That is, when you have to check on your bank balance, or speak to your landlord, do you change how you normally speak? Compare how you speak to young children with the way you speak to your friends. Or compare how you speak to teachers with how you speak to family members. Not only may your choice of words change from situation to situation, but the actual sound of your voice may change. Just as a speaker may use many voices, so may a writer.

Your Voice and Tone

In writing, the use of vocabulary to create effects is called **voice**; and the attitude or emotion that a writer reveals is called **tone**. Just as speakers show emotions and attitudes—even when they might not want to—a writer's voice and tone can reveal (or hide) feelings and attitudes.

See what you can learn about the writer of the following passage:

> What is most amazing to me is how the dorm residents continue to cook and eat in that filthy kitchen. They prepare their meal over the mess the person before them has left behind; it's disgusting. The kitchen has been so dirty that it seems to me a person could catch a disease just by walking in and getting ice from the refrigerator. These slobs have no respect or consideration for others.
>
> Lynkita Roberts, student

Do you get a good idea of how this writer feels? What do you think the "slobs" would say if they read this? Consider another example:

> It's just so ridiculous seeing professional players asking for so much money and then getting it. All they doing is play a game. There are those people who bust their butts behind a desk, run the world, and save other people's lives, and they only get paid one-half of a player's salary. It just isn't fair!
>
> Michael Herrity, student

Even though you may agree with what Michael says, his vocabulary and tone may get in the way of his message. Is he complaining because he is envious? Or does he intend to sound angry? Either way, his tone gets more attention than his point does.

In contrast, the following writer makes his point in a very low-keyed way:

> Late Friday morning, September 28, King addressed the convention's final session from the stage of the L. R. Hall Auditorium. During his remarks, a young white man who had been sitting in the sixth row rose suddenly and approached King. Without warning, the man punched King in the face.
>
> David Garrow, *Bearing the Cross*

Were you surprised by the last sentence? Because the writer's tone is so calm, we are not ready for the act of violence. Should we conclude that the writer is simply being an objective historian by not revealing his attitude toward what he relates? Or is it his lack of emotion that lets us fully experience the shock of this event?

In the next passage, the writer gives us a strong sense of her attitudes toward child-care policies and sexism in the United States by comparing the situation in England. How would you describe her tone? Do you think it supports or weakens her point?

> I saw Great Britain as being rather backward on women's issues and decidedly "unliberated." Why, English people still talked about manpower and chairmen when they referred to women and weren't even self-conscious about doing it! I could not imagine that progressive America had anything to learn from the Old World. In spite of all my American advantages, however, it was clear that I had not been able to cope successfully with the dual roles I had so joyfully undertaken.
>
> Sylvia Hewlett, *A Lesser Life*

Sometimes writers think that they need to impress their audience by using big words and stuffy language. (That was Dawn's problem when she tried to describe the demonstrators at the White House; she was trying to impress her teacher.) Many writing tasks do require language that is more formal than speech. But when a writer uses very formal language that doesn't come naturally, it can backfire. Writing that is dull and lifeless hardly invites us to keep reading; instead, it encourages us to do anything *but* read further. Here is an example taken from business:

> Unimpeachable business integrity in our business dealings with others will produce results of a more substantial nature.

The writer could say the same thing more effectively by using a normal vocabulary:

> Honesty in our business dealings is more productive than deception.

When you get rid of all the fancy words and stuffy tone, the message is most clear:

> Honesty is the best policy.

The following example of fancy words and a stuffy tone comes from a student's first draft:

> Race is an important factor in adopting because the transracial adoptee faces the stigma of growing up with a white family in a racist society. This stigma manifests itself in such ways as rude stares and insensitive comments from uncaring or curious individuals. Another problem is the common lack of exposure adoptees have to other blacks. Simple events like family gatherings can become uncomfortable ordeals if the adoptee is the only black present. Similarly, black functions become places of rejection for the adoptee who cannot feel comfortable or fit in with other blacks.

It is true that this topic should be treated formally. But it still can be interesting and inviting. After discussing her voice and tone with her teacher, the student revised the draft as follows:

> When a white couple considers adopting a black child, the couple should first think about the possible stigma of growing up with a white family in a racist society. Uncaring or curious strangers can make life difficult for the child by their rude stares and insensitive comments. Simple events like family gatherings can become uncomfortable ordeals if the adopted child is the only black person present. The adopted child faces another problem as well. If the child does not have a chance to meet and socialize with other blacks, the child might also find all-black social situations uncomfortable, too.
>
> Marjorie Hunt, student

The revised draft does not sacrifice the seriousness that Marjorie wants to convey to her readers, and it is much clearer.

Our last example illustrates a good match between the writer's subject and voice:

> Weight Watchers here I come! Ever since I left home, I have been eating nonstop. I know for a fact that if I don't slow down I'm not going to be able to fit into my dorm room. Eating—and cooking—seems to be the only thing that I have learned since coming to college.
>
> Barbara Lesane, student

When to Revise Your Voice and Tone

The passages in this section show how a writer's voice and tone can be used to present a message clearly and to connect with readers. Your choice of words (voice) and the attitudes you reveal (tone) are part of your message, and readers will react to them. You should write with your real voice, not with the voice you think you should be using.

But what *is* your real voice, and how can you tell if readers will hear it? After all, when you're writing, *you* know what you mean, and *you* know how you feel about it. But how can you know what your readers will think about your language and tone?

First of all, don't worry about your voice and tone until after you have written your discovery draft. *After* you have gotten your ideas on paper, read your draft aloud, and ask yourself whether this is the way you want to sound to others. Do you sound natural? Or stuffy? Do your words sound sincere, or are you trying to impress someone with fancy language? When you read your draft out loud, do you feel comfortable, or do you get all worked up?

If you can't answer questions like these about your own voice, ask a friend or a classmate to listen to you as you read the draft aloud. If your listener thinks you sound natural and is not confused by the points you make, your voice and tone are probably about right. In any case, get your ideas on paper first. Then use your discovery draft to "discover" the best voice and tone for your audience.

Reading and Writing Assignment ■

Read the following two accounts, written by British soldiers, of the Battle of Lexington fought in Massachusetts at the beginning of the War of Independence.

Passage 1 was written by a British lieutenant, Edward Thornton Gould, who was wounded and captured at the Battle of Lexington. As you will see, he is unclear about what actually happened. Notice that Gould calls the American soldiers "provincial troops"—as a member of the highly disciplined and uniformed British army, he does not recognize the Americans as soldiers like himself, but sees them as a rather disorganized body of men.

De Berniere, the author of passage 2, is more positive about who fired the first shot. In his account, the number of Americans has increased from 60 or 70 to 150, and De Berniere simply calls the soldiers "rebels."

Passage 1

> On our arrival at that place [Lexington] we saw a body of provincial troops armed, to the number of about sixty or seventy men; on our approach they dispersed, and soon after firing began, but which party fired first I cannot exactly say. . . .

Passage 2

The troops received no interruption in their march until they arrived at Lexington, a town eleven miles from Boston, where there were about 150 rebels drawn out in divisions. . . . Major Pitcairn came up immediately and cried out to the rebels to throw down their arms and disperse, which they did not do; he called out a second time, but to no purpose; upon which he ordered our light-infantry to advance and disarm them, which they were doing, when one of the rebels fired a shot, our soldiers returned the fire and killed about fourteen of them. . . .

In small groups, discuss the differences that you find between these two accounts, and try to explain why the differences exist. Take notes about the group's discussion using the right-hand side of your journal.

Now, read the following passage. As you might imagine, the Americans have a different view of things. The Reverend Clark writes of how the American officer, Captain Parker, dispersed his men when he saw the British troops advancing:

Passage 3

huzza'd:
cheered or
shouted
triumphantly

. . . but, many of them not so speedily as they might have done, not having the most distant idea of such brutal barbarity and more than savage cruelty, from the troops of a British king, as they immediately experienced!—!—For, no sooner did they come in sight of our company, but one of them supposed to be an officer of rank, was heard to say to the troops, "Damn them; we will have them!"—Upon which the troops shouted out loud, huzza'd and rushed furiously toward our men.—About the same time, three officers . . . advanced, on horse back, to the front of the body, and coming within 5 or 6 rods of the militia, one of them cried out, "ye villains, ye Rebels, disperse; Damn you, disperse!"—or words to this effect. One of them . . . said, "lay down your arms; Damn you, why don't you lay down your arms!"—The second of these officers, about this time, fired a pistol towards the militia, as they were dispersing. The foremost, who was within a few yards of our men, brandishing his sword, and then pointing towards them, with a loud voice said to the troops, "Fire!—By God, fire!"—which was instantly followed by a discharge of arms from the said troops, succeeded by a very heavy and close fire upon our party, dispersing, so long as any of them were within reach.—Eight men were left dead upon the ground! Ten were wounded.—The rest of the company, through divine goodness, were (to a miracle) preserved unhurt in this murderous action!—

As we can see, Reverend Clark is much more emotional in his account of the battle, and he puts the blame on the British. Notice that he describes the supposed insolence of the British officers, and he writes that the British are cruel, barbaric, and murderous.

Now, in small groups, discuss the differences between the British accounts (passages 1 and 2) and the American account (passage 3). How do you think the different writers' ideas of their audience affected what they wrote? What personal beliefs or biases might have affected each writer's reporting? Can you think of a recent news item that has been reported from different points of view? How do you account for the differences? On the right-hand side of your journal, summarize your group's discussion.

Reading and Writing Assignment ■

Look over the various passages written by students and professional writers included in this book. In small groups, discuss how various writers address their audiences and the ways they convey their personalities. Using the right-hand side of your journal, take notes about your group's discussion.

Revising Assignment ■

Use Worksheet 2 at the end of this book to analyze one of your longer drafts in terms of audience and tone. In the margin of your draft, make notes about how you would revise the way you address your audience.

Writing Assignment ■

Take a moment to review what you learned in this chapter. What new things did you learn about your readers and how to approach them? What did you learn about using language to convey your voice and tone? On the right-hand side of your journal, summarize the new things you learned about how to address your audience.

chapter 4

■

Revising Your First Draft

In Chapters 2 and 3 you wrote a discovery draft on your own. In the planning stage, you used such strategies as freewriting, brainstorming, and listing to explore your topic. Then you thought about your audience, and you adjusted your voice and tone to fit your subject and readers. At this point in the writing process, you have a first draft.

This first draft is certainly important, because it's a way to make "invisible" things—your ideas—"visible" on paper. But this is hardly the end of the writing process. Once you have something on paper, a whole new process of discovery begins. Now, you are ready to *rethink* your ideas by revising your draft.

Revision

A **revision** is just that—a *re-vision*, a looking again at your first draft. Some writers think of revision as *rehearsing*—as practicing and perfecting writing until it is ready for the audience to read.

In this book, the terms *revision* and *revising* refer to the process of rewriting a whole paper. We might call revision a complete overhaul, because every idea and word in the first draft is examined closely. In contrast, **editing** is the process of fine-tuning grammar, spelling, and punctuation without really changing the basic ideas or structure of the paper. But there's little point in fine-tuning until the ideas and structure are solid. Revision is the opportunity to think through your ideas one more time, and to make them as effective as possible.

If you're like most writers, you probably have already done some revising and editing as you wrote your first draft. Throughout the writing process (see Figure 1 on page 46), we start, stop, circle back, make mistakes, and revise again and again. Finally, we reach a point—and that point varies from writer to writer—when we say "done."

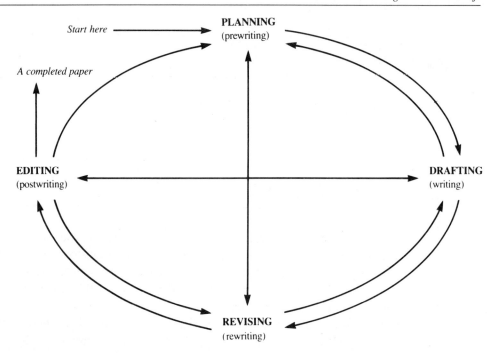

Figure 1   The writing process

However, what we consider to be "done," a teacher or another reader might consider to be the place where revision begins. Revision is rewriting. We may add ideas, and perhaps more details. We may delete (cut out) ideas that don't strengthen the main point. And we may change or rearrange sentences and paragraphs. During revision we reread and rework the entire paper and consider how to turn the draft into an essay suitable for our readers.

In some cases, your second draft may bear little resemblance to your first draft. This happens when a writer decides that the entire approach to the subject needs to be rethought. For example, one student wrote a discovery draft that discussed the growing number of students who were abusing alcohol on campus. But after finishing the draft, the writer realized that she was really more interested in analyzing how some college activities encourage students to drink. When she revised her first draft, her new approach led to a completely different paper.

Sometimes, during revision, a writer may decide that the draft is aimed at the wrong audience. For an essay assignment, one student wrote a letter trying to convince his classmates that overcrowded classes were a major problem at their university. During revision he realized that it would make more sense to address the letter to the Dean of Students; he then rewrote it using more formal language and slightly different arguments.

Revision also might lead a writer to change strategies—in other words, to change how the essay is structured. (We will look closely at writing strategies in Chapter 13.) A student who was drafting a paper about rap music spent a lot of time defining the terms "rap music" and "hip-hop." In revising the draft, she pursued a different strategy. Rather than structuring the paper through definitions, she traced the origins of rap music back to Africa.

In effect, during revision writers often draft an entirely new essay on the same topic using some of the ideas they already developed. But they change the focus by aiming at a different audience, or using a different strategy, or incorporating different examples and details.

One of the hardest things for writers to do is to let go of material they have already written. It takes guts to cross out whole sections on a page, or to watch sentences and paragraphs disappear forever from the computer screen. Most writers feel that it was work enough just *creating* a first draft; now they must start over.

Because professional writers seldom show us their revisions, we might think that they produce perfect prose the first time around. By comparison, our scribbled-over drafts may seem worthless. But very few writers can generate polished prose in one draft, and even good writing should be tested by the revision process. Writers who understand this have already taken their first step toward becoming better writers.

Working on a Paper in Progress

If you run into trouble during revision, don't give up. A short break may help. Sometimes you need to be a stranger to yourself in order to revise, and the best way to put some distance between you and your writing is to give yourself some time between looking at drafts. (This is one reason to allow plenty of time to complete a writing assignment.) Even if you don't have a great deal of time, a short break may help you to find places in your writing that can be improved.

When you are blocked and don't know how to go on, turn the problem into a revision tool. Ask yourself what the cause of your frustration is. Perhaps the trouble comes from not understanding the assignment. Or maybe your purpose for writing is unclear. Think of revision as a time to explore, and remember that you are not alone: Few people know what they mean until they write it.

Have you ever had the experience of not knowing that you knew something until someone asked you about it? Our heads are full of "passive" knowledge that we've absorbed from the world around us. We draw on such knowledge, for example, when we play trivia games—we often surprise ourselves with what we know. Or, we might tell a stranger how to find a street or a restaurant that we've never been to; somehow, we know where it is. Writing often works the same way. Without realizing it, we're full of opinions and ideas that become clear only whcn we are asked to write about them.

Writing takes a good deal of commitment, and it requires us to think carefully about a subject. Learning through writing—or during writing—is part of the writing experience. If you get frustrated during revision, that means you still have to talk to yourself some more. You still have some discoveries to make. In fact, the more interesting your ideas are, the more they will be improved through revision.

The Dead-End Draft

There may be times, during revision, when you look at your draft and decide that you aren't interested in pursuing the topic after all. Or, you may feel that you have reached a dead end. However, one thing that you need to learn about is the difference between a dead end and a temporary block. Sometimes, if you put aside a draft for a few hours (or for a few days, if time allows), you might return to it with a fresh outlook. Or, try writing your way out of a block by freewriting. Before deciding that you are really stuck, try to revise without even looking at your draft. Sometimes the draft itself can get in your way.

If you are not sure whether you are simply blocked or have reached a dead end, see your teacher, who may have some suggestions for you. Most likely, you will be able to change your topic if you lose interest or run out of steam. This happens to all writers at one time or another. Remember that writing is like exploring—it is a way to discover what you know and what you are interested in. Even reaching a dead end is a part of the discovery process; it can often lead to what you really want to write about. When you meet with your teacher, be prepared to say what you would rather write about, and why.

Reading and Revising Assignment   ■

Review the topics covered in the last two sections. What did you learn that you can apply to your own draft? Are you satisfied with how your draft is going? Or do you feel you have reached a dead end?

If you are not satisfied with your draft, try five or ten minutes of freewriting to see if you can identify your problems. Discuss them with your teacher or with a classmate.

In the margin of your draft, or on the page opposite it in your journal, jot down some notes that you can use when you revise.

Revision and Your Audience

As we discussed in Chapter 2, the act of writing an essay is an act of discovery—especially as you begin to write. During brainstorming and freewriting and drafting, you have to think about what you really want to say. Many writers write a discovery draft very quickly, because they are in a hurry to put down on paper everything that is in their mind.

During revision, however, a writer begins to think more about the intended audience. As you revise, you become more aware that you are writing for someone other than yourself, and you make sure that your ideas, voice, and tone fit the readers you wish to reach. (At this point you might want to review the questions for discovering an audience in Chapter 3; also see Worksheet 2 at the end of the book.) Unless the assignment requires you to aim your writing at a special audience, think about revising your *audience* along with your draft.

Revising Assignment ■

Look over your draft to see if you have lost track of your audience. Have you written about things your readers might not understand? Do you expect your readers to know more about your subject than they actually do? Use Worksheet 2 at the end of the book to assess how well your draft fits your audience.

In your journal, plan how you will revise your draft to fit your audience better.

Revision and Your Main Idea

Somewhere in a writing class right now, a student is probably raising a hand and asking, "But *why* do I have to have a main idea in my essay? My main idea is in the title. And besides, the essay is so short that any reader can figure out what I'm trying to say!"

In writing workshops, when students exchange papers, they may read each other's work and understand it perfectly well—even without some statement of the main idea. Why, then, do teachers often insist that the main idea be written out in a sentence or two?

To answer this question, just consider spoken language. Whether we are aware of it or not, we follow many "rules" and conventions in speaking, no matter how formal or informal the situation is. Part of the social behavior we agree to as members of a community is to observe certain rituals. For example, we learn when we should say "Please" and "Thank you" and "Excuse me." We usually reserve such politeness for strangers and formal situations, and we tend to be more relaxed with people we know well.

Other examples of ritualized behavior include saying "Thank you" to a clerk who waits on us in a store. Because this is expected, we indicate displeasure with the clerk's service if we do not say it. If the service was good and we don't say "Thank you," *we* are at fault. In the same way, we say "How do you do?" when we meet a professional person; but when greeting a good friend, such formal speech would be considered strange, if not rude! Whether we shake hands politely or exchange high fives, we do what is expected in the situation.

The same kinds of conventions are found in written language, and readers expect a clear expression of the main idea in an essay. Remember, we are readers as well as writers. Imagine reading an essay, and instead of taking in information, we are forced to hunt for it. That is what happens when a writer doesn't state a main idea, or provide details and transitions to move from one idea to another. When you write a paper or an essay exam, certain information and patterns are expected by your readers. It's rude to make them hunt for your main idea, as though it were a secret.

Another reason to express the main idea is that it helps *you*, during the discovery stages of writing. Even stating a possible main idea asks you to commit yourself to your writing. You can change your mind as you write your discovery draft, and then you can change your main idea. But instead of thinking of that as some kind of failure, look at it as a successful step toward finding out what you really mean to say. By checking your main idea as you draft, you will stay on track and won't drift away from your purpose.

How is the main idea different from the subject, or topic, of an essay? Basically, the **main idea** (or **thesis**) tells the reader *why* you are writing about the subject or topic. It states your purpose for writing.

A subject may be only a vague idea during the early planning stages of writing:

> *Subject*: Growing up in a large city

Next, a writer might focus in on this subject in the discovery draft:

> Growing up in a large city has its advantages and disadvantages.

Finally, this subject becomes the main idea when the writer states what is important about it:

> While growing up in a large city [*subject*] such as Detroit has often been difficult, I wouldn't trade the experience for anything else because urban life has taught me to be independent [*main idea about the subject*].

Think of your subject or topic as an area of discussion that can be summed up in a word or a phrase, like a title. But your main idea or thesis is a statement or a claim that you make about that topic. Here's another example:

Subject: An important mode of thought is the scientific method.

The subject simply tells you *what an essay is about*. After reading the above, you expect the essay to *be about* the scientific method as a way of thinking, and the statement commits the writer to showing that the scientific method is important. But the sentence doesn't tell you what the writer *thinks about* the scientific method. You have simply discovered the topic of the essay, not its main idea. Here's one way the sentence could be revised to state a main idea:

An important mode of thought is the scientific method [*subject*]. Moving from what we observe in the world to some conclusions about the world in our daily lives is exactly the kind of thinking that a scientist applies in research [*main idea about the subject*].

Now we know what the writer thinks about the topic, and we expect the essay to show how scientific thinking can be applied to everyday life.

Here is another example of a topic that has not yet been stated as a main idea:

My hiking trip in the Alleghenies taught me a lot about nature.

We know that the essay is *about* a camping trip and nature, but we don't know anything else. Revised, this sentence becomes a main idea:

My hiking trip in the Alleghenies taught me how much we depend on nature to provide food and shelter.

Readers usually expect the main idea to be stated near the beginning of an essay. This allows readers to predict what will follow. The better they can predict, the better they will understand the entire text. A statement of the main idea early in an essay is a widespread convention of college or academic writing. In the following example, see what happens when your expectations as a reader are frustrated:

Will Russ die? This is a question that lurks around your television set almost every afternoon. It is amazing how Russ can recover from his fatal disease, have an affair with Jack's wife, run an illegal casino, be head of the underworld, and fool around with Jack's wife's best friend all in one episode of "As the Ram Yearns."

This humorous description depicts the imaginary happenings in the world of soap operas. This is the place where you can find out that your sister is really your mother; your father is a former spy and your brother is addicted to Trivial Pursuit. To top things off, your dog is seeing a psychiatrist because it has a desire to be a cat. Even though soaps have some outrageous story lines, as this imaginary example shows, they do tend to relate some important messages to their audiences. I have noticed that soaps are turning to some of the more current issues in today's society. They no longer center mainly on topics such as divorce, infidelity, and sex. Soaps have gone into the closet and unleashed some of society's skeletons.

The introductory paragraph of this essay leads you to expect one thing, but the second paragraph gives you something entirely different. You have to hunt for the main idea—if you can find it at all. Now compare the revised essay:

Will Russ die? This is a question that lurks around your television set almost every afternoon. It is amazing how Russ can recover from his fatal disease, have an affair with Jack's wife, run an illegal casino, be head of the underworld, and fool around with Jack's wife's best friend all in one episode of "As the Ram Yearns." Even though soaps have some outrageous story lines, as this imaginary example shows, they do tend to relate some important messages to their audiences. I have noticed that soaps are turning to some of the more current issues in today's society. They no longer center mainly on topics such as divorce, infidelity, and sex. Soaps have gone into the closet and unleashed some of society's skeletons.

Barbara Lesane, student

As these examples show, sometimes, a writer rereads the discovery draft and finds that it does not get around to stating the main idea until the reader has reached the conclusion of the essay. Only after writing a few drafts was this writer able to focus and clarify her ideas so that she could state exactly what she wanted to say. Compare the following two paragraphs from a student's discovery draft. The first paragraph is the introduction, and the second is the conclusion:

[*Introduction*] Listening to music and singing have always been an interest of mine; however, whenever I thought about performing in front of people, I wasn't sure I could do it. I had often wondered how those in the music business seemed to have the courage to get up before a large audience and perform, and after seeing the Jacksons in concert, I thought I had a pretty good idea about how to perform before many people. I felt that if the lead singer of the group, Michael Jackson, had performed so well, then maybe I could perform just as well.

[*Conclusion*] For a while afterwards, I felt very disappointed and extremely upset with the Jacksons because they had made performing in front of people look so easy. I later realized the art of performing in front of large audiences meant that their great show was a result of years of hard work. I soon realized that to have the ability and courage to get up in front of an audience took more than just an observation of professionals like the Jacksons; it took a lot of experience and practice which I had yet to attain.

The student combined these two paragraphs in the following revision:

Listening to music and singing has always been an interest of mine; whenever I thought about performing in front of people, I wasn't sure I could do it. However, after seeing the Jacksons in concert, I thought I had a pretty good idea abut how to perform before many people. I felt that if Michael Jackson, had performed so well, then maybe I could perform just as well. Well, after a disastrous performance of my own, I realized that the art of performing in front of large audiences is a result of years of hard work. I realized that to have the ability and courage to get up in front of an audience took more than just an observation of professionals like the Jacksons; it took a lot of experience and practice which I had yet to attain.

Dawn Gibson, student

After writing her first draft, Dawn had a better idea of what she wanted to say. She was able to focus on her purpose for writing as she explored her topic. Notice that in the introduction to her first draft she simply wonders what it would be like to perform in front of people. In the conclusion of her draft she comes to some sort of understanding about her experience. It is natural to discover the significance of a topic as you are writing about it. That is why writing is a *process*; by drafting and revising, you think about the topic and discover what you most want to say about it.

Keep in mind that you are not required to put your main idea in the first paragraph when you revise. Your topic, your introduction, and the writing process itself may lead you to place the main idea elsewhere. If you are unsure about where to place your main idea, ask a classmate or your teacher to respond to your first draft.

Some essays have more than one important idea. A successful essay can cover several related topics and an assortment of observations about them. But it takes skill and experience to write such an essay without losing your focus—and your readers. Generally, an essay that focuses on one main idea will have the strongest impact on your readers. If you are unsure about whether you need to revise an essay to make the main idea more clear, discuss your draft with your teacher or with any thoughtful reader.

Reading and Revising Assignments ▪

1. Review the suggestions made about the main idea in this section. Then, look over a few of the passages written by students or professional writers in this book. Locate the statement of the main idea in at least one of the passages, and discuss your findings in small groups. What have you learned that you can apply to your own draft?

2. Look over your draft and find your own main idea. Does the main idea go beyond simply telling readers what the topic is? Does it state your purpose or viewpoint in some way? Where did you place the main idea in your draft? Would it be more effective if you placed it somewhere else? In the margin of your draft, indicate other places that you could put it, and jot down notes to consider during revision.

3. Exchange your first draft with a classmate. Using Worksheet 11 in the Appendix at the end of the book, each of you should answer the questions about each other's main idea. Can you find your classmate's main idea? Can he or she find yours? Consider your classmate's answers when you revise your essay later.

Revising the Organization of Your Draft

When you write a discovery draft, you are concerned mainly with getting things down on paper. And when you develop your discovery draft into your first draft, you still are more concerned with ideas than with how you present them. Because you are the writer, your ideas make perfect sense to you as you read over what you have written. Because you know what you *intend* to write, you may think that you have, indeed, written in a way that anyone can understand. Often, however, that is not the case. In a first draft, sentences may not be closely connected and may not say exactly what you mean.

If your sentences and paragraphs do not follow one another logically, your readers may not understand how the ideas in your essay are related. When you revise, pay close attention to the logical relationships between your ideas and to the connections you provide to move your readers from one idea to the next.

If you don't provide **transitions** (links between sentences, ideas, and paragraphs), you put a burden on your readers by forcing them to make connections for you. Readers can only read what is on paper; they can't read your mind. Most writers are blind to problems of logic and organization because they are too close to their own writing. They fill in the gaps in a draft in much the same way as they might finish the sentences of a close friend. A writer can discover the gaps by asking someone to read the draft and by putting it aside for a while.

The **organization**, or **unity**, of a piece of writing is difficult to define, but it results when the relationships between ideas are logical and when the writer provides transitions. When writing has unity, readers will say that it flows, or that it feels complete, or even that it satisfies. In Chapter 2 we noted that the writing process is a way of thinking. We can continue this comparison between writing and thinking by saying that writing makes relationships or connections between ideas. The process might be described as having three stages:

1. Making relationships

2. Combining those relationships into a pattern

3. Revealing the relationships and the pattern to readers

Let's look at a few examples of how writers achieve unity. First, notice how the following two paragraphs are linked by a question:

> In December, the month before Kennedy's inauguration, civil rights activists had won a victory in the Supreme Court when the justices ordered integration of bus stations and terminals serving interstate travelers. That court triumph made Kennedy's first few months in office all the more disappointing to blacks. But civil rights leaders still believed that Kennedy was a friend at heart and they knew he owed blacks a political debt. Eisenhower had been reluctant to use federal force after Little Rock. But Kennedy, civil rights leaders hoped, would not back down. Without enforcement from the executive branch, in this case in the form of a ruling from the Interstate Commerce Commission ordering compliance, the Supreme Court ruling would be meaningless. <u>Just how far would Kennedy go to enforce the nation's civil rights laws?</u>
>
> <u>The Congress of Racial Equality (CORE) intended to find out.</u> In 1947 CORE had organized the "Journey of Reconciliation" after the Supreme Court ruled that segregated seating on interstate buses and trains was unconstitutional.
>
> Juan Williams, *Eyes on the Prize*

Next, here's an example of a paragraph that is held together in the middle by a single word—*but*:

> The civil rights movement in America began a long time ago. As early as the seventeenth century, blacks and whites, slaves in Virginia and Quakers in Pennsylvania, protested the barbarity of slavery. Nat Turner, Sojourner Truth, Frederick Douglass, William Lloyd Garrison, John Brown and Harriet Tubman are but a few of those who led the resistance to slavery before the Civil War. After the Civil War, another protracted battle began against slavery's legacy— racism and segregation. <u>But</u> for most Americans, the civil rights movement began on May 17, 1954, when the Supreme Court handed down the Brown

v. Board of Education of Topeka decision outlawing segregation in public schools. The Court unlocked the door, but the pressure applied by thousands of men and women in the movement pushed that door open wide enough to allow blacks to walk through it toward this country's essential prize: freedom.

                                                    Juan Williams, *Eyes on the Prize*

This paragraph is unified by following a three-part order. The first half of the paragraph supports the topic sentence: *The civil rights movement in America began a long time ago.* The writer then gives proofs to support that idea: *As early as the seventeenth century, blacks and whites, slaves in Virginia and Quakers in Pennsylvania, protested the barbarity of slavery. Nat Turner, Sojourner Truth, Frederick Douglass, William Lloyd Garrison, John Brown and Harriet Tubman are but a few of those who led the resistance to slavery before the Civil War.* Notice that these supporting ideas are arranged in chronological order, from earliest to latest. Then the writer moves on to the second part: *After the Civil War, another protracted battle began against slavery's legacy—racism and segregation.* Finally, the third part begins with that all-important *But*.

In the next example, unity is again achieved through chronological order:

India has been the top producer of dried ginger since the dawn of the spice trade, though Indians use mostly the fresh rhizome in their own cooking. Their main market has always been the Middle East, which consumes the lion's share of this spice. Europe's frenzied use of ginger throughout the Middle Ages kept Indian growers busy until the sixteenth century, when Spain and Portugal decided to grow their own ginger in Jamaica and West Africa. Only recently, India has become the main supplier to the United States.

                                                    Bruce Cost, *Ginger East and West*

Notice all the cues that signal time: *has been, since the dawn, throughout the Middle Ages, until the sixteenth century, when,* and *recently.* All these cues help to unify the paragraph. In later sections we will study specific words and phrases that help to unify an essay by providing cues to its logic and organization. But unity is not a mechanical process of arranging sentences in a certain order according to some formula. Rather, unity is a balance of all the factors in a piece of writing. It comes with practice and experience.

The next chapter will look closely at the elements of a paragraph and how they can help you achieve unity during revision.

Reading and Revising Assignments ■

1. Review the suggestions that this section made about an essay's organization. Then, look over a few of the passages written by students or professional writers in this book. Analyze the organization of at least one of the passages, and discuss your findings in small groups. What have you learned about organization that you can apply to your own draft?

2. Look over your draft again, and focus on its organization. Are your ideas clear and logical? Did you provide transitions to help readers understand how one idea relates to the next? In the margin of your draft, jot down some notes about how you can improve the organization or strengthen transitions when you revise.

3. Exchange your draft with a classmate. Using Worksheet 13 in the Appendix at the end of the book, each of you should answer the questions about each other's organization and transitions. Consider your classmate's answers when you revise your essay later.

Writing Assignment ■

Review the topics covered in this chapter. What did you learn about revising that you didn't know before? On the left-hand side of your journal, summarize what you learned about revision as it relates to your audience, your main idea, and your essay's organization. Then, on the right-hand side of your journal, make notes to help you apply this information when you revise your own draft.

chapter 5

Developing Your Ideas

In Chapter 4 we looked at the broad things a writer must consider during revision—the audience, the essay's main idea, and its organization. At this point in the revision process, you probably know what you want to say, how you want to say it, and to whom you want to say it.

Now, in this chapter, you'll examine your revised draft even more closely. By looking carefully at each paragraph and by working further on your topic sentences, examples, and details, you will improve the unity of your essay and make its ideas more interesting (and more effective) for your readers.

The Paragraph

A **paragraph** is a way to signal small beginnings and endings to readers. Paragraphs organize your ideas into logical, manageable units. Flip open any page in this book and begin reading. Most likely, your eye led you to the beginning of a paragraph, because you are used to thinking of the indented space as a place to start. Imagine having to wade through pages and pages of type with no breaks!

The symbol for a paragraph [¶] was originally a punctuation mark, just like a comma or a period. It was used to mark a break in the flow of writing, first in handwritten manuscripts, and then in the early years of printing (until around the middle of the seventeenth century). Today, we don't use this symbol. Instead, we indicate a paragraph by indenting the first word. On a typewriter, we indent five spaces from the left, but printed books often indent fewer spaces.

You can use paragraphs to control the way your readers start, stop, and concentrate on the ideas in your writing. Each paragraph groups related ideas into a unit, and there is no formula to determine how long a paragraph should be. A paragraph may be one word long or may cover several pages, depending on the effect a writer wants to create.

You may have noticed that advertising often uses many short paragraphs to catch our attention and control how we read. Paragraphs are strong signals in such ads. Read the following advertisement, and notice how the paragraphs make you start and stop as you read:

> Hearing the cheers of the gallery can be music to a golfer's ears. I can hear them much better now, since I got help for a hearing loss.
>
> You know, nearly 20 million Americans with hearing problems needlessly miss life's precious sounds. Why needlessly? Because virtually all of them can *now* be helped—medically, surgically, or like me, with hearing aids.
>
> If you suspect a hearing loss, or thought nothing could be done about it, ask your family doctor who can guide you. Thanks to significant advances in the hearing field, there are many hearing health care professionals who can help you.
>
> So if you or someone you love doesn't hear well, arrange for a hearing test today. For hearing help information, call toll-free Hearing HelpLine at 800/ EAR WELL.
>
> Because you should *hear* what you're missing!
>
> Reproduced with the permission of the Better
> Hearing Institute, Washington, D.C.

Newspaper paragraphs also tend to be very short, partly because short paragraphs are easier to read in narrow columns of type. In the following introduction to an article in *The Wall Street Journal*, notice how each paragraph makes a fresh start:

> One hand on the steering wheel, Trudi Richards hangs out the window of her four-wheel-drive Daihatsu, peering at animal tracks in the Tasmanian soil.
>
> As the vehicle lurches to a halt in front of a mud patch, she jumps out, drops to a crouch, and stalks—bent double—through the damp woods. "Nothing but wombat prints," she mutters. "I think we can conclude that a tiger didn't pass this way last night."
>
> Actually Miss Richards is well aware that a Tasmanian tiger probably hasn't passed this way in 50 years. The species is thought to have become extinct in the 1930s. But tiger searchers, such as Miss Richards, don't let technicalities get in their way.
>
> "Australians Have a Devil of a Time Tracking
> (Extinct) Tasmanian Tiger"

The short paragraphs in advertising and newspapers make material seem interesting and easy to understand. But long paragraphs also can be effective. When a writer wants to link a lot of closely related details, a single long paragraph may be the best solution. (Look ahead at the next three examples to see how effective a long paragraph can be in grouping details.)

As you create a first draft, you may not be indenting and thinking about paragraphs at all. In fact, paragraphing is really part of the revision process, not part of drafting. As groups of related material become clear, during revision you may decide to break long paragraphs into smaller ones, or to combine short paragraphs into a single one. You also may need to add transitions or topic sentences to paragraphs; we'll discuss those aspects of revision in the sections that follow this assignment.

Reading and Revising Assignments ■

1. Select one of the longer examples in this book (that is, a passage which includes a number of paragraphs), and analyze the writer's use of paragraphs to group material. Do you think the passage would be better if it were a single long paragraph? Why or why not? In small groups, discuss how various writers use paragraphs. On the right-hand side of your journal, record what you have learned about paragraphs.

2. Analyze your own use of paragraphing in your draft. Do you have too many paragraphs? Too few? In the margin of your draft, jot down some notes for revising your use of paragraphs.

3. Exchange your draft with a classmate. Using Worksheet 12, each of you should answer the same questions about each other's use of paragraphs.

The Topic Sentence

Usually, a paragraph contains a **topic sentence**, which indicates its subject or main idea or provides a transition from one idea to the next. If writing can be viewed as a dance between writer and reader, it is clear that the writer leads, but always with the partner, the reader, in mind. The writer provides signals for the reader to follow. One very common signal for readers is the topic sentence; it is the glue that binds paragraphs together.

Topic sentences are used more often in nonfiction writing, such as essays and reports, than in fiction. Let us look at the use of topic sentences in various paragraphs (the topic sentences are underlined):

> The cowboy hat, originally part of the practical working garb of men who had to ride long distances in an extreme climate, has over the past century become heavy with symbolic meaning. Basically it suggests toughness and independence, but many subtle variations of this message are possible, depending among other things on the color and shape of the hat and its trimmings. The Hollywood convention White Hat = Good Guy, Black Hat = Bad Guy still operates: men who wish to appear as rebels or desperate characters prefer the

darker shades, and straight arrows the lighter ones. Ambiguous, subtle or se-
cretive types may favor grayed hues, while the more common tans and browns
that repeat the colors of Western landscape are worn (or thought to be worn)
by natural, down-to-earth men. Plain leather hatbands, no doubt on the principle of contagious magic, suggest the simple approach to life and physical energy of the beef cattle to which the leather once belonged; expensive hand-
tooled bands and decorations of silver and feathers imply a high-flying life style
and an extensive bank account. The shape of the Western hat is also a form of
communication. In general, the higher the crown, the higher the self-esteem of
the wearer; the wider the brim, the closer his connection to the realities of
outdoor life on the Western plains, where shelter from sun, rain, dust and wind
are of primary importance.

Alison Lurie, *The Language of Clothes*

In this example, the topic sentence points clearly to the subject matter of
the whole paragraph. The topic sentence lets readers anticipate what will come
next. But sometimes the topic sentence can appear in the middle of a paragraph,
as in the following example:

The total number of languages in the world is large: say between 4,000
and 4,500. But, considering the total world population of 4 billion and 19
million, this seems to be a small number. If we divide this number by 4,500
languages, we have approximately one language for every 893,111 people,
but that is not exactly how human languages are distributed. There are only
five languages that can claim a really large number of speakers, namely, Chinese (811 million), English (363 million), Hindi-Urdu (271 million), Russian
(240 million), and Spanish (219 million). Of these languages, only English can
claim to have attained the enviable position of a more or less universal language. A universal language is one which, in its various forms and functions, is
used by a large portion of the human population for easy communication between peoples of diverse cultural and language backgrounds. Esperanto is an
example of a man-made, artificial international language. Other examples are
Novial, Occidental, Interlingua, Volapük, and Ido.

Braj B. Kachru, "American Englishes and Other Englishes"

Why would a writer put the topic sentence anywhere except at the beginning of a paragraph? In this case, the writer helps readers fully appreciate that
English has the status of a universal language. He builds up to his main point in
the topic sentence by first listing statistics about other languages and the number
of speakers. By the time we learn that only English can claim to be a universal
language, we realize how important that fact is.

In the next example, the writer organizes his paragraph by time, and so the
main point comes last, at the end of the piece:

Late Friday morning, September 28, King addressed the convention's final session from the stage of the L. R. Hall Auditorium. During his remarks, a young white man who had been sitting in the sixth row rose suddenly and approached King. Without warning, the man punched King in the face. A shocked stillness came over the crowd, which watched in amazement as King stood his ground and accepted several blows. As one eyewitness described it, King made no move to strike back or turn away. Instead, he looked at his assailant and spoke calmly to him. Within seconds, several people pulled the attacker away. While others led the crowd in song, King and his colleagues spoke with the assailant at the rear of the stage. Then King returned to the podium to tell the audience that the man, Roy James, was a twenty-four-year-old member of the Nazi party from Arlington, Virginia. King said he would not press charges against him. Birmingham police arrived and insisted that the city would press charges even if King chose not to. Without delay, James was hustled before a local court Judge, convicted of assault, and sentenced to thirty days in jail and a $25 fine. Birmingham's segregationist mayor, Art Hanes, visited the courtroom to tell James to his face never again to set foot in Birmingham. The entire incident, from assault to sentencing, took barely four hours. It left most onlookers stunned and impressed by King's lack of fear when confronted by direct physical violence.

David Garrow, *Bearing the Cross*

Notice that the sentence "Without warning, the man punched King in the face" comes early in the paragraph; this sentence tells us what *happened*. But the writer is more interested in telling readers the *effects* of what happened. By reporting the events in the order they happened, Garrow prepares readers to understand King's philosophy of nonviolence.

Some paragraphs do not have topic sentences. The following description of a concert by B.B. King in the Soviet Union has no real topic sentence, although the last part of the last sentence moves toward being one. Nevertheless, we have no trouble understanding what the author wants to say:

A slick-haired Soviet M.C. announced B.B. King ("A great Negritanski musician"), and then King was onstage with his well known guitar—Lucille—and a ten-man ensemble. As King and the ensemble swung into "Why I Sing the Blues," one could sense the puzzlement of the Soviet audience. "Negro" music to them meant jazz or spirituals, but this was something else. Also, there was the question of response. B.B. King is a great, warm presence when he performs, and he asks his audience to pour themselves out to him in return. King teases his audiences, urging them to clap along, to whistle, to hoot their appreciation, like the congregations in the Southern churches in which he grew up. But to Russians, such behavior suggests a lack of culture and an almost frightening disorder. Though obviously impressed the audience at first kept a respectful silence during the numbers, as it might at the symphony. (Only the foreigners shouted and stomped out the beat; we found the Russians around us staring at us open-mouthed.) Then King played an irresistible riff, stopped and leaned toward the audience with his hand cupped to his ear. The audience caught on and began to clap. King changed the beat, and waited for the audience to catch up. Then he changed it again. Soon the whole place was clapping along to "Get off My Back, Woman," and there were even a few timid shouts and whistles. King, who carried the blues to Europe, Africa, and the Far East, had broken the ice one more time.

Andrea Lee, *Russian Journal*

Reading and Revising Assignments   ■

1.   Compare some of the longer passages (having several paragraphs) and some of the single-paragraph passages included in this book. In small groups, discuss how various writers used their topic sentences. On the right-hand side of your journal, record what you learned about topic sentences.

2.   Analyze how you used topic sentences in your draft. Do your paragraphs have topic sentences? If you don't have many topic sentences, do you think you should add them to some of the paragraphs? Do you have paragraphs that act as transitions to move readers from one idea to the next? If not, do you see places where you could use them? In the margin of your draft, jot down some notes for revising your use of topic sentences.

3.   Exchange your draft with a classmate. Using Worksheet 12, each of you should answer the same questions about each other's use of topic sentences.

Details and Examples

In any essay, details and examples will help you (1) clarify your general ideas, (2) explain the nature or character of something, and (3) support your opinions. By illustrating your points with examples, you give readers specific ideas or pictures for them to visualize.

Writers use examples to support their claims or assertions, to illustrate abstract ideas and make them more real, and to draw readers into a subject. For instance, if you and a friend were talking about violence in films, you could explain your points better if you named some films and specific scenes that you considered violent. To say that your roommate is absent minded is not as believable (or as interesting) as giving an example to prove it—such as the time she thought she had lost her contact lenses, but they were actually in her eyes! In writing, especially, illustrations like these catch your readers' interest and help them to understand your point.

In the following passage, notice how the examples are used to support the topic sentence (underlined):

Although American women have never been officially involved in combat, a surprising number of them have distinguished themselves in wartime. Deborah Sampson Gannett disguised herself as a man, enlisted in the Continental Army, and fought in several engagements before her true sex was discovered. Bridget Divers, wife of a Civil War private in the First Michigan Cavalry, often rode with the men on scouting and raiding expeditions. Once, traveling with a wagon train that was attacked by Confederate cavalry, she took command of the poorly armed teamsters and fought off the rebel assault. Jacqueline Cochran ferried planes to the U.S. Eighth Air Force in England during World War II.

Margaret Truman, *Women of Courage*

The three examples of specific women in wartime not only help persuade us that the topic sentence is true, but they also allow us to translate the abstract idea (women doing heroic deeds in wartime) into specific terms that we picture as real. The passage is much more interesting because we can imagine Deborah Sampson Gannett disguising herself as a man in order to fight, or Bridget Divers taking command in a battle. Instead of dry, abstract facts, the writer uses examples to make the point more interesting and more memorable.

Consider another passage:

Dedication and commitment played a major part on our wrestling team. For example, we made a promise to practice together at certain times, and there were no exceptions. If someone would come late to practice or not come at all, he would have to do extra work. One time, a guy on our team missed two practices in a row. He had to run five extra miles and wrestle the whole team after practice.

Daniel Fabbri, student

In his first draft, Daniel had used no examples to illustrate what he meant by dedication and commitment. But these abstract terms mean different things to different people, and only Daniel could say what they meant to his wrestling team. When he revised his draft, he included examples that readers could picture and understand.

Examples are very useful when your topic is difficult to understand or is something abstract that you cannot point to; it just exists as an idea. A good lecturer, for example, always tries to connect the subject to something specific and concrete that listeners can follow—we remember better when we can picture something concrete.

The following paragraph is missing some sentences. See whether you can understand it:

> When we hear or look at a display of speech or writing, the dimension we are most conscious of is a horizontal one—the stream of time in speech, the span of time in writing. Almost everything that we put in a message has to go to the right or left of something else. Much that happens when a language changes is due to collisions or confusions along this course. Changes in meaning may worm their way into such a change in form.

The passage is hard to follow, isn't it? Now read the entire paragraph, with the author's examples underlined:

> When we hear or look at a display of speech or writing, the dimension we are most conscious of is a horizontal one—the stream of time in speech, the span of time in writing. Almost everything that we put in a message has to go to the right or left of something else. There is no "above" or "below," "behind" or in "front." Much that happens when a language changes is due to collisions or confusions along this course. It may be only a lapse, as when a speaker, intending to say *discussing shortly*, says *discushing*, bringing a sound that belongs to the right over to the left. Or it may be permanent, as in *horseshoe*, in which everybody makes the *s* of the first element like the *sh* of the second. Changes in meaning may worm their way into such a change in form. For example, speakers distinguish *got to* "had the privilege of" and *got to* "be under obligation to" by using the unchanged form for the first meaning and a changed one for the second: *I got to get off, I gotta get off.*
>
> Dwight Bolinger, "Some Traits of Language"

This difficult passage about language would be nearly impossible to follow without the examples, which help clarify the material. Even if a reader has difficulty with the abstract ideas in the passage, at least the examples of those ideas can be understood.

Reading and Writing Assignments   ■

1. In a textbook for another class, find some examples of abstract ideas that you have to understand. Did the writer include some examples to nail the point down? If not, what kind of help do you think the author could have given you? In small groups, discuss the textbook passages you have found, and say whether or not the author has helped you to understand the abstract ideas.

2. Perhaps you can recognize an abstract idea in someone else's writing but have trouble knowing when *your* writing is too abstract. It is easy to realize in a philosophy class that "soul" and "mind" are abstract concepts. But do you see that your own experiences and ideas may be abstract to other people?

Examine one of your drafts, and look for any abstract ideas that your readers may not understand. What examples can you add during revision to make your point more interesting and more clear? In the margin of your draft, make notes about examples you can add during revision.

3. On the left-hand side of your journal, write a short entry that uses examples to illustrate something abstract about yourself. For instance, if your topic sentence says that you are very "resourceful," your examples should show that you can take care of yourself in an emergency. Telling about how you got lost in the woods on a camping trip, and how you were the only one who kept your head, would be more effective than just stating that you are good in a crisis. Make sure that your examples prove your point.

Examples and Your Topic Sentence

After you develop a main idea in a draft, then you can decide what examples or details best illustrate your point. Be careful not to add examples for their own sake, because that just distracts readers from your main point. For instance, in an essay about the causes of divorce, you might use specific examples of people you know who have gone through a divorce. But if you add details about the children of divorce, or about the effects of divorce on the whole family, you no longer would be writing about the causes of divorce. Your examples would steer readers *away* from your main point.

As you probably realize by now, there is a strong connection between a topic sentence and the examples that support it. Examples are meaningless if they do not illustrate your point, and a topic sentence is not very helpful if it is not developed in some way. Read the following passage, and notice how each example relates to the topic sentence (underlined):

The evolution of predominantly Black urban areas in northern cities is traceable by an examination of the migratory patterns of Blacks from southern regions of the United States. From the 1790s to the early 1900s, 90 percent of the Black population lived in the South. In 1910, 89 percent continued to live in the South, but the percentage began to decrease in each succeeding decade to 85 percent in 1920, 77 percent in 1940, and 60 percent in 1960. Precise causes of the migration of Blacks to the North are unknown; however, certain social and economic factors influenced the movement. The first was the severe devastation of southern cotton by the boll weevil following on a series of bad crop years. The second was the development of labor needs in factories of the North. With the onset of World War I the immigration of Europeans to the United States was abruptly curtailed. Industry, which previously provided hundreds of thousands of jobs each year for new immigrants, now had its labor supply curtailed during a period of great demand for labor. Many firms sent recruiters to the South to encourage Blacks to come North. Many Black southerners who migrated North later encouraged friends and relatives to join them, and the move became easier with someone at the other end to help find a job and a place to live. After World War I, immigration from Europe resumed, only to be curtailed permanently by restrictive legislation in the early 1920s. Black Americans then established a secure position in the northern industrial scene.

Elizabeth Whatley, Language Among Black Americans

This paragraph is quite long, but it starts out solidly with a strong topic sentence. After that, supporting examples make up most of the paragraph, and a strong concluding sentence wraps up the whole thing. Now examine the first sentence more closely:

The evolution of predominantly Black urban areas in northern cities [*subject*] is traceable by an examination of the migratory patterns of Blacks from southern regions of the United States [*main idea about the subject*].

This topic sentence accomplishes two purposes. First, it states the subject: the development of black urban areas in northern cities. Second, it tells us that the writer can trace why blacks have migrated into these areas. We can anticipate what kind of information the paragraph will include.

The following passage, by a student writer, clearly illustrates how a topic sentence (underlined) and examples are related in a well-written paragraph:

The first couple of days the kitchen remained decent and usable; if students cooked themselves a meal they cleaned up their mess. <u>As the days went by, the kitchen began to look as if a cooking tornado had passed through and dropped off all of its leftover debris.</u> The trashcans were overflowing with empty containers and excess food, and the stove and countertops looked as if a group of children had been fingerpainting with grease and food droppings. Furthermore, the smell of old and soured food was overwhelming when you walked down the hall to your room or to the bathroom. The kitchen had become a haven for bugs and flies; if they weren't on the stove and countertops or buzzing around the trashcans, they were lurking on the walls just waiting for their time to snack.

Lynkita Roberts, student

The writer first leads readers into her subject by saying that the kitchen started out clean. Then she moves into her main point by saying how dirty the kitchen became. She follows that topic sentence with specific examples of the mess in the kitchen. Readers can visualize the overflowing garbage cans and the food everywhere, and perhaps they can even summon up a memory of a stale-smelling kitchen. The examples prove the writer's point and also convey her disgust.

Here is another passage in which the topic sentence is followed by examples:

> There are narrow margins for success and failure here because a parent rewarding dependence is seen as loving whereas his consistent training for independence can be perceived as rejection. For example, when a child comes home and says, "Somebody hit me!" the mother who responds with "Oh, my poor dear" fosters dependence, and the mother who says "Who hit first?" may be fostering guilt, and the mother who says "What happened?" and hasn't taken sides may be fostering independence.
>
> Judith Bardwick, *Psychology of Women: A Study of Bio-Cultural Conflicts*

In the last three passages that show the connection between topic sentences and examples, notice that the topic sentence is at the beginning of each paragraph. We saw earlier, however, that the topic sentence may come in the middle or at the end of a paragraph. Wherever the writer puts it, the supporting examples must be connected to it—otherwise, they belong in a different paragraph. Look at how easily we can rewrite the last passage and move the topic sentence to the end; but also notice that the examples still support the topic sentence:

> When a child comes home and says, "Somebody hit me!" the mother who responds with "Oh, my poor dear" fosters dependence, and the mother who says "Who hit first?" may be fostering guilt, and the mother who says "What happened?" and hasn't taken sides may be fostering independence. *Thus* there are narrow margins for success and failure here because a parent rewarding dependence is seen as loving whereas his consistent training for independence can be perceived as rejection.

Local (Specific) Detail

Cat.

Did you think of a cat when you read the word above? What did the cat look like? How do you know that the cat you thought of is the same cat that the writer thought of? You have your own idea of *cat*—or maybe no idea at all, if you don't think in pictures. In any case, without specific details, you cannot think of the exact cat that the writer had in mind. As a result, the "passage" has not communicated much.

In Chapter 3 we considered how the audience shapes our writing. Now we'll explore how writers shape the audience's responses by supplying sensory details. *Sensory* details appeal to our senses, allowing us to visualize something, or even to imagine a texture, a smell, a taste, or a sound. As we continue to discuss using examples to clarify our writing, we'll look closely at **local**, or

specific, **detail**—detail that leaves no doubt about what the writer wanted the reader to "see."

Let's begin by looking at how local detail helps a writer control the writing situation. Read the following sentence:

> The cat lay in the sun.

Now compare these sentences:

> The tabby sprawled in the late afternoon sun.

> The yellow tiger, Shasta, curled up on the chair, basking in the summer sun.

> The Siamese kitten inched his way across the couch, trying to capture every bit of the morning sun.

Each of these three sentences represents a different choice and provides a vivid picture of the cat. The abstract idea of *cat* becomes more concrete with each detail. Because the writer controls the language, the writer also controls how readers will picture the cat. Of course, there are also situations where the first option—"The cat lay in the sun"—would be most suitable.

Here is how one student revised her first draft in order to include local detail:

First draft
> Since I had eaten all the spaghetti in the house, I decided to make frozen fried chicken—the closest thing to a real meal I could think of.

Revised draft
> Having exhausted my supply of Franco-American, the following evening I decided to cook a real meal—frozen fried chicken. Getting "the child-resistant seal" off the box of Banquet's frozen chicken parts was a real challenge.
>
> Barbara Lesane, student

The revised passage is more specific, mentioning *Franco-American* instead of simply *spaghetti*, and *child-resistant seal* instead of *hard-to-open package*. Of course, there are no child-resistant seals on frozen foods, but the writer wanted to make it clear that she is *totally* helpless in the kitchen. Not only is a package of frozen chicken quite a treat, it is also difficult for her to handle.

Here is another example of how local detail can enliven writing:

First draft
> About five minutes later the lights were shut off, and I became aware of how smoky and dusty it was. The pushing got worse when the concert began, and it got very crowded.

Revised draft

About five minutes later the lights were shut off, and I became aware of the thick layer of cigarette smoke and stage dust that floated above the heads of everyone who stood on the floor of the coliseum. The pushing got worse when the concert began, and I felt like a slimy sardine among all of the tightly packed bodies of enthusiastic people.

Dawn Gibson, student

Notice how particular words and phrases like "tightly packed" and "thick layer of cigarette smoke" help make the scene easy to imagine. Anyone who has been to a rock concert may nod in recognition; readers who have never had that experience should be able to imagine it better. And any reader should be able to imagine feeling "like a slimy sardine."

In adding local detail to your own writing, keep in mind that details should support your main idea just as examples should; they both give readers a deeper understanding of the writer's views.

Writing that lacks details is often too abstract to interest readers much. To illustrate, we'll look at part of an essay by a student who wanted to write about love but who hadn't narrowed the topic down. The writer had not fully considered how abstract the concept of love is, and how it differs from person to person. In this introduction to the paper, he tried to define what love is:

Love is a mixture of feelings and emotions a person has inside for another person or thing. Love is something that two people have for each other. It is a special feeling.

Although the definition sounds right, it is much too vague. In fact, watch what we can do to it:

Hate is a mixture of feelings and emotions a person has inside for another person or thing.

Anger is a mixture of feelings and emotions a person has inside for another person or thing.

So the definition really says almost nothing. The writer goes on:

Love is something that two people have for each other. It is a special feeling.

Again, the writer has said very little, because readers can fill in anything:

Love is something that lovers/sisters/friends have for each other. It is a special feeling.

At this point, readers know what the essay is about, but they don't know anything about the writer's experiences of love, or about the point of the essay. No doubt a concept like love is difficult to define, even for professional writers. Two of them try, in the next passage, and they point to the problem in a humorous way:

> The word "love" is used loosely by writers, and they know it. Furthermore, the word "love" is accepted loosely by readers, and *they* know it. There are many kinds of love, but for the purposes of this article I shall confine my discussion to the usual hazy interpretation: the strange bewilderment that overtakes one person on account of another person. Thus, when I say love in this article, you will take it to mean *the pleasant confusion we know exists.* When I say passion, I *mean* passion.
>
> James Thurber and E. B. White, *Is Sex Necessary?*

Thurber and White make an important point about abstract ideas. Readers and writers often do agree to leave such things vague, knowing that they can be understood only within the context of each person's experience. But that is the challenge of writing—and the pleasure of reading—to try to share our worlds and understand each other's experiences. Personal details help us to do that.

Feeling discouraged, our student writer tries again:

> The love of a sister [The writer decides to limit the topic.] is a special kind [Meaning?] that creates security [The reader begins to pay attention.] and is protective. Sisterly love creates [Repeats the verb—how boring] a bond that brings happiness [Uses an abstract word to describe an abstract word—now the reader is lost] and true understanding. For example, [Oh, good—some real stuff] when my sister broke off her engagement, I understood why. [Is that all? No explanation? The reader is disappointed!]

Now, the writer seems confused. Does he want to write about how he feels about his sister, or about how she feels about him? Notice that his subject is "the love of a sister," but his example is about *his* response to *her* broken engagement. By now, as you might imagine, the student wants to give up. But he revises one more time:

> The love of an older brother toward a sister is protective. [OK, now it's clear.] For example [Will the reader be disappointed again?] when we were in grade school together, I always made sure she got to her classroom on time. [Well?] I would meet her after school so that she would not get lost on the way home. [The reader begins to get interested.] Actually, we only lived around the block from school! [A surprise!]
>
> Connor Jennings, student

The writer has finally found a way to explain his particular understanding of love by using an example that shows it, rather than simply telling readers about it. He gained control of the writing situation by providing details that led readers in a very specific direction.

Following are three versions of an introduction to a student essay. Notice that each revision gets more vivid:

First draft

I once went to a party, and the guy I was dating had invited his old girlfriend from another school and all her friends. John didn't know how much this girl hated me until she poured beer down my back, and my friends and I started a fight. We had to hide up on a store roof to get away from those girls!

Second draft

I was nervous about attending my boyfriend John's party because his old girlfriend was going to be there. I had never told him about the time she tried to run me over with her car. What would she pull this time in her territory among her friends? I found out when she poured beer "accidentally" down my back.

Third draft

All I felt was a cold stream down my back. At first, I didn't know what it was, but the smell soon told me that beer was dripping off my back, into my jeans, and over my shoes. What had happened? I was at my boyfriend's house for a party, and someone had dumped a beer all over me. I whirled around, and there Anita stood—my boyfriend John's ex-girlfriend and my arch-enemy. She smiled in triumph at my shock and embarrassment.

Paula Lesack, student

With each revision the writer adds local detail, and in the third draft she turns the sequence of events around so that we begin with the event itself.

Reading and Revising Assignments

1.   Look over some of the reading passages in this book. In small groups, discuss how various writers use examples and local detail to connect with readers. On the right-hand side of your journal, record what you have learned about using examples.

2.   Analyze your draft to see how you use examples and local detail. Do you use too many examples or too much detail? Not enough? In the margin of your draft, jot down some notes to help you revise your use of examples.

3.   Exchange your draft with a classmate. Using Worksheet 14, each of you should answer the same questions about each other's use of examples and details.

part **three**

Your Purposes for Writing

Writing to Express Yourself
Writing to Inform
Writing to Persuade

Introduction

Most writers don't plan out the kind of writing they do. They don't sit down at their computers and say, "Let's see—I haven't written a really good persuasive essay in a while." Instead, they think about their *purpose* for writing—what they want to accomplish. For example, a writer says, "If I want to get the city to improve the trash pickup in my neighborhood, how should I go about it?"

You already have found many purposes for writing: to apply for college or a job, to contact an old friend who has moved away, to report on laboratory research, to complain to your landlord, to give directions to a party, to express your feelings in a poem, to convey your knowledge, to organize your ideas, and to find out what you think. Whatever your purpose, you know that each writing task asks you to do something different. (Your letter to apply for a job is not the same as one you would write to a friend.) You know that there is no one formula for writing.

Chances are, if you listed all your purposes for writing, they would fall into one or more of these three categories:

1. To *express* yourself in an imaginative or personal way

2. To *inform* someone or to explain something

3. To *persuade* someone to agree with you

During the planning stages of writing, you might wonder what comes first—the purpose for writing or the subject. Often the answer isn't very clear; nor should it be.

Suppose a writer wants to describe his or her experience growing up in a small town. The subject then is "life in a small town." A number of choices follow. The writer could tell a humorous story about what life is like when everyone knows each other, or could describe what the main street looks like (all three blocks of it). In this case, the purpose would be to express a point of view or to convey personal memories. But the writer also might want to inform readers about how small-town life is disappearing or about people's values in a small town. The writer also might want to persuade readers to consider moving to a small town, because they would enjoy the way of life.

A writer's purposes, then, often overlap. In this example, an entertaining account of small-town life would certainly contain some information; and an explanation of people's values in a small town might be a very persuasive argument for moving to such a place. Chapters 6, 7, and 8 will help you look closely at a writer's three main purposes: to express, to inform, and to persuade.

Writing Assignment   ■

What purposes for writing have you had over the years? What other purposes for writing are you likely to have in the future, in college or on the job? On the left-hand side of your journal, list the types of writing you have already had to do; on the right-hand side, list the new kinds of writing you expect to do.

The Essay

Once you have a subject and a purpose for writing, then you need to decide on the *form* you should use—how the writing should look to fit your subject and purpose. Sometimes a poem is the best form; sometimes a diary entry or a report or an essay is the form your writing should take. So far, most of your writing has been journal entries. Now you will focus on the essay.

The essay form has been stretched and pounded and squeezed into a number of shapes over the years. In general, though, an **essay** is a brief prose discussion of a topic. A writer might examine the topic thoroughly in an essay, or might investigate only parts of the topic, to explore it.

One way to define the essay is to describe its overall structure: Most essays have an introduction, a discussion, and a conclusion. To be more exact, an essay has an introduction that states a main idea and outlines supporting facts or arguments; a transition to the discussion of facts and examples; and then a transition to the writer's conclusion.

This basic structure can be found in an enormous variety of essays. A writer may use it in a letter; a narrative of personal experiences; a description; a critique of a film, book, or restaurant; an ongoing column in a newspaper; an editorial or an article in a magazine; a critical discussion in an academic journal; a sermon; a lecture; and so on.

Beyond all the choices open to the writer of an essay, there is also the choice of how formal or informal to be. A formal essay is characterized by seriousness, an apparent logical organization, and language that is more appropriate to writing than to speech. In contrast, an informal essay is quite relaxed in language, style, and structure, and it often focuses on personal experiences.

Like a writer's purposes, the issue of formality depends a good deal on the topic and the intended audience. Unfortunately, there are no hard-and-fast rules to guide you in all situations. Each writing task calls on you to think about your purpose, your topic, and your audience. The chapters that follow will help you to consider your options as a writer.

Reading and Writing Assignment

Look over the essays at the ends of Chapters 6, 7, and 8 to get a sense of the various forms an essay can take. Which essays are formal? Which are informal? How can you tell?

Examine your other textbooks and the magazines or newspapers that you read regularly. How many different kinds of essays do they include?

Bring the most interesting essay you find to class. Be prepared to say what kind of essay it is, how formal it is, and what you think the writer's purpose is.

In your journal, make notes about what you have learned about the essay as a form of writing.

chapter **6** ■

Writing to Express Yourself

What Is Expressive Writing?

Perhaps the chief characteristic of **expressive writing** is the sense of self. The writer freely expresses his or her personal recollections, ideas, and observations.

Examples of expressive writing include letters, diaries, journals, auto-biographies, and prayers. (An *autobiography* is the story of one's own life; a *biography* is the story of someone else's life.) A narrative or a description is also usually expressive, since the story teller or observer puts it into his or her own words.

Of course, all writing begins with an individual. But expressive writing *demands* that one begin with the self—an *I*. (How else would one write letters or a journal except to use the first person?) Keep in mind that a label like *expressive writing* is a convenience; it allows us to group together certain kinds of writing that share common features. With expressive writing, the most common feature is *the sense of the writer's self.*

Expressive writing has some connections with an oral tradition, which you already know and use. For example, your daily conversation is a long personal narrative addressed to many different audiences. Your conversation is an oral expression of your personal thoughts and feelings.

You tell *anecdotes* (short, amusing or interesting stories) about yourself and your family and friends all the time. Family life is full of such stories. By retelling the family's history and past events—such as what old Uncle Fred did at cousin Amanda's wedding that was so embarrassing—we create continuity from one generation to the next. Family stories also may include friends: "Re-member that girl your brother Angus brought to the senior prom?" Such a question may send insiders into peals of laughter. Stories like these become family legends.

Alex Haley's novel *Roots* is an example of expressive writing in which one man collected together all the oral narratives that his family had cherished and passed down through the generations. These family stories allowed Haley to trace his ancestors back to the time of slavery, and even earlier, to Africa.

Reading Assignment ■

Bring an example of expressive writing to class, and share it. Ask your classmates whether the example is purely expressive, or whether it contains elements of other kinds of writing—such as informative or persuasive writing.

Assignment ■

In class, pair up with another student, and, on audiotape or videotape, record a conversation about something that happened to you or to someone you know. Describe an incident that is humorous or sad, or that shows some strong emotion like fear or anger. It's important to talk to your partner, not to the recorder, so that your conversation sounds as natural as possible, and you will be more involved in telling the story because you have a real audience. Save the tape until later in this chapter for another assignment.

Reading Expressive Writing

Before we discuss how to read expressive writing, let's look at the results of little experiment. Read the following passage:

> I remember the train whistle. It blew with a rush of steam. Hurriedly, Daddyji drew my palms together within his own huge ones, said the Hindu farewell, "*Namaste*," lifted me through the compartment window, and handed me to Cousin Prakash.

One group of students, with no other information about the writer or the passage, came up with the following guesses about it:

1. The writer must be recalling something from childhood. The story is in the past tense, and the writer begins by saying, "I remember." And the child must be small—at least, the father's hands seemed "huge."

2. The story takes place in a train station, and the train is about to leave. There's the sound of a whistle, and the child is lifted "through the compartment window." We really can't tell who is coming or going. Probably the child is going, because why would the child (boy or girl?) be handed through the window? (Some students thought the father was going away.)

3. The story must be set in India, because the people speak Hindu. (But one student noted that this could be any city where Indian people lived, anywhere in the world.)

4. The time of the scene may be in the past—at least thirty (?) years ago. The whistle is a steam whistle, so maybe the train has a steam engine. (But maybe the setting is in part of the world that still has steam-powered trains. We're not sure about this.)

5. The event was probably an important occasion or parting, and that is why the writer recalls it at all. The child and father loved each other—it might have been a sad parting. (The class disagreed about this.) The child was going to live with Cousin Prakash.

Notice how short the passage is, compared with the amount of information the students gathered. Their reading of the passage raised all that speculation. What does this tell you about the act of reading?

In a way, reading is the making of meaning *beyond* the words on the page. As you already know from Chapter 2, reading involves active participation in a piece of writing; when we read, we call up our own experiences and knowledge. We certainly have knowledge about content—as in the students' remarks about train stations and goodbyes. But we also have knowledge about how texts work, about how words come together. When we read, our expectations about a piece of writing are first raised and then fulfilled.

The students made some very good guesses in interpreting the passage. The writer, Ved Mehta, has written several books about his childhood in India. The passage you just read is from the beginning of *Vedi,* the book recalling his years at a school for the blind in Bombay. The year was 1939. (He wasn't going to live with his cousin; Prakash was accompanying him on his journey to the school.)

As readers we may have our own reasons for wanting to read a particular meaning into something. "What do you mean by that?" we ask, expecting the words to mean more than they appear to, or something different from what they seem to mean. Have you ever tried to read between the lines of a letter you received? Perhaps you stared at the closing: "Love ya!" Hmm . . . real love? Or friendly, this-is-the-way-to-sign-a-letter love? Have you ever gotten an assignment back from a teacher with a mysterious comment on it? "Kathleen, you have a journalistic style." What is *that* supposed to mean? Is it good or bad to have a "journalistic style"?

Often, words *do* mean more than—or something else than—they appear to mean. For example, here is the beginning of a letter that Groucho Marx wrote to Katherine and Arthur Murray (of dancing studio fame):

May 23, 1951

Dear Katie and Arthur:

Your announcement that your daughter Jane is marrying an obscure quack named Heimlich on June 3rd saddened me considerably.

Did you feel a twinge of shock? How could anyone be so rude? Do you believe Groucho meant what he said? Why or why not? Read the next part of the letter:

I've had my *eye* on Jane for a long time and always hoped that some day you would wind up as my in-laws. Well, she made her choice—one that, I believe, she will ultimately regret.

Well? Continue reading:

With me, each day would have been 24 hours of gaiety and laughter; with Heimlich she will have a life of viruses, vaccines, surgical instruments and rubber gloves. Only time can decide whether she made the right decision.

Even though I am a bitter, disappointed and disillusioned man I send them both my heartiest congratulations.

Best,

Groucho

P.S. Note to Jane: See that all his nurses are ugly.

If you didn't know who Groucho Marx was, perhaps you believed him. Or, if you knew he was a comedian, maybe you were suspicious. In this case words *do* mean something other than they appear to mean. Groucho isn't saddened or disappointed; he feels just the opposite. But how does the reader know that?

Reading and Writing Assignment   ■

Study Groucho's letter, and record on the right-hand side of your journal all the clues that tell you its real meaning. Then, on the left-hand side of your journal, jot down your ideas about how humor works in the first place. How do you know if someone is serious or is making a joke? What happens when we misread someone's intention? Record an example of when you misread someone, or someone misread you. Share your example with the class.

Besides the clues in the letter itself, we know that Groucho is having fun with the Murrays because we depend on our life experiences and our reading experiences to help us figure out the meaning. From life we know that people usually don't write rude things to their friends—or, at least, that people aren't supposed to. From reading we know that words *can* mean many things. When we bring our experiences to bear on this letter, it makes sense.

Reading and Writing Assignment

Go to the library, and find a collection of letters written by someone famous who interests you. You might start with the Library of Congress heading for the individual; then look under "Correspondence." One helpful source is *American Letter Writers 1698-1943,* by Harry B. Weiss. Or, look the individual up in any biographical dictionary or encyclopedia to find information about collected and published letters. (See the librarian if you need help.)

On the right-hand side of your journal, write a page or so about what you discover about the person through the letters. Also record what you discover about letters as a form of writing. Be prepared to report your findings to the class.

Of course, not everyone writes letters like the one by Groucho Marx. Do you think that he and other famous people whose letters were published thought that other people might read them someday? Would your own letters be any different if you thought they might be published and read by strangers? In what ways would they be different or the same?

Many of the skills and techniques that we use to write personal letters are also used in writing an autobiography. For that reason we will turn next to autobiography as an example of expressive writing. (Remember that an *autobiography* is the story of one's own life; a *biography* is the story of someone else's life.)

Write Before Reading

Before you read the following passage from Malcolm X's autobiography, think about any autobiographies you have read. On the right-hand side of your journal, make a list of any that you remember. Then, on the left-hand side of your journal, jot down your ideas about the following questions:

1. Why would someone write an autobiography?

2. As a reader, what do you expect from an autobiography?

I saw that the best thing I could do was get hold of a dictionary—to study, to learn some words. . . .

riffling: shuffling
or thumbing
through the
pages of a book

I spent two days just riffling uncertainly through the dictionary's pages. I'd never realized so many words existed! I didn't know *which* words I needed to learn. Finally, just to start some kind of action, I began copying.

I suppose it was inevitable that as my word-base broadened, I could for the first time pick up a book and now begin to understand what the book was saying. Anyone who has read a great deal can imagine the new world that opened. Let me tell you something: from then until I left that prison, in every free moment I had, if I was not reading in the library, I was reading on my bunk. You couldn't have gotten me out of books with a wedge. . . . I had never been so truly free in my life.

Notice that Malcolm X addresses the reader directly ("Let me tell you something"). Although we cannot always tell if the writer of a journal or diary expects others to read it, we do expect the writer of an autobiography to be very conscious of his or her audience. In the passage above, Malcolm X describes how he acquired, as he says, a "homemade education" in prison. Do you think he is making a point about prison or about education when he says that?

We read autobiographies of famous people—celebrities, politicians, artists—with various amounts of curiosity and eagerness. Sometimes a person tells us more than we want to know—sometimes less.

We already looked at the beginning of the next passage, by Ved Mehta. Now, let's read it in a larger context:

Daddyji: The
ji is a mark of
respect; see
Mamaji below,
as well.

I remember the train whistle. It blew with a rush of steam. Hurriedly, Daddyji drew my palms together within his own huge ones, said the Hindu farewell, "*Namaste*," lifted me through the compartment window, and handed me to Cousin Prakash. "You are a man now," he said. This sentence of my father's was to become the beginning of my clear, conscious memory. In later years, I would recall it again and again, as if it were the injunction of my destiny. Cousin Prakash held me out just in time for Mamaji to kiss me before the train started moving.

What Daddyji would later remember about my going away in the train was the chill of the February day. Mamaji, however, would remember that she was oblivious of the cold as she held me tight against her chest at the station and felt my tears streaming down her neck; I seemed to sense that something awful was about to happen to me. "Vedi's not yet five," she said to Daddyji.

By comparing Malcolm X's and Ved Mehta's autobiographies, we can see that not all autobiographies, or personal reminiscences, are alike. We might expect this, of course, since no two people's *lives* are alike.

Sometimes writers write about particular experiences, rather than their lives as a whole. The next few examples show that kind of expressive writing.

Write Before Reading ■

Before reading the next excerpt, from war correspondent Michael Herr's narrative of his experiences in Viet Nam in 1967, use the right-hand side of your journal to record anything that you know about Viet Nam. Also write about how you learned what you know—from reading about it, from popular or documentary films, or from talking with someone who was there.

tracers: bullets that leave a smoky trail
flex guns: machine guns that can swing in any direction
Huey: HueyCobra, a high-speed helicopter

At 800 feet we knew we were being shot at. Something hit the underside of the chopper but did not penetrate it. They weren't firing tracers, but we saw the brilliant flickering blips of light below, and the pilot circled and came down very fast, working the button that released fire from the flex guns mounted on either side of the Huey. Every fifth round was a tracer, and they sailed out and down, incomparably graceful, closer and closer, until they met the tiny point of light coming from the jungle. The ground fire stopped, and we went on to land at Vinh Long, where the pilot yawned and said, "I think I'll go to bed early tonight and see if I can wake up with any enthusiasm for this war."

Michael Herr, *Dispatches*

Write After Reading ■

Do you think that the source of your knowledge about Viet Nam influenced how you read the passage? Discuss this question in class, and, on the left-hand side of your journal, record the results of the conversation.

Read the next passage:

opalescent: shimmering like an opal
asymmetry: not balanced, out of proportion

Ten days after having my breast removed, I went to my doctor's office to have the stitches taken out. This was my first journey out since coming home from the hospital, and I was truly looking forward to it. A friend had washed my hair for me and it was black and shining, with my new grey hairs glistening in the sun. Color was starting to come back into my face and around my eyes. I wore the most opalescent of my moonstones, and a single floating bird dangling from my right ear in the name of grand asymmetry. With an African kente-cloth tunic and new leather boots, I knew I looked fine, with that brave new-born security of a beautiful woman having come through a very hard time and being very glad to be alive.

I felt really good, within the limits of the grey mush that still persisted in my brain from the effects of the anesthesia.

When I walked into the doctor's office, I was really rather pleased with myself, all things considered, pleased with the way I felt, with my own flair, with my own style. The doctor's nurse, a charmingly bright and steady woman of about my own age who had always given me a feeling of no-nonsense support on my other visits, called me into the examining room. On the way, she asked me how I was feeling.

"Pretty good," I said, half-expecting her to make some comment about how good I looked.

prosthesis: an artificial replacement; in this case, an artificial breast

"You're not wearing a prosthesis," she said, a little anxiously, and not at all like a question.

"No," I said, thrown off my guard for a minute. "It really doesn't feel right," referring to the lambswool puff given to me by the Reach for Recovery volunteer in the hospital.

Usually supportive and understanding, the nurse now looked at me urgently and disapprovingly as she told me that even if it didn't look exactly right, it was "better than nothing," and that as soon as my stitches were out I could be fitted for a "real form."

"You will feel so much better with it on," she said. "And besides, we really like you to wear something, at least when you come in. Otherwise it's bad for the morale of the office."

I could hardly believe my ears! I was too outraged to speak then, but this was to be only the first such assault on my right to define and to claim my body.

Audre Lord, *The Cancer Journals*

Write After Reading ■

Serious illness is often a deeply emotional, difficult topic to write about. On the left-hand side of your journal, describe your response to Audre Lord's passage about breast cancer. What do you think of the way she handled the topic? What kind of person do you think she is, based on your reading?

The next example of expressive writing is a personal recollection that is almost like a fable. The author, Karen Fields, was collaborating with her ninety-year-old grandmother, Mamie Garvin Fields, on Mamie's memoirs of her life as a black schoolteacher in Charleston, South Carolina, during the Depression. In doing so, Karen got a unique opportunity to get in touch with memories of her own childhood:

One summer [my grandfather] took me out, day after day, for lessons on a new two-wheeler. The day I got the knack, I ran yelling into the house, "I DID it! I did it ALL BY MYSELF." Spoken like a true American, but the sentiment did not suit him: in Dixie nobody got by as an isolated individual, "all by myself," if they truly did anywhere else. My grandfather let me spout on until at last I noticed that he was taking no part. He let me know, without smiling, that it was sure very nice that I could ride now. But listen here, didn't my Uncle Al hold me up sometimes? Well, yes. And wasn't it my parents who bought the training wheels? Yes. Didn't other children try to show me what to do? Uh huh. So why did I want to say, now, "all by myself"? Grandfather Fields' tone of voice made the whole editorial comment on the facts just elicited. But just as the atmosphere became unbearably grave, he found a way to wink, twinkle, and dispel it. My grandfather always taught in that deliberate, methodical way.

Karen Fields, *Lemon Swamp and Other Places: A Carolina Memoir*

Reading and Writing Assignment

Go to the library, and find an autobiography written by someone famous who interests you. You might start with the Library of Congress heading for the individual under "Autobiography," or look in the card catalog under the person's name. *A Bibliography of American Autobiographies* (1961) and *American Autobiographies 1945–1980* are other sources. (See the librarian if you need help.)

On the right-hand side of your journal, write a page or so about what you discover about the person through his or her autobiography. Also record what you discover about autobiography as a form of writing. Be prepared to report your findings to the class.

An interview is often an exercise in gathering facts about a person. But sometimes people being interviewed will talk about themselves in the same way they might write about themselves in an autobiography. Following is an interview with Gabriel García Márquez, a Colombian writer who won the Nobel Prize for Literature in 1982. Notice how autobiographical—and expressive—the interview is:

Interviewer: How did you start writing?
García Márquez: By drawing. By drawing cartoons. Before I could read or write I used to draw comics at school and at home. The funny thing is that I now realize that when I was in high school I had the reputation of being a writer, though I never in fact wrote anything. If there was a pamphlet to be written or a letter of petition, I was the one to do it because I was supposedly the writer. When I entered college I happened to have a very good literary background in general, considerably above the average of my friends. At the university in Bogotá, I started making new friends and acquaintances, who introduced me to contemporary writers. One night a friend lent me a book of short stories by Franz Kafka. I went back to the pension where I was staying and began to read *The Metamorphosis.* The first line almost knocked me off

the bed. I was so surprised. The first line reads, "As Gregor Samsa awoke that morning from uneasy dreams, he found himself transformed in his bed into a gigantic insect. . . ." When I read the line I thought to myself that I didn't know anyone was allowed to write things like that. If I had known, I would have started writing a long time ago. So I immediately started writing short stories.

Writers at Work: The "Paris Review" Interviews

Good examples of expressive writing can also grow out of people's travel experiences. A few years ago, writer Paul Theroux decided to walk around the coast of England. Some of his reactions to what he saw and the people he met are expressed in this passage:

bobble-hats: woolen caps with pom-poms on top

Once, from behind a closed door, I heard an Englishwoman exclaim with real pleasure, "They are *funny*, the Yanks!" And I crept away and laughed to think that an English person was saying such a thing. And I thought: They wallpaper their ceilings! They put little knitted bobble-hats on their soft-boiled eggs to keep them warm! They don't give you bags in supermarkets! They say sorry when you step on their toes! Their government makes them get a hundred-dollar license every year for watching television! They issue drivers' licenses that are valid for thirty or forty years—mine expires in the year 2011! They charge you for matches when you buy cigarettes! They smoke on buses! They drive on the left! They spy for the Russians! They say "nigger" and "Jewboy" without flinching! They call their houses Holmleigh and Sparrow View! They sunbathe in their underwear! They don't say "You're welcome"! They still have milk bottles and milkmen, and junk-dealers with horse-drawn wagons! They love candy and Lucozade and leftovers called bubble-and-squeak! They live in Barking and Dorking and Shellow Bowells! They have amazing names, like Mr. Eatwell and Lady Inkpen and Major Twaddle and Miss Tosh! And they think *we're* funny?

Lucozade: a glucose drink like Gatorade

Paul Theroux, *Kingdom by the Sea*

Theroux counters the Englishwoman's statement that Americans are funny—in the sense of strange—by giving examples of how the English are equally funny, based on his own experiences with them. His examples are clear enough that readers get a good idea of the habits of the English (in Theroux's view). Notice that Theroux doesn't really discuss what happened to him. This example of expressive writing does not focus on the "I." Instead, the writer's observations and unique vision make the passage expressive.

In the next example the writer also begins with personal experience, but she moves entirely beyond the self. She never uses the word *I,* and yet the passage is expressive:

Shopping malls have become gathering places, places to socialize as well as shop, all over the country. People of all backgrounds meet on the wide avenue that runs the length of the mall. For example, a woman with a screaming baby in a stroller rolls right over the feet of a vice-president of a local bank, who in turn bumps into two punks with Mohawks and torn jeans, who admire the outdated polyester suit of a middle-aged widow, who stands in line for ice cream behind a gay man with three earrings. All these people are forced to listen to the lady playing a huge organ in the middle of the mall. They all must eat at MacDonald's, the only restaurant there, if they get hungry. And they all probably forgot where they parked.

Cynthia Wong, student

Even though this writer doesn't mention herself in describing the shopping mall, we know that she has observed the scene and has selected the details and words that describe what she experienced. The self in this passage is *implied*; readers know that the writer is expressing herself through her observations.

Observations about other people can also be expressive, as in the following description of President Lyndon Johnson's personality. Again, the writer does not say *I* and does not focus on the self, but the opinions and details that he records are expressive:

consummate: supremely skilled
kaleidoscopic: constantly shifting, like the patterns formed by mirrors and colored glass in a kaleidoscope
derision: scoffing, ridicule
fathomed: understood

Lyndon Baines Johnson, a consummate politician, was a kaleidoscopic personality, forever changing as he sought to dominate or persuade or placate or frighten his friends and foes. A gigantic figure whose extravagant moods matched his size, he could be cruel and kind, violent and gentle, petty, generous, cunning, naive, crude, candid, and frankly dishonest. He commanded the blind loyalty of his aides, some of whom worshipped him, and he sparked bitter derision or fierce hatred that he never quite fathomed. And he oscillated between peaks of confidence and depths of doubt, constantly accommodating his lofty ideals to the struggle for influence and authority. But his excesses reflected America's dramas during his lifetime, among them the dramas he himself created. Or, as Hubert Humphrey, the vice-president he both respected and abused, put it, "He was an All-American president. He was really the history of this country, with all of the turmoil, the bombast, the sentiments, the passions. It was all there. All in one man."

Stanley Karnow, *Vietnam: A History*

As the last two passages show clearly, expressive writing sometimes has much in common with fiction, which is writing from the imagination rather than from history or real life. Poems, plays, short stories, novels, and screenplays are common forms of fiction.

For one thing, the goals of a fiction writer and of a nonfiction writer (a diarist, say) may be similar. Both may want to discover something about themselves or the world, and they understand that writing is a way to do so. Both fiction and nonfiction (such as autobiographies and narratives) are valid ways to express truth about human nature and human experience. After all, the stuff of both fiction and nonfiction is always rooted in human experience—in the writer's experience.

Second, whether writers explore their personal experiences or make things up, they borrow ideas from wherever they can. In a novel a fiction writer may invent diaries and letters and treat them as real. A screenwriter may begin a story by insisting that it is true. A poet may write a poem about a real person or event. On the other hand, a diarist or a letter writer might do so as though all the world were looking on, and the writer's consciousness of an audience might make her or him much more careful or more poetic. For the same reason, in writing an autobiography one may record events in the same sort of order as the plot of a novel—selecting and arranging incidents into a unified whole. Life, as you know, is never as neat as that. But sometimes that act of writing about one's life might help a writer to give it order and meaning.

Reading and Writing Assignment ■

Read the following passage from a work of fiction, *Meridian*, by Alice Walker. Then, in small discussion groups in class, answer the questions that follow the passage.

> One day when Meridian was seven she found a large chunk of heavy metal. It was so thickly encrusted with dirt that even when she had washed it the metal did not shine through. Yet she knew metal was there, because it was so heavy. Finally, when she had dried off the water, she took a large file and filed away some of the rust. To her amazement what she had found was a bar of yellow gold. Bullion they called it in the movies. She filed a spot an inch square and ran with it (heavy as it was) to her mother, who was sitting on the back porch shelling peas.
>
> "I've found some gold!" she shouted. "Gold!" And she placed the large heavy gold bar in her mother's lap.
>
> "Move that thing," her mother said sharply. "Don't you see I'm trying to get these peas ready for supper?"
>
> "But it's gold!" she insisted. "Feel how heavy it is. Look how yellow it is. It's gold, and it could make us rich!"
>
> But her mother was not impressed. Neither was her father or her brothers. She took the bar of gold and filed all the rust off it until it shone like a huge tooth. She put it in a shoe box and buried it under the magnolia tree that grew in the yard. About once a week she dug it up to look at it. Then she dug it up less and less . . . until finally she forgot to dig it up. Her mind turned to other things.
>
> Alice Walker, Meridian

Questions for discussion

1. Where do you think this family lives (North, South, West Coast, East Coast)? Do they live in the country, a town, or a suburb?

2. What social and economic status does the family have?

3. Is Meridian younger or older than her brothers? Does her age matter in the story?

4. How would you describe the relationship between Meridian and her mother, father, and brothers?

5. What do you think the gold means to Meridian?

6. Why does Meridian bury the gold in the yard?

7. Why does she continue to dig the gold up?

8. Why does she stop digging it up?

9. Who is telling this story? Is Meridian or someone else the narrator?

10. Who makes the comment about bullion in the first paragraph?

11. Who makes the comment that the family "was not impressed" in the last paragraph?

12. Can gold rust? What do you believe Meridian found?

13. What do you think the "other things" are that Meridian's mind "turned to" at the end of the story?

On the right-hand side of your journal, summarize how you and your group arrived at your readings or interpretations of this story. Did you read it the same way that you read Ved Mehta's piece at the beginning of this chapter? Or was there something different about how you approached this story?

Writing Assignment

On the left-hand side of your journal, write a story that describes what you think would happen if Meridian came home from school with a perfect score on a math test. Base your story on what you learned about Meridian and her family from the passage and questions above.

As you read the following piece, try to determine where it came from—a newspaper, a letter, a novel, or some other source.

THE AGING MOTHER AT THE GRANDMOTHER'S DEATH SAID

No flowers, and she meant it. The undertaker said, whatever you wish, of course, but, you know, people wish to do *something*; the priest said, maybe some just from the family?

But no, the aging red-haired daughter said, no, by God: mother hated flowers at funerals. No flowers—put it in the paper.

But the flowers came anyway, to the funeral home and to the church and to the daughter's home—to which, by fumbling, the others were also sent—they came in baskets, pots, bouquets, vases, wreaths and sprays.

They were put in the living room late in the morning of the funeral day, the red-haired daughter upstairs with her private grief for the old woman who loved flowers and hated the high stink they made of death.

At noon she came down the stairs, white and forgetful until she saw the funeral of cut flowers in her living room.

And then—how the strong face worked, how she stood in the back porch yelling bring them, all of them, bring them here, how she threw them, all of them, out into the back yard, each flung stronger, crying hard: no flowers, *no* flowers, no *flowers,* spray, pot, baskets, vases, wreaths, bouquets, how the containers tumbled quick and down, the flowers separating, lifting, pausing, swaying to the air and down, like a wake.

Then she was herself again all day, easy and calm, having done homage in this way, having raged a little and cried, and having thrown things hard, she was calm and easy with all who came, without quite thanking anyone for flowers.

Roland Flint

"The Aging Mother at the Grandmother's Death Said" was published in a collection of poems. The poet, Roland Flint, focuses on everyday events in *other* people's lives and manages to find poetry that expresses his own feelings. In another poem he says: "When people say listen to this, this would make a perfect Flint poem, I do listen—for friendliness and because you never can tell."

Now read the next example of expressive fiction:

The pass was high and wide and he jumped for it, feeling it slap flatly against his hands, as he shook his hips to throw off the halfback who was diving at him. The center floated by, his hands desperately brushing Darling's knee as Darling picked his feet up high and delicately ran over a blocker and an opposing linesman in a jumble on the ground near the scrimmage line. He had ten yards in the clear and picked up speed, breathing easily, feeling his thigh pads rising and falling against his legs, listening to the sound of cleats behind him, pulling away from them, watching the other backs heading him off toward the sideline, the whole picture, the men closing in on him, the blockers fighting for position, the ground he had to cross, all suddenly clear in his head, for the first time in his life not a meaningless confusion of men, sounds, speed. He smiled a little to himself as he ran, holding the ball lightly in front of him with his two hands, his knees pumping high, his hips twisting in the almost girlish run of a back in a broken field. The first halfback came at him and he fed him his leg, then swung at the last moment, took the shock of the man's shoulder without breaking stride, ran right through him, his cleats biting securely into the turf. There was only the safety man now, coming warily at him, his arms crooked, hands spread. Darling tucked the ball in, spurted at him, driving hard, hurling himself along, his legs pounding, knees high, all two hundred pounds bunched into controlled attack. He was sure he was going to get past the safety man. Without thought, his arms and legs working beautifully together, he headed right for the safety man, stiff-armed him, feeling blood spurt instantaneously from the man's nose onto his hand, seeing his face go awry, head turned, mouth pulled to one side. He pivoted away, keeping the arm locked, dropping the safety man as he ran easily toward the goal line, with the drumming of cleats diminishing behind him.

Irwin Shaw, "The Eighty-Yard Run"

There is no doubt that this paragraph is about a football game, even if it is an imaginary one. Note that Shaw says the center "floated" by, and he describes Darling as having an "almost girlish run." Would you call this language "poetic"? If you found such language on the sports page, what would you call it? (Consider the effect of this language on different audiences. How would an athlete respond to it, as opposed to someone who doesn't know much about the game? Would women respond differently than men?)

For another example of how expressive writing and imaginative fiction overlap, compare the following descriptions:

Samuel Spade's jaw was long and bony, his chin a jutting v under the more flexible v of his mouth. His nostrils curved back to make another, smaller, v. His yellow-grey eyes were horizontal. The v *motif* was picked up again by thickish brows rising outward from twin creases above a hooked nose, and his pale brown hair grew down—from high flat temples—in a point on his forehead. He looked rather pleasantly like a blond Satan. He said to Effie Perine: "Yes, sweetheart?"

Dashiell Hammett, *The Maltese Falcon*

Mr. Ambrose wore his hair parted on the left side, almost to his ear. A fine powder covered his hair, like dust: the result of too much hair spray. His eyes were deep-set, and peered over a pinched nose that grew white around the nostrils when he got angry in class. His ears were unusually large, and curled around the edges like old leaves. He usually wore a musty brown velour shirt, back to front, unzippered. His arms swung self-consciously at his sides, and his hands were small and paw-like, very brown on the outside, and white on the inside. His blue corduroys bagged at the knees, so much so that his legs looked unnaturally bent. He wore black, carefully polished boots with unfashionably high heels.

Cynthia Wong, student

Sam Spade, a tough detective, was created by writer Dashiell Hammett in his suspense novel *The Maltese Falcon* (and was played by Humphrey Bogart in the film version). Mr. Ambrose is a real person described by a student. However, the fact that one man exists only in imagination while the other is real and can be observed does not prevent each writer from using expressive language to describe them.

Fiction has shaped our expectations as readers in many ways, and our expectations often influence how we read expressive writing. For that matter, film and television have also shaped our ways of reading. We have come to expect—and look for—pattern and symmetry, and we often impose patterns where none can be proved. Whereas a *writer* might look at her or his experiences and not find much unity, a *reader* searches for unity once those experiences are written down.

So far, we have been discussing various ways that readers make a text mean something. But writers certainly do their share, too. Next we will examine how writers provide cues that help readers create meaning.

Reading for Specific Cues

In Chapter 2 we talked about the strategies that writers can use to help their readers in subtle ways. When you are writing, ask yourself, "What can I do to help readers understand what I have written?" Keep this question in mind as we look first at words and phrases and then at sentence patterns that can help readers understand what you mean.

Some Words and Phrases That Help Readers

Sometimes writers assume that their readers know as much as they do. Even worse, writers sometimes don't give any thought to what a reader may or may not know. Look over the following list:

Jimmy Page	Veronica Lake	foul line
Mario Lanza	majolica	MLA
Lithuania	the Big Board	barrister
agoraphobia	kiddush	Margery Kempe

Chances are, you do not recognize all these names and words. If you came across them while reading and were given no explanation, you would probably be annoyed—if not upset. However, if the writer gave you cues like the following, you would be a wiser and much-relieved reader:

— former Led Zeppelin guitarist Jimmy Page
— Mario Lanza, the legendary opera singer
— Lithuania, a Soviet Socialist Republic located on the Baltic Sea
— agoraphobia (fear of open spaces)

Considerate writers supply such cues and information, showing that they are thinking of their readers. They do not assume that all readers are walking encyclopedias who know everything. Instead, they provide brief explanations that serve to guide their readers.

Let's begin with some examples of cues in expressive writing. Pay close attention to the underlined words:

> One night, in a Chinese restaurant, Sarah became a fancier of roast squab.
>
> Calvin Trillin, *Alice, Let's Eat*

The phrase "in a Chinese restaurant" makes it clear where the writer is. Whatever may happen next in the story will make sense because readers know the context.

The next passage is full of important cues:

> A slick-haired Soviet M.C. announced B.B. King ("A great Negritanski musician"), and then King was onstage with his well known guitar—Lucille—and a ten-man ensemble.
>
> Andrea Lee, *Russian Journal*

Here, as in the previous example, we learn the context of the narrative: B.B. King is giving a concert in the Soviet Union. The Russian-style introduction in parentheses tells us who King is. And we also learn the name of his guitar and how many people are in his band.

In the next passage, the cues combine to reveal that the writer is in a difficult situation:

> Fifty miles down a dirt road in Wyoming one time, the old bus suffered two flat tires, which was one flat tire too many. We sat there for an hour wondering what to do about it before a rancher came along in his pickup truck.
>
> Charles Kuralt, *On the Road*

Readers who pay attention to the details will understand that the writer is far from a gas station—and even far from a telephone to call for help. Kuralt and his colleagues feel so helpless that they do nothing for an hour.

In the next passage, the writer uses an imaginative parenthetical cue to help readers locate Queens, New York:

> I trusted the United States Army to relocate me satisfactorily. It did, in 1946, choosing to establish me in Queens (then but a five-cent subway ride from the clamorous glamour of Manhattan).
>
> Larry L. King, "Playing Cowboy"

So far, we have looked only at examples of cues in expressive writing, which focuses on the self and personal experiences. Keep in mind, however, that writers try to use cues in other kinds of writing as well. Words, phrases, and sentence patterns that help readers are also found in informative writing (such as lab reports and accounts of historical events) and in persuasive writing (such as editorials and advertising). In the rest of this section, we will look at cues in all three kinds of writing, beginning with an informative passage:

> Several black men accompanied Pathfinder John C. Frémont during three expeditions into the far West.
>
> William Loren Katz, *The Black West*

The passage makes it clear that Frémont was some sort of Western explorer—and that's all we need to know for the moment. The next passage goes further. The writer uses cues to establish the subject's identity and credentials (qualifications):

> A few years ago, Dr. Mary Calderone, executive director of SIECUS, the Sex Information and Education Council of the U.S., and one of the nation's leading authorities on sex education, was answering questions from an audience of Chicago high-schoolers.
>
> Norman M. Lobsenz, "Sex and the Senior Citizen"

This writer wants to make sure that we understand why Dr. Calderone is an authority, and why her views are to be valued.

In the next passage the writer uses dashes to set off a short summary of a novel:

> The Mists of Avalon—a novel based on the legend of King Arthur, but told through the eyes of the women central to the story—was published by Knopf in 1983 and became a runaway bestseller.
>
> Lois Rosenthal, "From the Mists Comes Marion Zimmer Bradley"

Notice how much information is embedded in this passage. Besides telling us what the novel is about, the writer also gives us the name of the publisher and the year the novel was published.

Several cues about age in the next passage help readers to pinpoint the exact age the writer is discussing:

> No one has met a child under three years old who wants to do something a few days in the future. However, at the preschool age, a great many unrealizable tendencies and desires emerge. . . . Suppose that a very young (perhaps

two-and-a-half-year-old) child wants something—for example, to occupy her mother's role.

Vygotsky, "The Role of Play in Development"

In the next example the writer gives two cues to identify the period of history he wants readers to consider:

> The civil rights movement in America began a long time ago. As early as the seventeenth century, blacks and whites, slaves in Virginia and Quakers in Pennsylvania, protested the barbarity of slavery. Nat Turner, Sojourner Truth, Frederick Douglass, William Lloyd Garrison, John Brown and Harriet Tubman are but a few of those who led the resistance to slavery before the Civil War.

Juan Williams, *Eyes on the Prize*

Williams does assume that readers will know the approximate dates of the Civil War. But the writer of the next passage takes no chances. He is very much aware that he is writing for nonspecialists, and so he carefully defines his terms and gives examples of them:

> The various fields of science have a well-defined pecking order. There is a range from "soft" science to "hard" science. In the United States, molecular biology, biochemistry, astrophysics, and high-energy physics are now at the hard end. They have great authority in the scientific and general communities, and they are seen as somehow more rigorous and precise than other sciences. At the other end of the spectrum are fields like ecology, paleontology, and behavioral biology.

David Raup, *The Nemesis Affair*

The following passage is trickier than the earlier ones, because readers must balance several cues at once. And they *still* may need to turn to a dictionary for help:

> Somebody once observed to the eminent philosopher Wittgenstein how stupid medieval Europeans living before the time of Copernicus must have been that they could have looked at the sky and thought that the sun was circling the earth.

James Burke, *The Day the Universe Changed*

If readers don't know when Copernicus lived (1473–1543), they might be cued by knowing what time period *medieval* refers to (the centuries from 500 to 1500). In addition, alert readers should be able to figure out that Copernicus believed the earth revolved around the sun.

Reading and Writing Assignment   ■

Read any one of the essays in this book, and identify any words or phrases that help you to create meaning. On the right-hand side of your journal, describe how these cues helped you to understand what the author meant.

Then look at one of your longer journal entries (on a left-hand page). What cues did you use that might help your readers? What cues might you add so that readers can understand you better? Directly opposite your journal entry—on the right-hand page—jot down some ideas about how to cue your readers better.

Besides cues that define or explain the meanings of specific words, writers also help readers by carefully using pronouns. A **pronoun** substitutes for and points backward to something that has already been specified or named. (Grammarians refer to the already-named person, place, or thing as the *antecedent; ante* is a Latin word meaning "before.") Without pronouns, we would have to write sentences like the following:

> . . . Jackson was permitted to dig out that amount, a feat Jackson accomplished in a few days. Jackson immediately left for Missouri and a family reunion of free people.

Sentences like these may remind you of the books you used as a child in learning to read: "Dick and Jane went out to play. Dick and Jane played ball. Dick and Jane had fun playing ball." For most readers, the constant repetition of names—and the short sentences—is tiresome. Pronouns, then, link sentences together and provide variety. They also help readers to follow the writer's thoughts.

Read the following passage, and pay close attention to the underlined words:

> Several black men accompanied Pathfinder John C. Frémont during three expeditions into the far West. One, Mifflin Gibbs, later became a businessman, newspaper publisher and civil rights activist in gold rush California. Another, Saunders Jackson, joined Frémont's last expedition because he needed seventeen hundred dollars to purchase his family from their Missouri slave master. When gold was discovered on Frémont's California land, Jackson was permitted to dig out that amount, a feat he accomplished in a few days. He immediately left for Missouri and a family reunion of free people.
>
> William Loren Katz, *The Black West*

This passage moves from the general phrase *several black men* to naming two specific men. After naming Jackson, the writer then substitutes *he* and *his*. He uses pronouns instead of repeating the name. The pronouns link the passage together and provide a thread for the reader to follow.

In the next passage, a single **possessive pronoun** (*their*) is used to show ownership. The writer does not have to repeat the names of the three owners:

> Another time, when Frémont, Dodson and another man galloped 120 miles in one day, Dodson was responsible for roping fresh horses when their steeds became exhausted.
>
> William Loren Katz, *The Black West*

Sometimes **demonstrative pronouns** (such as *this, that, these,* and *those*) can be used to refer back to whole phrases, not just to particular words. In the following examples, the antecedents and the demonstrative pronouns are underlined:

> Adult children of alcoholics over-react to changes over which they have no control.
> This is very simple to understand.
>
> Janet Geringer Woititz, *Adult Children of Alcoholics*

> The softer sciences also tend to have more observational data, and this has the irony of making it more difficult to construct simple, unifying theories.
>
> David Raup, *The Nemesis Affair*

In these two passages, the things already specified are not just one word, but several. We also could rewrite the sentences like this:

> That adult children of alcoholics over-react to changes over which they have no control is very simple to understand.

> That the softer sciences also tend to have more observational data is ironic, and makes it more difficult to construct simple, unifying theories.

Reading and Writing Assignment ▪

Read any one of the essays in this book, and identify how pronouns help you to create meaning. On the right-hand side of your journal, describe how these cues helped you to understand what the author meant.

Then look at one of your longer journal entries (on a left-hand page). What pronouns have you used that might help your readers? What pronouns might you add so that readers can understand you better? Directly opposite your journal entry—on the right-hand page—jot down some ideas about how to use pronouns better.

Repetitions That Help Readers

When we talk, we sometimes repeat ourselves to emphasize an important point:

> It's far, far, too expensive.

> I agree with every word you've said—every single word.

As in speech, the use of repetition in written language can ensure that readers will get the message. There also are times when pronouns will just confuse things—when it is better for the writer to repeat key words. Read the following passage, for example, and pay attention to the underlined words:

> My American friends are always telling me that they cannot cook rice. They can hardly be blamed for their phobia. It starts, I think, with inadequate—inaccurate, in fact—instructions on rice packages that invariably suggest using far more water than rice actually requires. The rice ends up by being mushy and the people who are cooking it often think that it is their fault. It is not.
> There are, actually, many methods of cooking rice well.
>
> Madhur Jaffrey, *Indian Cooking*

It would be difficult to write this passage effectively without repeating the word *rice*. (Note that Jaffrey does substitute the pronoun *it* once, for variety.)

In the next example, the repetition of the word *portrait* and the words that refer to related concepts help to hold the passage together:

> . . . The portrait was acquired by a Venetian merchant and eventually found its way to the National Gallery in London.
> A portrait was indeed something new in the Islamic world. The holy law of Islam has been interpreted as banning the representation of the human image. This ban was totally effective against sculpture, which did not begin to penetrate the Islamic world until the late nineteenth century and is still viewed with strong disapproval by purists. Two-dimensional painting was, however, widely practiced, especially in the Persian and Turkish lands. It differed from Western painting in two important respects. One was that it was limited in the main to book illustration and miniature, occasionally also to mural painting. The practice of hanging paintings on the wall was Western and was not adopted by Muslims until the late nineteenth century. The other was that the

figures depicted in these paintings were mostly literary and historical. <u>Portraiture</u> does occur in classical Islamic art, but it is exceedingly rare and subject to strong disapproval.

Bernard Lewis, *The Muslim Discovery of Europe*

In this case, repeating *portrait* at the end of the first paragraph and in the first sentence of the next paragraph links the two ideas—even though the writer moves on to another, related subject. Also notice that the writer uses many terms that are related to portrait painting. By repeating key words and related terms, the writer achieves a strong sense of unity. As the following passage shows, unity may depend wholly on repeated chains of ideas:

<u>Each change</u> brings with it <u>new attitudes and institutions</u> created by <u>new knowledge</u>. These <u>novel systems</u> then either oust or coexist with the structures and attitudes held prior to the <u>change</u>. Our modern view is thus a mixture of <u>present knowledge and past viewpoints</u> which have stood the test of time and, for one reason or another, remain valuable in <u>new circumstances</u>.

James Burke, *The Day the Universe Changed*

Notice how one sentence flows smoothly into the next. The writer achieves this unity by building thematic associations through repetition. In this case, repetition is helpful in guiding the reader through the passage.

Reading and Writing Assignment ∎

Read any one of the essays in this book, and identify how repetitions help you to create meaning. On the right-hand side of your journal, describe how these cues helped you to understand what the author meant.

Then look at one of your longer journal entries (on a left-hand page). What repetitions have you used that might help your readers? What repetitions might you add so that readers can understand you better? Directly opposite your journal entry—on the right-hand page—jot down some ideas about how to use repetitions better.

Some Sentence Patterns That Help Readers

In speaking, the way we say, or stress, certain words creates different meanings or effects. For example, how many meanings can you give to the following common remarks just by changing the stress from one word to another?

Oh, sure.

Are you going now?

I love it.

In writing, too, we can create various effects by how we arrange the words in a sentence. By repeating that arrangement, or sentence pattern, we can provide cues for readers. For example, the writer of the following passage from a piece of expressive writing repeats a particular pattern of words to achieve an emphatic tone—that is, we are very sure of what she means:

> There were <u>no special effects to entice the audience's attention</u>, <u>no extraordinary lights to enliven the bland walls</u>, and definitely <u>no squealing from the audience to distract me</u>.
>
> Dawn Gibson, student

Notice that the word *no* is repeated throughout. But there is another, less obvious pattern as well: *to entice, to enliven, to distract*. We might say that these words are **parallel**; that is, they share the same pattern (in this case, *to* + verb). By repeating the two patterns throughout the sentence, this writer achieved unity and a very strong tone.

Here's another example of how a sentence pattern provides cues in a piece of expressive writing:

> These unhealthy kitchen conditions could be improved <u>if</u>, and only <u>if</u>, the unhappy students would stand up for their rights and say something about it, <u>if</u> the counselors would report the condition of the kitchen, and <u>if</u> the housekeeper would complain to her boss.
>
> Lynkita Roberts, student

One word—*if*—holds this passage together. And, again, the writer used parallel verb forms: *would stand up, would report, would complain*.

As you read the next passage, notice how the sentence pattern guides you:

> <u>Whether</u> victims of sexual exploitation during slavery, <u>or</u> tragic mulattoes who tried to escape their blackness by passing, <u>or</u> extremely dark-skinned black women who suffered inter- and intra-racial prejudice, <u>or</u> matriarchs, <u>or</u> welfare recipients, <u>or</u> the new super black women of the 60's, black women have been treated as types.
>
> Trudier Harris, *From Mammies to Militants*

In this sentence, the word *or* is repeated faster and faster as the writer builds up to the main point at the end. Also notice the parallel patterns that follow *or*: "tragic mulattoes" is balanced with "extremely dark-skinned black women," "matriarchs," and so on.

Here's another example of how the sentence pattern sets up a rhythm:

> Our modern Sioux language has been white-manized. There's no power in it. I get my knowledge of the old tales of my people <u>out of a drum</u>, or <u>the sound of a flute</u>, <u>out of my visions</u> and <u>out of our sacred herb pejuta</u>, but above all <u>out of the ancient words from way back</u>, the words of the grand-fathers, the language that was there at the beginning of time, the language given to We-Ota-Wichasha, Blood Clot Boy. If that language, these words, should *ever* die, then our legends will die too.
>
> Leonard Crow Dog, in *American Indian Myths and Legends*

If you read the above passage aloud, you are likely to fall into a certain rhythm, emphasizing the word *out* in order to balance the phrases. A second pattern is at work here, too, in the renaming of the ancient language:

> . . . out of the <u>ancient words</u> from way back, the <u>words of the grand-fathers</u>, the <u>language that was there at the beginning of time</u>, the <u>language given to We-Ota-Wichasha, Blood Clot Boy</u>.

No underlined cues are provided in the next passage. See what you can make of it:

> The voyages of Gama and Magellan had been preceded by uncelebrated pioneers on trading voyages across the Mediterranean and by those who inched down around the coast of Africa. There were countless pioneers in the voyages toward evolution. Columbus knew there was a Japan to be reached, Gama that India was there. The pioneers of evolution were en route to an unknown destination.

You probably had to reread this passage as you tried to discover the links between ideas. You may even have silently supplied a *but* at the beginning of the last sentence. Now read the passage as the author wrote it, paying attention to the underlined words:

> <u>Just as</u> the voyages of Gama and Magellan had been preceded by un-celebrated pioneers on trading voyages across the Mediterranean and by those who inched down around the coast of Africa, <u>so too</u> there were countless pioneers in the voyages toward evolution. <u>But while</u> Columbus knew there was a Japan to be reached, Gama that India was there, the pioneers of evolution were en route to an unknown destination.
>
> Daniel Boorstin, *The Discoverers*

Now you can see that the writer is comparing actual sea voyages by famous explorers to the "voyages" of scientists who study evolution. The corrected passage has only six more words. It also makes the last sentence part of the preceding one. With these few changes in sentence structure, the ideas are balanced and become clear.

Following are two more examples of how parallel structure helps the writer to communicate.

Not parallel

Slowly, with ease, soundless, the Opeyo Dancers moved off the stage. The drums and guitar pounded, did throb, were rising and falling.

Parallel

Slowly, easily, soundlessly, the Opeyo Dancers moved off the stage. The drums and guitar pounded, throbbed, rose and fell.

Demeatrice Johnson, student

Not parallel

At sixteen, I was full of wildness, outspoken, and I was a selfish person. When the teacher left the room, I talked loudly, was fighting with my classmates and would throw spitballs and even climbed on the desk. When I disobeyed, my mother punished me: no going out, I couldn't talk on the telephone, and I was not allowed to have company.

Parallel

At sixteen, I was wild, outspoken, and selfish. When the teacher left the room I talked loudly, fought with my classmates and threw spitballs and even climbed on the desk. When I disobeyed, my mother punished me: no going out, no telephone, no company.

Ocky Chung, student

See if you can find the parallel elements in this example:

He took us to a gas station on the highway, waited until the flats were fixed, drove us back to the bus, and helped us jack up the wheels and change the tires. . . . His wife cooked us elk steaks for dinner, tucked us under warm quilts for the night, and sent us off full of flapjacks and sausage the next morning.

Charles Kuralt, *On the Road*

Here is how the passage looks if we line up the parallel elements:

He

    took us to a gas station on the highway,

    waited until the flats were fixed,

    drove us back to the bus, and

    helped us jack up the wheels and change the tires. . . . His wife

      <u>cooked us</u> elk steaks for dinner,

      <u>tucked us</u> under warm quilts for the night, and

      <u>sent us</u> off full of flapjacks and sausage the next morning.

Finally, here is an example of a passage with several parallel elements. As you read it, notice that the cues do not depend on what you may know about the various subjects discussed. Instead, the cues depend on your knowledge of *how texts are made*.

> When <u>they try to dress</u> themselves, <u>comb</u> their hair, <u>color</u> a picture, <u>clean</u> their room, <u>finish</u> a puzzle, <u>they are not only mimicking</u> adult behavior, <u>identifying</u> with suitable people, <u>improving</u> specific skills—<u>they are also</u>, in numerous and diverse ways, <u>teaching</u> themselves <u>that they have</u> skills and <u>that they can</u> cope (more or less) all by themselves. . . . The child <u>who is</u> confident in his abilities and <u>who explores</u> the world and his skills from the basis of a secure parental affection is less likely to use dependent behavior as a means of <u>punishing</u>, <u>exploiting</u>, and <u>manipulating</u>. <u>That child will</u> be slower to use dependent behavior in order to master tasks because he will try to perform the tasks himself before asking for help. And <u>that child will</u> enjoy affection but he will not need it in continuous doses in order to reassure himself that he exists and is estimable.
>
> Judith Bardwick, *Psychology of Women: A Study of Bio-Cultural Conflicts*

Reading and Writing Assignment ■

Read any one of the essays in this book, and identify how sentence patterns help you to create meaning. On the right-hand side of your journal, describe how these cues helped you to understand what the author meant.

Then look at one of your longer journal entries (on a left-hand page). What sentence patterns have you used that might help your readers? What sentence patterns might you add so that readers can understand you better? Directly opposite your journal entry—on the right-hand page—jot down some ideas about how to use sentence patterns better.

How to Draft Expressive Writing

By now you should have a good idea of what expressive writing is. You have read several kinds of expressive writing, and have written some of your own. You can build on what you have done so far by reading a few more examples and by considering the writing situation and the audience. Then you will be ready to do one of the writing assignments at the end of this chapter.

In defining what expressive writing is, we noted that you do it all the time when you speak. You tell stories—about what you did the night of your prom, about how you won that race, about what happened in your English class. People constantly begin conversations by saying something like, "I remember one time when I . . ." or, "Did you hear what happened on Leon's date? Well, . . ." You use the same story-telling traditions when you write something about yourself and your experiences. But the expectations of a *listening* audience are very different from those of a *reading* audience. To demonstrate this point, the next writing assignment returns to what you did at the very beginning of this chapter—you told a story.

Writing Assignment   ■

As your first assignment in this chapter, you tape-recorded yourself or someone else telling a story. Now, transcribe that tape by writing down exactly what you hear. (You may want to include your transcription in your journal, on a left-hand page.) Is the written version any different from the spoken version? Is it as complete and as clear? As interesting? What does this tell you about the importance of facial expressions, gestures, and tone of voice? In small groups, share your observations with your classmates. Then, on the right-hand side of your journal, opposite your transcription, make notes about what you have discovered.

Next, exchange the written versions of your stories, and discuss how they might be improved. What kinds of cues do they need to be as effective as the spoken version? (Put your story aside for now; you may be able to use it for your writing assignment at the end of this chapter.)

Perhaps the most important thing to keep in mind in a piece of expressive writing is focus, focus, focus. Don't try to write about everything. Instead, concentrate on one incident, one idea, one emotion. Look over the selections in this chapter, and notice how short most of them are. Even the longer pieces still focus on just one incident.

Consider the following description of a concert in the Soviet Union:

> A slick-haired Soviet M.C. announced B.B. King ("A great Negritanski musician"), and then King was onstage with his well known guitar—Lucille— and a ten-man ensemble. As King and the ensemble swung into "Why I Sing the Blues," one could sense the puzzlement of the Soviet audience. "Negro" music to them meant jazz or spirituals, but this was something else. Also, there was the question of response. B.B. King is a great, warm presence when he performs, and he asks his audience to pour themselves out to him in return.

King teases his audiences, urging them to clap along, to whistle, to hoot their appreciation, like the congregations in the Southern churches in which he grew up. But to Russians, such behavior suggests a lack of culture and an almost frightening disorder. Though obviously impressed, the audience at first kept a respectful silence during the numbers, as it might at the symphony. (Only the foreigners shouted and stomped out the beat; we found the Russians around us staring at us open-mouthed.) Then King played an irresistible riff, stopped and leaned toward the audience with his hand cupped to his ear. The audience caught on and began to clap. King changed the beat, and waited for the audience to catch up. Then he changed it again. Soon the whole place was clapping along to "Get off My Back, Woman," and there were even a few timid shouts and whistles. King, who carried the blues to Europe, Africa, and the Far East, had broken the ice one more time.

Andrea Lee, *Russian Journal*

For all the detail in this passage, it really focuses on just one thing—the audience at King's concert. By focusing on the audience, the writer is able to describe the cultural context that gives this event its meaning. The passage also shows that expressive writing need not be "I" centered. Although this description is based on personal experience, it moves outward from the writer to make observations about the world.

In contrast, the next passage is entirely "I" centered. It was written by Redmond O'Hanlon, a specialist in natural history (the study of the origins, descriptions, and relationships of things in nature). In this passage he describes one predicament that he and a companion, James Fenton, met with in the jungles of Borneo:

undulating: moving in a smooth, wavelike motion
anterior: placed in front
posterior: placed in back
via: by way of

I looked at my legs. And then I looked again. They were undulating with leeches. . . . They were edging up my trousers, looping up toward my knees with alternate placements of their anterior and posterior suckers, seeming, with each rear attachment, to wave their front ends in the air and take a sniff. They were all over my boots, too, and three particularly brave individuals were trying to make their way in via the air-holes. There were more on the way—in fact they were moving toward us across the jungle floor from every angle, their damp brown bodies half-camouflaged against the rotting leaves.

"Oh God," said James, *"they are really pleased to see us."*

Redmond O'Hanlon, *Into the Heart of Borneo*

This is a vivid account of what must have been an unpleasant, if not frightening, experience. But it is also rather funny, given James Fenton's response to the situation. Although it is a brief description, it is very expressive because its focus is so clear.

Our final example of focused writing comes from a technical writer who also writes poetry:

I had a friend who used to grab onto my heel and make me look like a crooked flamingo on somebody's front lawn. At first I'd laugh, but when I realized what I was feeling, that I felt like a crooked flamingo, I'd get embarrassed, even angry. And, pink with anger, of course I looked all the more like a flamingo. And when she let go, I felt like the owner, standing on the front lawn, straightening the flamingo and shaking my fist at some harmless kid.

Joseph Kilbridge

This writer is having some fun with the picture of himself looking like a flamingo. (He even gets pink like one!) Notice the series of emotions that he feels: first silly, then embarrassed, then angry, and finally harassed. An ordinary situation—goofing around with a friend—has been transformed by its focus on the writer's emotions.

Writing Assignment ■

Before going on to the assignments to write your own expressive essay, look back through this chapter. What did you learn about expressive writing that you didn't know before? On the right-hand side of your journal, summarize what you have learned about the main kinds of expressive writing; about the cues and patterns you can use to guide readers; and about how to focus your writing. In small groups, share your journal notes with your classmates.

Assignments in Expressive Writing

The following pages guide you through three different expressive writing assignments. Here is a brief description of them:

1. Remembering the Past: Your Life   This assignment invites you to write about yourself and the events of your life.

2. Remembering the Past: Other People   This assignment invites you to write about your memories or perceptions of another person.

3. Remembering the Past: Your Family   This assignment invites you to write about yourself and your relationship with your family.

To help decide which assignment interests you most, first read the preliminary assignment below, and then quickly read what each assignment is about and how you might approach it. Also look over your journal and the expressive writing you have already done in this chapter. Perhaps you can develop one of your earlier drafts further, or can adapt it to fit one of the following assignments. If you still can't decide which assignment seems most interesting, consult with your teacher.

When you have picked an assignment, turn to Chapter 2 for some tips about how to discover your ideas. Then, after you have written your discovery draft, Chapters 4 and 5 and Worksheets 1 through 6 will help you plan and edit your final draft.

Just as you enjoyed reading the expressive writing in this chapter, your classmates and teacher look forward to reading what you write about yourself, someone you know, or someone in your family.

Preliminary Assignment

Before you begin one of the following assignments, read the following comments about writing an autobiography:

polyglot:
speaking, writing, composed in many languages
ubiquity:
existence everywhere at the same time
mode:
customary fashion or style

A powerful need to listen to each others' personal histories (and thus to learn more about our own) runs throughout our mobile, polyglot culture. This helps explain the ubiquity and popularity of autobiographical acts, which in many variations of narrative mode have flourished since the early years of the republic, and even before. Certainly autobiography in its many forms is widely produced and enthusiastically consumed today. One finds personal histories everywhere one finds books: on library shelves and in the syllabi of college courses; at the checkout counters of drugstores and supermarkets; on bestseller lists, as book club selections, and in reviews (almost weekly, it seems) of the *New York Times*; in the knapsacks of high school students and hitchhikers. The paperback revolution has made it possible, on the one hand, for a poet's or movie star's memoir to rival the latest detective story and, on the other hand, for the account of a forgotten runaway slave's life to be relived in a class on Afro-American history.

Albert Stone, *Autobiographical Occasions and Original Acts*

1. On the right-hand side of your journal, summarize what is most significant about this passage; on the left-hand side, directly opposite, write a response to the above comments. Pay special attention to the following remark: "A powerful need to listen to each other's personal histories (and thus to learn more about our own) runs through our mobile, polyglot culture."

2. In small groups, discuss what Albert Stone believes about the importance of writing an autobiography. Why do we want to read about the details of others' lives?

3. On the right-hand side of your journal, make a list of autobiographies that you have read, or a list of people whom you know have written autobiographies. Share your list with your group. What makes the autobiographies alike or different? Make notes about the group's discussion on the right-hand side of your journal.

Assignment 1.   Remembering the Past: Your Life

In this assignment, you are invited to write about yourself and the events of your life. Begin by reading the following comment by someone who has written an autobiography:

> These memories of mine have been collected slowly, over a period of years. . . . Many a time, in the course of doing these memoirs . . . the temptation to invent has been very strong, particularly where recollection is hazy and I remember the substance of an event but not the details—the color of a dress, the pattern of a carpet, the placing of a picture. My memory is good, but obviously I cannot recall whole passages of dialogue that took place years ago. Only a few single sentences stand out: *"They'd* make you toe the chalk line," "Perseverance wins the crown," "My child, you must have faith." . . . Then there are cases where I am not sure myself whether I am making something up. I *think* I remember but I am not positive.
>
> Mary McCarthy, *Memories of a Catholic Girlhood*

Guidelines for Assignment 1   ■

1. On the left-hand side of your journal, write a response to the above comments about writing autobiography. Pay special attention to the following remark: "Many a time, in the course of doing these memoirs . . . the temptation to invent has been very strong, particularly where recollection is hazy and I remember the substance of an event but not the details." How would you relate this to the statement you read in the preliminary assignment: "A powerful need to listen to each other's personal histories (and thus to learn more about our own) runs through our mobile, polyglot culture"?

2. In small groups, discuss Stone's and McCarthy's different views about the process of writing an autobiography. Stone sees autobiography as a personal act that has public consequences. On the other hand, McCarthy, who wrote many autobiographical essays, isn't very interested in what others may think. She realizes that autobiography always begins with private memories which may be distorted by time. How do we reconcile these two views about the public and private functions of autobiography? How might you relate both writers' ideas to writing about yourself? Make notes about the group's discussion on the right-hand side of your journal, opposite your response.

3. Pick an event from your own life that you would like to write about. It doesn't have to be an earthshaking event. It could be just a vague memory that you can clarify through writing. (Before you pick a topic and begin to write, reread your journal for ideas. You may already have a topic that you would like to pursue.)

Reflect on what it means to write about yourself as you write. The psychologist Carl Jung, in writing about himself, said, "The older I have become, the less I have understood or had insight into or known about myself." Do you agree? McCarthy compares writing about yourself to being an amateur archaeologist. Is that a useful comparison?

4. Consider your responses to the above passages. As you explore your topic in a draft, compare your own attitude toward writing about yourself with the attitudes of Stone, McCarthy, and Jung. Refer to these writers specifically in your own writing.

Following are two examples from students' papers that will give you ideas about how to write about yourself and the ideas of others at the same time:

> When thinking about the past, my mind goes in all different directions. A number of images race through my head in a matter of seconds—people, places, things—things that trigger thoughts about events that took place so long ago. There are so many untold stories that mean so much to me, but mean so little to someone else. After all, I'm not a famous person, and I think that Albert Stone is only talking about famous people.
>
> If I see a particular flower, it could bring me back to another time—just as if I were an archaeologist, as Mary McCarthy says. But to another person, it's just a flower.

My memories are under lock and key. Only I can go through my past. I could share them with others, but they might not understand them or appreciate them in the same way that I do. In one perspective, memories are an escape from everyday life which take us back to a time of happiness or sorrow. Somehow memories lead us back to reality. We can't live in our memories, even though it would be nice to try. Memories are remembered as possible dreams or goals we once had, which help us live in the present to progress toward the future.

Mary Warry, student

Mary McCarthy writes, "Many a time, in the course of doing these memoirs . . . the temptation to invent has been very strong, particularly where recollection is hazy and I remember the substance of an event but not the details." I think this is probably true of most people who try to remember their past. When I try to recall things that happened to me when I was ten or eleven or younger, I remember things but they do not seem real; it seems like I'm just telling a story or it happened to someone else.

Kari Packer, student

Assignment 2.   Remembering the Past: Other People

In this assignment, you are invited to write about your memories or perceptions of someone who is not related to you.

The goal in this assignment is to describe someone from memory. When you describe another person, you often say a good deal about yourself as well. For example, you may want to explain why that person had an impact on your life. In a way, writing about another person is another way to write an autobiography.

Lillian Hellman, an American playwright, wrote a collection of sketches of people who were important to her at different points in her life. She introduces these sketches with the following words:

Old paint on canvas, as it ages, sometimes becomes transparent. When that happens it is possible, in some pictures, to see the original lines: a tree will show through a woman's dress, a child makes way for a dog, a large boat is no longer on an open sea. That is called pentimento because the painter "repented," changed his mind. Perhaps it would be as well to say that the old conception, replaced by a later choice, is a way of seeing and then seeing again.

That is all I mean about the people in this book. The paint has aged now and I wanted to see what was there for me once, what is there for me now.

For Hellman, the *act* of remembering people and examining how she remembered them is as significant as the individuals themselves.

Guidelines for Assignment 2 ■

1. On the left-hand side of your journal, write a response to Hellman's idea of pentimento. Pay special attention to this comment: "I wanted to see what was there for me once, what is there for me now." Then, on the right-hand side of your journal, make a short list of people whom you might write about as Hellman did—people who were important at different times in your life. You might even list someone you don't know—perhaps someone famous—but who has had an impact on your life in some way.

2. In small groups, discuss how the act of remembering can change what is significant about a memory. Then relate this idea to Stone's comments about how popular autobiographies have become. Do you think that anyone can write about himself or herself without thinking about possible readers? Make notes about the group's discussion in your journal, on the right-hand side.

3. Choose a person from your list to write about. (Reread your journal entries for ideas.)

Don't just settle for a physical description of the person, or say in a vague way how nice or bad the person was. Consider writing about him or her *doing* something—dancing, talking, working, and so on. (Look back at the descriptions of Mr. Ambrose and Darling, the football player, in the examples of expressive writing.)

Another good way to describe someone is to focus on what is unique about him or her. Perhaps your subject collects something unusual, or lives somewhere special that might reveal something significant. For example, one student wrote about a friend who collects decks of playing cards. The student described how the friend makes a point of buying playing cards wherever she travels, how people give them to her, and how she keeps notebooks to record them in. This is an unusual hobby, and it made the description more interesting and appealing.

4. As you explore your subject in a draft, consider Hellman's passage again, and refer to it specifically. How has your perception or memory of the person changed? Jean Jacques Rousseau, the eighteenth-century philosopher, said, "I may omit or transpose facts, or make mistakes in dates, but I cannot go wrong about what I have felt, or about what my feelings have led me to do." Can you relate this idea to how you remember this particular person?

Following are two examples of how students used Hellman's pentimento idea in their essays:

> When I decided to write about Mr. Hayden, my high school basketball coach, I asked my brother Nick what he remembered about him. We discov-

ered that we had two different memories of the same events. For example, I remember enjoying eating lunch in the cafeteria with him—Mr. Hayden would quiz me about what I had done in school that day, and he always seemed impressed with what I had done on a science project, or what short story we had read in English class. He made me feel like I was smart and interesting. Nick, however, hated it when Mr. Hayden would ask us about our classes. He felt he was just checking up on us.

I guess this is what Lillian Hellman meant about "a way of seeing and then seeing again." I had to rethink just how things were. I don't care if my brother is right and I am wrong. I want to keep my memories of those lunches, because that is what is "there for me now."

Walter Healy, student

Writing this essay turned out to be a chance to look inside myself and sort out my feelings. When I began writing, I was angry at my girlfriend for telling my mother I had been drinking, but as I revised and reflected on that Saturday night, I realized I was wrong to be upset because she really helped me in the end. I guess remembering and writing *can* change the significance of an event, as Hellman says.

Nikki Hall, student

Assignment 3.   Remembering the Past: Your Family

In this assignment, you are asked to write about yourself and your relationship to your family. ("Family" can be defined broadly here. Besides people who are actually related to you, it can include foster parents, legal guardians, or other people who have helped to raise you and have come to be thought of as family.)

Writing about your family is another way to write your autobiography, because your family has such a great influence on who you become.

Write Before Reading   ■

On the right-hand side of your journal, list all those whom you consider to be part of your family. Record some significant event or memory about each person and how it affected you.

Now read the following passages about remembering, family life, and growing up:

Mussolini:
Italian dictator
during World
War II

It is our parents, normally, who not only teach us our family history but who set us straight on our own childhood recollections, telling us that *this* cannot have happened the way we think it did and that *that*, on the other hand, did occur, just as we remember it, in such and such a summer when So-and-So was our nurse. My own son, Reuel, for instance, used to be convinced that Mussolini had been thrown off a bus in North Truro, on Cape Cod, during the war. This memory goes back to one morning in 1943 when, as a young child, he was waiting with his father and me beside the road in Wellfleet to put a departing guest on the bus to Hyannis. The bus came through, and the bus driver leaned down to shout the latest piece of news: "They've thrown Mussolini out." Today, Reuel knows that Mussolini was never **ejected** from a Massachusetts bus, and he also knows how he got that impression. But if his father and I had died the following year, he would have been left with a clear recollection of something that everyone would have assured him was an historical impossibility, and with no way of reconciling his stubborn memory to the stubborn facts on record. . . .

ejected: thrown out forcefully

As orphans, my brother . . . and I have a burning interest in our past, which we try to reconstruct together, like two amateur archaeologists, falling on any new scrap of evidence, trying to fit it in, questioning our relations, belaboring our own memories.

Mary McCarthy, *Memories of a Catholic Girlhood*

Happy or unhappy, families are all mysterious. We have only to imagine how differently we would be described—and will be, after our deaths—by each of the family members who believe they know us. The only question is, Why are some mysteries more important than others?

lavished: gave generously
Lincolnesque: like Abraham Lincoln
gaunt: thin, bony

The fate of my Uncle Ed was a mystery of importance in our family. We **lavished** years of speculation on his transformation from a brilliant young electrical engineer to the town handyman. What could have changed this elegant, **Lincolnesque** student voted "Best Dressed" by his classmate to the **gaunt**, unshaven man I remember? Why did he leave a young son and a first wife of the "proper" class and religion, marry a much less educated woman of the "wrong" religion, and raise a second family in a house near an abandoned airstrip; a house whose walls were patched with metal signs to stop the wind? Why did he never talk about his transformation?

Gloria Steinem, "Ruth's Song (Because She Could Not Sing It)"

Write After Reading

Perhaps reading these passages about family life has stirred up new memories for you. On the left-hand side of your journal, write some notes about anything else you remembered.

Guidelines for Assignment 3

1. On the left-hand side of your journal, write a response to the above passages.

2. In small groups, discuss how thinking and writing about an experience can help define it and give it new meaning. How can an experience you had live on in your memory? Pay especial attention to McCarthy's story about her son, and to Steinem's idea about family "mysteries." Make notes about the group's discussion in your journal, on the right-hand side.

3. Choose a family event to write about. It doesn't have to be an earthshaking event. It could be just a vague memory that you can clarify through writing. (Reread your journal for ideas.)

4. Consider your responses to the above passages. As you explore your subject in a draft, compare what happened to these writers or how they felt with your own life, and refer to the passages specifically in your own writing. Following is an example of how you might incorporate other ideas with your own:

> Thanksgiving around our house can be a traumatic time because my mother gets so uptight about making sure everything is perfect. Of course, in a house with four teenage kids, something is bound to go wrong—my sister decided to stay out with her boyfriend past her curfew on the night before Thanksgiving one year, which really sent my mother up the wall, and last year, I broke my mother's antique serving platter while setting the table. However, every year, the story we tell about The Most Disastrous Thanksgiving Ever concerns my brother Mark and a can of whipped cream.
>
> Like Reuel's experience with the bus, I'm sure that what actually happened is very different from the story as we tell it now. After reading the things by McCarthy and Steinem, I became interested in why my family keeps telling this story. I sat down with my brothers and sister and had an interesting discussion, which I'll tell about.
>
> Maria Calvado, student

chapter **7**

Writing to Inform

In this chapter we will focus on two closely related kinds of prose: informative writing and explanatory writing. Keep in mind that labels like these are only a convenience which lets us group together certain kinds of writing that have common features and purposes. Because writing that informs and writing that explains are so similar, we will refer to both of them as informative writing.

What Is Informative Writing?

As you might guess, we can broadly define **informative writing** as writing that conveys information. But the word "information" is itself tricky to define. For example, your name and address are one kind of information; your recipe for chili is another kind; and your reaction to country music is another kind altogether.

Purely informative writing is rare. For example, although a computer manual may tell you *how* to carry out a certain operation, it is also likely to explain *why* you should do it that way. Similarly, a historian not only describes *what* happened at a particular time but also explains *why* it happened as it did. It is often hard to present just the facts without trying to explain them in some way. Most papers or reports require that the writer go beyond the facts to some kind of explanation. Thus, informative writing often ends up as **explanatory writing**—writing that explains the information presented.

Informative writing, like expressive writing, can take on many forms, and it can be simple or highly complex, depending on the subject. On one end of the scale, we might find directions for operating some kind of a machine—a bicycle, a stereo, or a computer, for example.

Most textbooks would fall in the middle of our scale, because they are packed with information. What seems to be important to most readers of textbooks is the *arrangement* of material: Is the information presented in a clear and

117

organized way? Is it interesting to read? We'll return to this idea of arrangement later in the chapter.

News articles and historical writing might fall on the other end of the scale. Some such writing is as simple as an outline of events. But something like a biography of a president—which is loaded with information—is also likely to include explanations and the opinions of the writer. Informative writing can even be the basis for persuasion, if that is the writer's main purpose. (Chapter 8 examines persuasive writing; what you learn about informative writing will be very useful later.)

Reading Assignment   ■

Bring an example of informative or explanatory writing to class, and share it with your classmates. In small groups, discuss whether the examples are purely informative, or whether they have other purposes as well. Did anyone find a purely informative example?

Writing Assignments   ■

1.   On the left-hand side of your journal, write a short essay in which you simply provide information about something that happened to you.

2.   Write a second version of your informative essay, but this time explain *why* the event happened.

3.   On the right-hand side of your journal, say which of your two essays you prefer, and why.

Reading Informative Writing

In the essay "Four Kinds of Reading," poet and teacher Donald Hall defines reading for information as

> reading to learn about a trade, or politics, or how to accomplish something. We read a newspaper this way, or most textbooks, or directions on how to assemble a bicycle. With most of this sort of material, the reader can learn to scan the page quickly, coming up with what he needs and ignoring what is irrelevant to him, like the rhythm of the sentence, or the play of metaphor. Courses in speed reading can help us read for this purpose, training the eye to jump quickly across the page. If we read a newspaper with the attention we should give a novel or a poem, we will have time for nothing else, and our mind will be cluttered with clichés and dead metaphor. Quick eye-reading is a necessity to anyone who wants to keep up with what's happening, or learn much of

what has happened in the past. The amount of reflection, which interrupts and slows down the reading, depends on the material.

Donald Hall, *"Four Kinds of Reading"*

Since the selections in this chapter are primarily informative, your reading may well be "quick eye-reading." This is different from the way you had to read the expressive selections in Chapter 6, where you were responding to the writer's personality or to the use of detail. You may find that you will read more slowly in the next chapter, too, because it deals with persuasive writing, and you will have to reflect on what the author is saying.

Just as writers have different purposes for writing, so do readers have different purposes for reading. At times, we need to read a piece of writing more than once, or to adjust our speed of reading to match our purpose. Even though informative writing is often easy to read quickly, there is much to be gained from reading a selection more than once. Remember: One good reason for reading in this writing course is to examine how others write. After your first quick reading, reread the selections in this chapter more slowly a second or third time so that you can see how the writers convey their information.

By now you are an expert on reading for information, which you have been doing in school ever since you began to read—and began to take tests. But if you ever thought that all you had to do as a reader was to absorb facts and then recite them back on a test, you may have been disappointed with the results. Reading is always an active process. As the reader of informative writing, you must decide what is important to remember as you read along. Moreover, studies have shown that simply underlining what seems important is not as effective as taking notes and attempting to summarize the material in your own words.

Writing Assignment ■

The ability to summarize material is useful because then you can keep track of all the different things you have to read in college and on the job. A summary helps you find information when you need it. Following is one example of a summary—an abstract of an article found in a sociological journal. (An *abstract* is a summary of a piece of writing that highlights all the important points.)

An examination of prize-winning picture books reveals that women are greatly underrepresented in the titles, central roles, and illustrations. Where women do appear their characterization reinforces traditional sex-role stereotypes: boys are active while girls are passive; boys lead and rescue others while girls follow and serve others. Adult men and women are equally sex stereotyped; men engage in a wide variety of occupations while women are presented only as wives and mothers. The effects of these rigid sex-role portraits on the self image and aspirations of the developing child are discussed.

Lenore J. Weitzman, et al., *"Sex-Role Socialization in Picture Books
for Preschool Children"*

Notice that this summary simply states what the article is about; the writer offers no opinion about the topic or about the results of the study. If you wanted to do research into children's books or gender stereotyping, this abstract would help you decide whether or not to read the whole article.

Your assignment is to write a similar summary of any one of the essays in this book. In order to guide other readers, you will have to read the essay carefully, perhaps several times. If you don't understand the essay, your audience won't be able to follow your summary.

Concentrate on the overall meaning of the essay. Can you say what it is about in one sentence? The meaning may not be obvious at first, but in writing a summary, your job is to make the meaning clear for other readers.

Here are some guidelines to follow in your summary:

1. Put the name of the author and the title of the essay near the beginning of your summary.

2. Use the present tense throughout your summary. Instead of writing "says" over and over, look for substitutes like "asserts," "believes," "claims," and so on when they are appropriate.

3. Summarize the content—what the essay is about—not the structure. There is no reason to include phrases like "In the third paragraph. . . ."

4. State the writer's ideas in your own words. Save quotations for when the author says something unique or when your words cannot convey what the author means.

5. Be objective in reporting the author's ideas. You will have the opportunity to react to the essay later, either in class discussion or in your journal or an essay.

Informative writing makes you incorporate new ideas into your own knowledge of the subject. If you are reading actively, you will constantly compare new information with what you already know. Some writers make this easier by giving readers clues. For example, the writer might set off important words or phrases by underlining them or using different typefaces. Textbooks like this one are arranged so that readers can quickly grasp their organization. Headings and the layout of type steer readers to the main points. The following example is from a psychology textbook:

Looking Ahead

In this chapter we address a number of questions about memory that psychologists are investigating: What is memory and how does it operate? Are there different kinds of memory? How are we able to recall material from long ago yet forget information to which we have been exposed a few moments earlier? Can we improve our memories?

We begin the chapter by examining the issue of how information is stored and recalled in memory. We discuss evidence showing that there are actually three separate types of memory, and explain how each type operates in a somewhat different fashion to allow us to remember material we have been exposed to. Next, the problems of retrieving information from memory and the reasons information is sometimes forgotten are examined. We also consider some of the biological foundations of memory. Finally, we discuss some practical means of increasing one's memory capacity.

After reading and studying this chapter, then, you will be able to:

— List and describe the three kinds of memory
— Explain the phenomena involved in retrieving what is stored in memory
— Identify and describe the major causes of forgetting
— Outline four methods for improving your memory
— Define and apply the key terms and concepts listed at the end of the chapter

Robert S. Feldman, *Understanding Psychology*

The writer of this textbook is trying to help students study efficiently by outlining what is important before they read the chapter. By listing what students should be able to do after reading the chapter, the writer has guided them to the points they should focus on.

Writing Assignments ■

1. Go to the library, and read an encyclopedia article about a topic that interests you. On the right-hand side of your journal, take notes about how the writer arranges the information. Are sections introduced with short titles? Are there diagrams or pictures? Does the author define any special terms? After taking notes, use the left-hand side of your journal to write a short summary of the topic in your own words.

2. Do you know what your name means? Both your first name and your family name (surname) may have interesting meanings. Here's how to find out:

a. Begin by asking your parents, grandparents, other relatives, or whoever raised you, whether they know anything about the meaning and history of your names. Some families pass names along—even surnames, as in Thomas *Tramble* Turner and Emily *Taliefarro* Smith, or *Charleton* Heston.

b. Your first, middle, and last names may all be listed in a standard dictionary. Start, but don't stop, there. Your dictionary may even have a section about names in the appendix.

c. Look in a name dictionary or in an etymological dictionary (having to do with the history and meaning of words) for the meaning of your name. Ask the reference librarian to help you find these books, or check the card catalog to locate them.

d. If your names have an interesting ethnic origin, you may have to consult a foreign language dictionary for their meanings.

e. Are your names biblical? To find out, see if they are listed in the concordance found at the end of a standard Bible. (A *concordance* is an alphabetical list of all the words in a book). Then look up the passages in which your names occur to find out about the people you may have been named for.

3. On the right-hand side of your journal, take notes about what you learned about each of your names. Then, on the left-hand side, write a brief report to explain the significance of your names. Share your report in class.

Reading for Transitions

Readers can get confused when separate, unrelated ideas appear in a sentence or a paragraph and the writer has not connected them. Good writers try to help readers by providing **transitions**—words and phrases that signal how one idea relates to the next. Transitions are found in all kinds of writing, but they are especially important in informative writing. After all, if readers get lost and don't see how one idea relates to the next idea, how much information can they get? (Pages 126 and 127 list some common transition words.)

As a writer, your own writing makes perfect sense to you when you stop and read over parts of a draft or the whole draft. Because you know what you *intend* to write, you may think you have, indeed, *written* it in a way anyone could understand. But the ideas in a first draft are often unconnected, and sentences might not say exactly what you intend. Consider the following first draft:

> The quickest way to identify a novice in the laundry room is to look for the person who reads *every* label on *every* stitch of clothing. With a little amount of bleach and a lot of prayer, I was able to escape having a one-color wardrobe.
>
> Barbara Lesane, student

' We know that the general topic of this essay has to do with laundry. The writer tells us how to spot someone doing laundry for the first time, and she also says that she managed to do her laundry correctly. But certain information seems to be missing. For one thing, we have questions about *content*: Is the writer herself a novice at doing laundry? Is she herself that person who reads the labels on her clothes? And we also have questions about *structure*: What is the connection between these two sentences? Can something be added to make the connection clear?

Similar questions of content and structure arise in the following passage, which also lacks transitions:

> Europe used ginger in a frenzied manner. Europe kept Indian growers busy. Spain and Portugal decided to grow their own ginger in Jamaica and West Africa. India has become the main supplier to the United States.

Readers have no idea when these events occurred (a content question), or what the relationship must be between ideas (a structure question). Also, notice that the sentences are very short; read the passage out loud, and listen to how each sentence ends with a dull thud. The passage reads better and makes much more sense in its complete version, below. Notice how all the references to time help you to understand how the ideas are connected:

> Europe's frenzied use of ginger <u>throughout the Middle Ages</u> kept Indian growers busy <u>until the sixteenth century, when</u> Spain and Portugal decided to grow their own ginger in Jamaica and West Africa. Only <u>recently</u>, India has become the main supplier to the United States.
>
> Bruce Cost, *Ginger East and West*

Now read the revised passage out loud, and notice how the transition words also make the writing flow smoothly. The sentences no longer bump into each other, and readers are guided through the passage.

Here is another example in which time is used to provide transitions between ideas:

> <u>In December, the month before Kennedy's inauguration</u>, civil rights activists had won a victory in the Supreme Court <u>when</u> the justices ordered integration of bus stations and terminals serving interstate travelers.
>
> Juan Williams, *Eyes on the Prize*

Another way that transitions can hold a piece of writing together is by summing up information or providing an explanation before moving on to the next point:

preemie:
premature baby

> In recent years we have become penny-wise and dollar-foolish, saving a few dollars on food subsidies for pregnant poor women and then spending $40,000 to $100,000 of public money to care for each underweight preemie

that is born to many of these same women. <u>But besides incurring these direct costs</u>, by neglecting our children we are compromising the educational standards and future productivity of our nation.

Sylvia Ann Hewlett, A Lesser Life

In the next passage, the writer points out that what we know is a combination of inherited knowledge and new knowledge; again, a transitional summary phrase connects the ideas:

> Each change brings with it new attitudes and institutions created by new knowledge. These novel systems then either oust or coexist with the structures and attitudes held prior to the change. <u>Our modern view is thus</u> a mixture of present knowledge and past viewpoints which have stood the test of time and, for one reason or another, remain valuable in new circumstances.

James Burke, The Day the Universe Changed

Even a single transitional word can change the meaning of a passage. Compare the following two examples:

> The social sciences could be added at the "soft" end. Many of the sciences higher on the pecking order do not even recognize fields like economics and sociology as sciences.

> The social sciences could be added at the "soft" end, <u>although</u> many of the sciences higher on the pecking order do not even recognize fields like economics and sociology as sciences.

David Raup, The Nemesis Affair

In the second version of this passage, *although* tells us that there may be different views of the subject; the author signals that others may question whether such social sciences as economics and sociology should be ranked among the sciences at all.

Sometimes, as in this example, a writer can show the relationship between ideas and make connections between sentences just by adding one transitional word. Both as a reader and as a writer, you should be aware of the power of such words as *and*, *but*, *or*, *nor*, and *yet*. These **coordinate conjunctions** *connect* two or more equally important ideas. In contrast, words like *that*, *who*, *which*, and *where* are **subordinate conjunctions**; they indicate that one idea *depends* on the other (is subordinate to it). In the following passage, notice that *yet* and *but* each introduce a contrasting idea in the second part of those sentences:

> At the time, I was studying agricultural slavery in the profitable 1850s. I had found that in spite of the economic boom, something was amiss. Planters

in the coastal districts of South Carolina were making more money than at any other time in their lives; <u>yet</u> they were increasingly at odds with social currents in the rest of the Americas and Europe. They craved a literary and a technical culture worthy of their status, <u>but</u> they imported their books, tools, and simple machines from people hostile to their ideals. They wanted to modernize their industry, improve roads and waterways, and develop communications, <u>but</u> they were ideologically opposed to a strong central government with the means and authority to carry out the program.

Theodore Rosengarten, Tombee: Portrait of a Cotton Planter

While transitional words and phrases help us make sense of writing, sometimes we respond to a number of clues in combinations. Read the following passage:

My sons's early model Speak and Spell <u>had given</u> him what seemed to be hundreds of hours of enjoyment <u>when one day</u> the ENTER key broke off at its plastic hinge. <u>But since</u> Stephen could still fit his small finger into the buttonhole to activate the switch, he <u>continued to enjoy</u> the smart, if disfigured, toy. <u>Soon thereafter, however,</u> the E key snapped off, and <u>soon</u> the T and O keys followed suit. <u>Although he continued to use</u> the toy, its keyboard soon became a maze of missing letters and, for those that were saved from the vacuum cleaner, taped-on buttons.

Henry Petroski, To Engineer Is Human

First, look at the time relations indicated by the verbs (*had given, continued to enjoy, continued to use*). These words guide us through the order of events. Now, look at the other time words (*when one day, soon* and so on); they also help us in the same way. Finally, words like *but* and *since* don't tell us about the order of events, but they do tell us how the bits of information relate to each other.

The following example begins with a very bold transition (and notice that it is not even a complete sentence). The author abruptly turns from general comments about nutrition to look closely at the work of three writers:

Enough of generalities. The point can be made more vividly by looking at a handful of examples, past and present, and realizing how little has changed in the last 100 years. Listen for the common notes struck by these writers, three from before the age of vitamins, and one from the enlightened seventies.

Harold McGee, On Food and Cooking

Helping Readers Make Connections

Here is a list of some common transition words that help readers make connections.

To add material, to list ideas, and to show the order or steps in a sequence:

again	in addition	first, second, third
also	next	firstly, secondly, thirdly
and	in the first place,	finally
and then	in the second place	last

To show the order of importance:

besides	moreover	likewise
furthermore	equally important	too
further	most important	

To compare—to show similarities and likenesses:

in like manner	likewise	similarly
in the same way		

To contrast—to show differences:

yet	in contrast	nevertheless
and yet	in spite of	notwithstanding
but	on the other hand,	otherwise
for all that	on the contrary	still
however	although, though	

To give an example:

to example	specifically	in particular
for instance	in fact	indeed
to illustrate	that is	
to demonstrate	incidentally	

To indicate place:

opposite,	here	next to
on the opposite side	nearby	adjacent to
beyond		

Helping Readers Make Connections (*continued*)

To indicate purpose:

to this end	in order to	with this in mind
for this purpose	so that	

To show results or cause and effect:

hence	as a result	thereupon
accordingly	therefore	then
thus	consequently	

To summarize, to tie examples together, and to lead to a conclusion:

to sum up	in other words	in short
in brief	in essence	to be sure
on the whole	in sum	in any event

To indicate time:

meanwhile	recently, lately	later
immediately	at length	temporarily
after a while	soon	
afterward	in the meantime	

To concede—to admit that there are other points of view:

at the same time	this may be true	although
after all	of course	no doubt
admittedly	naturally	

To indicate transitions between paragraphs:

in addition to this fact	of course	it must be admitted,
as stated above	as a consequence	however
these circumstances	most important of all	in spite of
being true	on the whole	there are, of course, other
in conclusion	at the same time	for all these reasons

Reading and Writing Assignments ■

1. Read the following passage. On the right-hand side of your journal, list all the words that help you make transitions as a reader. On the left-hand side, describe how the transition words clarify the relationships between ideas.

> Current anthropological and sociological studies on aging support a policy of age-segregated housing for the elderly. Such residences are designed to encourage new social relationships which in turn develop social participation, morale, and self-esteem. Thus they counteract loneliness and isolation. The Knightsdale Estate has these virtues; but exactly which factors contribute to its success?
>
> Doris Francis, *Will You Still Need Me,*
> *Will You Still Feed Me, When I'm 84?*

2. Read any one of the essays in this book. On the right-hand side of your journal, list the words that help you make transitions as a reader. On the left-hand side, describe how the transition words help you to understand the relationships between ideas.

3. Examine how you use transition words in one of your own drafts. In the margin of your draft, make notes about how you would revise transitions to help your readers understand how ideas relate to each other.

How to Draft Informative Writing

Informative writing doesn't always require you to do library research or conduct interviews. When you write about yourself, or about things you know well, you already have the information you need. In the following paragraph, a Korean-American student explains her first reaction to hearing English spoken:

> When I first came to the United States, I spoke only fluent Korean. I thought that the Korean language was the only language spoken in the world, because even my American father spoke some Korean. The English that my father did speak, I decided, was just his way of being fancy or his way of communicating to my mom when my parents didn't want me to hear what they were saying. When I heard other American kids around me speak English, I thought that they, too, were talking about me, so I stayed away from American kids, and even formed a temporary prejudice against them.
>
> Cathy Johnson, student

In this example the writer tells us why she had a particular attitude about the English language. Her explanation—her information—is based on her own experience, not on research.

Writing Assignment ▪

You already have a great deal of information about all kinds of things that other people may not know. You may even be an expert about some things, such as your job, your hobbies and interests, or some talent you have. Select one thing that you enjoy and know how to do. On the right-hand side of your journal, list the important things that someone would have to know about your subject in order to do it well. On the left-hand side, write a paragraph telling someone about your subject.

When we meet someone for the first time, we often exchange factual information such as our names, occupations, ages, where we live, and so on. In this way we find some common ground and get to know one another. Each piece of information we exchange can trigger all sorts of interactions: "What an interesting name! How did your parents ever come up with that?" "*I'm* from Dallas, too—do you miss it?" "Isn't bridge work dangerous?" In fact, it's hard to limit our conversations to bare facts like name, occupation, and home town, because statistics don't really say much about a person. Given a fact or two, we seek further information; then we put it all together to understand and appreciate each other.

Writing Assignment ▪

Writing a biography of a classmate is good practice in collecting and arranging data in an orderly and interesting way. You have already collected data about your classmates just by getting to know them. The following guidelines will show you how to collect more information and organize it into a biography.

1. Find a biographical dictionary in the reference section of your library; a common one is the *Dictionary of American Biography*. Read about someone who interests you, and based on that entry, make up some questions you should ask your classmate about his or her life. In small groups, share the questions you have made up. In addition, make a list of people who know your subject— roommates, friends, relatives, teachers, counselors: What questions should you ask them to learn more about your subject?

2. Decide what kind of biography you want to write. Do you want to write a fact-based, straightforward biography as you found in the dictionary? Or would you like to do something more interesting? Magazines like *Rolling Stone, Interview, Ebony, Time*—even *People*—can give you ideas about how to focus on your subject. You may decide to concentrate on one or two important aspects of your classmate's life, rather than giving a complete history.

3. Interview your subject and any other people who might have information for your biography. Record what you learn carefully, and try to include some quotations about your subject; you may be able to use them when you begin writing.

4. Compare your information with the entry from the biographical dictionary. Will you use all the data you collected? List some categories under which the information can be organized, such as "early childhood," "education," and "most important events." Do you have too much information about some areas? Do you need to ask more questions about other things? If necessary, interview people again, with a new list of questions.

5. Write the biography of your classmate, and share it with the rest of the class.

Informative writing often begins as a list of facts or statistics, like the notes you take in class or on the job. In fact, the writing process itself may start as a list of ideas or facts that you want to use, as we saw in Chapter 2. Later, your lists and brainstorming begin to take shape through freewriting, and you draft a paper, or write a memo, or answer a question on an essay exam.

In the following example, the writer is simply making notes about important points concerning the "greenhouse effect." The notes will prompt the writer's memory during drafting, when the information comes together:

- definition: a long-term warming of planet caused by chemical changes in atmosphere
- atmospheric scientists: broad hist. cycles of warming & cooling
- experts: earth began warming after last ice age (18,000 yrs. ago)
- caused by carbon dioxide (CO_2) = the glass of a greenhouse—rays of the sun in, excess heat can't escape back into space
- humans: CO_2 from fossil fuels speeding warming trend—average temp. betw. 2° & 8° by 2050

After studying such notes, a writer rearranges them and makes connections between ideas. Most important, the writer aims what he or she says at a reader, and the result is informative writing like this:

> Scientists are also concerned about the "greenhouse effect," a long-term warming of the planet caused by chemical changes in the atmosphere. Atmospheric scientists have long known that there are broad historical cycles of global warming and cooling; most experts believe that the earth's surface gradually began warming after the last ice age peaked 18,000 years ago.

. . . [T]he greenhouse effect [is] caused in large part by carbon dioxide (CO_2). The effect of CO_2 in the atmosphere is comparable to the glass of a greenhouse: it lets the warming rays of the sun in but keeps excess heat from reradiating back into space. Indeed, man-made contributions to the greenhouse effect, mainly CO_2 that is generated by the burning of fossil fuels, may be hastening a global warming trend that could raise average temperatures between 2°F and 8°F by the year 2050. . . .

Michael D. Lemonick, "The Heat Is On"

Writing Assignment ■

Take a page or two of your notes from another class—based either on a lecture or on your reading—and write them up as an essay, using the left-hand side of your journal. Keep in mind that you are rewriting the notes for someone else to read and understand. After you finish the essay, think about what you do differently when writing for a reader other than yourself. Record your observations on the right-hand side of your journal.

Informative writing very often provides directions about how to build something (like a birdhouse), or cook something (like burritos), or operate a machine (like a computer). Think of how often you have had to read directions—about everything from how to bake a pizza to how to use your bank card. And think of all the directions you have had to give. As you know, it sometimes seems easier to give verbal directions than to write them out. In giving verbal directions, you can point, move your hands around, and make faces—all of which somehow helps your listener to understand. But we can't always give (or receive) verbal directions, and with today's technology we need instructions to operate many of the machines that make life easier. It's become almost impossible to depend on verbal directions.

Let's look at some simple directions first. A freshman wrote these instructions about what equipment to bring when camping:

To be properly prepared, you must know the basic items to take with you, such as warm clothes and good boots. A few years ago, I went on a trip to the mountains and forgot to pack my jacket. The temperature dropped from 70 to 40. By the time the weekend was over, I figured out a good motto: "It is better to pack something and not need it than to not pack it and need it." At all times of the year, a poncho or raincoat with a warm lining should be packed. It should be placed in the top of your pack so it will be easy to get to if you run into some rain while hiking. Bring good hiking boots so that you won't get blisters. Nothing ruins a camping trip more than having to sit by the campfire soaking your feet while your friends explore the woods.

John Hoyle, student

Notice that this writer directly addresses readers, because he intends for them to follow his directions. Do you think his information would be more effective as a simple list, or do the examples help you to understand why his suggestions are valuable?

The more complex a task is, the more complex instructions are likely to be. For example, the 1988 user's manual for Microsoft Word, a word-processing program, is over 450 pages long. Here is a short passage from this manual:

To start Word and display the document you last worked on

Follow either of the basic procedures above to start Word with a diskette or a hard disk system, except:

Instead of typing *word* at the prompt, type: *word/L*

/L is called a *switch*. You can type either a lowercase or uppercase L. When you quit Word, the path and filename of the document in window 1 is stored on the Word disk or directory. When you start Word with /L switch, Word checks for this information. If you move or delete the document from the disk or directory where it was when you quit, or accidentally delete the file (MW.INI) containing the information, Word starts up with a new untitled document instead.

Example Suppose you quit Word with README.DOC in window 1. Type *word/L* to start up with README.DOC in that window.

Of course, these directions are hard to follow if you aren't already familiar with computers. But notice that the writers of this manual try to be as clear as possible, and they give examples to explain the operations of the program.

In the college classroom, you are often expected to demonstrate in writing what you have learned. And very often the material is as new and difficult as the passage from this computer manual. In order to acquire new knowledge and *learn*, you must

1. Read the textbook and other materials, listen to lectures, ask questions, and participate in class discussions

2. Integrate the new information with your own experiences and what you already know—as you read, listen, and discuss and as you study on your own

If you view learning in this way, you will see that it is an active process, not a matter of passively "absorbing" information as it washes over you. One good way to become an active learner is to write *before* reading, and you have had some practice applying this strategy to expressive writing in Chapter 6. Now, let's use the same strategy to examine informative writing. Read the following selections as a writer who wants to learn about informative writing by studying how other writers convey information.

Write Before Reading ■

Before you read the next passage, use the right-hand side of your journal to jot down all that you know about human memory. Don't worry if you blank out. Just try to write down a definition of memory, and give one example of a time when you relied on your memory.

Our Working Memory: Short-Term Memory

sensory stimuli:
anything that can be perceived by the senses

Because the information that is stored briefly in our sensory memories consists of representations of raw sensory stimuli, it is not necessarily meaningful to us. In order for us to make sense of it and to allow for the possibility of long-term retention, the information must be transferred to the next stage of memory, short-term memory. Short-term memory, sometimes referred to as working memory, is the memory in which material initially has meaning, although the maximum length of retention is relatively short.

The specific process by which sensory memories are transformed into short-term memories is not yet clear. Some theorists suggest that the information is first translated into graphical representations or images, and others hypothesize that the transfer occurs when the sensory stimuli are changed to words (Baddeley, 1985). What is clear, however, is that unlike sensory memory, which holds a relatively full and detailed—if short-lived—representation of the world, short-term memory has incomplete representational capabilities.

In fact, the specific amount of information that can be held in short-term memory has been identified: seven bits, or "chunks," of information, with variations up to plus or minus two chunks. A chunk is a meaningful grouping of stimuli which can be stored as a unit in short-term memory. According to George Miller (1956), it could be individual letters, as in the following list:

C T N Q M W N

But a chunk might also consist of larger categories such as words or other meaningful units. For example, consider the following list of letters:

TWACIAABCCBSMTVUSAAAA

Clearly, because the list exceeds seven digits, it is difficult to recall them after one exposure. But suppose they were presented to you as follows:

TWA CIA ABC CBS MTV USA AAA

In this case, even though there are still twenty-one letters, it would be possible to store them in memory, since they represent only seven chunks.

Chunks can vary in size from single letters or numbers to categories that are far more complicated, and the specific nature of what constitutes a chunk varies according to one's past experience. . . .

Robert S. Feldman, *Understanding Psychology*

Write After Reading

1. Now that you have read the passage about memory, compare the notes you wrote before reading with what you learned from the passage. Did your reading confirm what you already knew, or do you need to revise your notion of memory? On the left-hand side of your journal, directly opposite what you wrote about memory, write a new paragraph that takes into account what you learned from your reading.

2. Notice how the author introduces the terms that psychologists use when discussing memory. On the right-hand side of your journal, use your own words to define *short-term memory, sensory stimuli*, and *chunks*. Try to give an example of each term.

3. In small groups, discuss the first paragraph of this passage as it applies to reading, studying, and learning. What does it tell you about how to approach new material? On the right-hand side of your journal, record the results of your group's discussion.

Historical writing is always informative, because it includes so many facts. As you read the following passage, ask yourself which facts are truly important:

Several black men accompanied Pathfinder John C. Frémont during three expeditions into the far West. One, Mifflin Gibbs, later became a businessman, newspaper publisher and civil rights activist in gold rush California. Another, Saunders Jackson, joined Frémont's last expedition because he needed seventeen hundred dollars to purchase his family from their Missouri slave master. When gold was discovered on Frémont's California land, Jackson was permitted to dig out that amount, a feat he accomplished in a few days. He immediately left for Missouri and a family reunion of free people.

But probably the most skilled of the black explorers with Frémont was Jacob Dodson, a young servant to Frémont's father-in-law, Senator Thomas Hart Benton. Frémont, at the outset of his expeditions in 1842, described Dodson as "only 18, but strong and active and nearly six feet in height." Young Dodson, according to another member of the expedition, became "expert as a Mexican with the lasso, sure as a mountaineer with the rifle, equal to either on horse or foot, and always a lad of courage and fidelity." Once, the party had to ride 840 miles from Los Angeles to Monterey and back in nine days. Another time, when Frémont, Dodson and another man galloped 120 miles in one day,

Dodson was responsible for roping fresh horses when their steeds became exhausted.

William Loren Katz, *The Black West*

The author packs a great deal of information into these two paragraphs about the black men who explored the West with Frémont. We learn not only what role they played in Frémont's company but also what two of them did after the expedition. If you were asked to summarize this passage, which facts would you emphasize, and which would you discard?

The next example of informative writing also presents many historical facts—who, what, where, and when—but it adds an explanation of why those facts were important to civil rights leaders:

In December, the month before Kennedy's inauguration, civil rights activists had won a victory in the Supreme Court when the justices ordered integration of bus stations and terminals serving interstate travelers. That court triumph made Kennedy's first few months in office all the more disappointing to blacks. But civil rights leaders still believed that Kennedy was a friend at heart and they knew he owed blacks a political debt. Eisenhower had been reluctant to use federal force after Little Rock. But Kennedy, civil rights leaders hoped, would not back down. Without enforcement from the executive branch, in this case in the form of a ruling from the Interstate Commerce Commission ordering compliance, the Supreme Court ruling would be meaningless. Just how far would Kennedy go to enforce the nation's civil rights laws?

The Congress of Racial Equality (CORE) intended to find out. In 1947 CORE had organized the "Journey of Reconciliation" after the Supreme Court ruled that segregated seating on interstate buses and trains was unconstitutional. Together, black and white CORE workers had traveled by bus throughout the upper South in an attempt to test the ruling. They were harassed and finally arrested in North Carolina for violating the state's segregation laws.

Juan Williams, *Eyes on the Prize*

In this passage we learn about the initial disappointment of the black leaders in President Kennedy, their ultimate faith in him, and their hope that he would stand firm on civil rights. At the same time, we learn what the leaders did to test Kennedy and the Supreme Court ruling.

Now compare another informative passage from the same book:

The civil rights movement in America began a long time ago. As early as the seventeenth century, blacks and whites, slaves in Virginia and Quakers in Pennsylvania, protested the barbarity of slavery. Nat Turner, Sojourner Truth, Frederick Douglass, William Lloyd Garrison, John Brown and Harriet Tubman are but a few of those who led the resistance to slavery before the Civil War. After the Civil War, another protracted battle began against slavery's legacy— racism and segregation. But for most Americans, the civil rights movement began on May 17, 1954, when the Supreme Court handed down the Brown v. Board of Education of Topeka decision outlawing segregation in public schools. The Court unlocked the door, but the pressure applied by thousands of men and women in the movement pushed that door open wide enough to allow blacks to walk through it toward this country's essential prize: freedom.

Juan Williams, Eyes on the Prize

This passage, again, includes many facts: that resistance to slavery began in the seventeenth century; that various individuals led the resistance before the Civil War; and that the battle was renewed after the Civil War, in the nineteenth century. But we also learn that, for most Americans, the civil rights movement began in the 1950s. Is that a fact, or is the author expressing an opinion? As a careful reader, *you* have to decide whether that statement is correct or not.

Reading and Writing Assignment ■

Go to the library, and read about the events that occurred on your birth date. (Most libraries have some major newspapers on microfilm, such as the *New York Times, Washington Post, Los Angeles Times*, and *The Wall Street Journal*.) Or, if you prefer and can do so, go to the office of your hometown newspaper and read about local happenings on the day you were born.

As you read, try to distinguish between the more important historical events and less important events. Are any of the events that were important on your birthday still important today? Can you find any events that have been resolved or have worsened since you were born? On the right-hand side of your journal, take notes abut what you learn. On the left-hand side, write a short essay about what the world was like on the day you were born.

Informative writing can have other purposes besides simply telling us something we should know or might want to know. The example that follows is from the 1948 edition of the *Scout Field Book* and is addressed to boys between the ages of eight and twelve.

Write Before Reading ■

Before you read the followng passage, use the right-hand side of your journal to jot down all that you know about snakes. Don't worry if you blank out. Just try to define what a snake is, and give an example of when you saw one—whether in the wild, on television, or at the zoo.

REPTILE FACTS

When you see a snake slithering off before you or swishing into a crack between the rocks, what do you do? Do you get scared? Do you grab for a stone to kill it? Or is your first thought to get closer to have a good look at it?

Well, if a fellow is scared of a snake, it is usually because he believes some of the crazy notions people have about snakes.

Somebody may tell you, for instance, that some snakes jump clear off the ground to strike at you. They couldn't if they tried! Snakes move on the ends of their ribs and have to brace themselves to lift any part of their body up in the air. Even the poisonous snakes can't strike much longer than about one-half the length of their body.

Or someone may yell: "Watch out! It has its tongue out to sting you!" The long, forked tongue is not a stinger. It's an antenna with which the snake can "taste" your presence.

Or: "Don't touch that slimy creature!" Snakes aren't slimy. They are covered with perfectly dry scales.

If you really want to find out about snakes, forget all the fables you may have heard about them, and get down to facts.

Now, if some fellow tries to kill every snake he sees, he is being just plain ignorant.

Most of our snakes are beneficial. The main diet of the smaller ones consists of snails, worms, insects, and their grubs. The larger ones go after rats, mice, and gophers. Even the poisonous snakes rid fields and woods of rats and mice.

So let's hope that there is neither fear of snakes nor ignorance in your Patrol, but a real desire to find out more about them. . . .

Our Poisonous Snakes

Get to know the poisonous snakes first.

Fortunately, we have only four kinds of poisonous snakes in the United States, and it is quite easy to tell them apart, if you will take the trouble to learn what they look like.

What makes them dangerous is the fact that they have glands in their heads that produce a strong poison, and pairs of grooved or hollow teeth, fangs, through which they can shoot this poison into the flesh of their victim with a well-directed thrust of a powerful head.

Rattlesnakes are found in all forty-eight states. They vary in size from babies, of about eight inches, up to eight feet. Their coloring and pattern depends to a certain extent upon where they live. Pale colored ones often live in deserts, darker ones in forests. The tail is provided with a queer "musical" instrument. This rattle is a horny, jointed structure which the snake can shake so fast that you can hardly see it. The buzz is a warning signal—one it is best to heed! The number of rattle-joints, by the way, does not tell the rattler's age. One is added whenever the rattlesnake changes its skin, and that may be three to five times a year.

Scout Field Book, 1948

Write After Reading   ■

Now that you have read the passage about snakes, compare the notes you wrote before reading with what you learned from the passage. Did your reading confirm what you already knew, or do you need to revise your ideas about snakes? On the left-hand side of your journal, directly opposite what you wrote about snakes, write a new paragraph that takes into account what you learned.

Although the writer is clearly trying to inform his audience, he also has another purpose in mind: to persuade young readers to respect snakes and to leave them alone. He does this in part by using facts—by shooting down some popular myths about snakes and by listing the benefits that snakes perform in the natural environment. Beyond facts, however, the writer also expresses some opinions, saying that anyone who would harm a snake is "being just plain ignorant." Since no one wants to be considered ignorant, this statement is persuasive, even though it is really an opinion. In addition, the passage is written in an amusing way, especially in the discussion of myths about snakes. Readers get a number of facts about snakes, but the facts and the writer's tone also serve another purpose: to persuade us not to harm snakes.

The last two examples—about the civil rights movement and about snakes—show that informative writing may do more than simply inform. Especially when you are learning new information, you have to be a careful reader to distinguish between facts and opinions. However, just paying attention to *content*, or subject matter, may not be enough. It is also important to watch how information is arranged. In the following passage, notice how the writer first defines his subject by giving some examples and by arranging them in a certain order. Then, in the second paragraph, he moves beyond facts to express some opinions that are based on the arrangement of information he himself has set up. As you read the passage, keep asking yourself whether the information is a fact or an opinion:

pecking order:
the order of
importance
among chickens

The various fields of science have a well-defined pecking order. There is a range from "soft" science to "hard" science. In the United States, molecular biology, biochemistry, astrophysics, and high-energy physics are now at the hard end. They have great authority in the scientific and general communities, and they are seen as somehow more rigorous and precise than other sciences.

paleontology:
the study of
fossils

At the other end of the spectrum are fields like ecology, paleontology, and behavioral biology. The social sciences could be added at the "soft" end, although many of the sciences higher on the pecking order do not even recognize fields like economics and sociology as sciences.

I think the differences between the hard and soft sciences are more matters of perception—and some good marketing—than fact. Some fields, like economics, are inherently more difficult than others, like physics, because they deal in complex systems with many more unpredictable elements. The softer sciences also tend to have more observational data, and this has the irony of making it more difficult to construct simple, unifying theories. All fields of science have some very soft spots not immediately obvious.

David Raup, *The Nemesis Affair*

Write After Reading

Look at the first sentence: "The various fields of science have a well-defined pecking order." This topic sentence tells us that the paragraph will be about the relationships among various sciences. What do you think of the phrase "pecking order"? Does it sound serious enough for the topic at hand? Why do you think the author used it? On what basis are the various sciences arranged into a "pecking order"? What makes a science "hard" or "soft"? And where do social sciences like sociology, economics, and psychology fall in this classification system?

In small groups, discuss these questions in class, and summarize the discussion on the right-hand side of your journal. Then, on the left-hand side, write a paragraph in which you agree or disagree with this method of classifying sciences; use examples to support your point of view.

Informative writing often includes many definitions, because the writer has to be sure that readers will understand basic terms and concepts. If readers don't understand what basic terms mean, they will not grasp the information. In fact, an important part of reading informative writing is recognizing when you have found a definition. Look again at this sentence from the passage we read earlier about memory:

Short-term memory, sometimes referred to as working memory, is the memory in which material initially has meaning, although the maximum length of retention is relatively short.

Notice that there are no clear signs that this *is* a definition. The term is not printed in bold type (**short-term memory** is . . .) or in italic type (*short-term memory* is . . .), as important terms often are printed in textbooks. Nor is the definition presented like an entry in a dictionary (as "pecking order" was presented in the last example). Instead, it is up to you, the reader, to recognize that the author is defining what he means by "short-term memory." If you don't notice his definition, you may not understand what the passage means.

The following passage is from a journal for teachers of reading. Professionals can understand its special vocabulary, but to most readers it may seem difficult and abstract. As you read, pay attention to the arrangement of ideas, as indicated by underlining. Also study the definitions in the margin:

Jean Piaget (1896–1980): a psychologist who specialized in child development

syncretism: the attempt to combine differing beliefs

juxtaposition: the act of placing things side by side

Piaget identified <u>three major areas</u> related to question answering which could explain a reader's inability to consider several items of information at the same time. . . . This inability may surface in various types of responses to a reasoning task. <u>These responses can be classified</u> according to the following dimensions of reasoning: <u>syncretism, juxtaposition, and selectivity.</u> Syncretism is the tendency to connect a series of separate ideas into one confused whole. <u>In other words,</u> the child does not try to change the knowledge already stored in his or her head to accommodate the real meaning of a concept or to understand the meaning of the question. The child selects one or two words from the question and free associates. <u>Juxtaposition</u> is the failure on the part of the child to consider the relationship of two events or ideas placed next to each other in a passage. The child considers only the isolated events or ideas and is apparently unaware of any relationship between them. <u>The third dimension, selectivity,</u> requires the child to systematically select the relevant from irrelevant

text implicit question: one that requires readers to make connections between ideas on their own

information in his or her memory store to answer the question. Although the child may remember most of the information read, he or she may not be able to select the particular facts which answer the question. As a result, the child may respond with accurate but irrelevant information. The poor readers' responses to text implicit questions reveal that all of these dimensions may be operating.

Betty C. Holmes, "The Effect of Prior Knowledge on the
Question Answering of Good and Poor Readers"

The underlining and the definitions in the margins were added to show that this writer *does* define important terms in the body of her text, but she leaves it up to the reader to find them. There are no big arrows pointing to definitions. But the writer has given an important clue to understanding the first term, *syncretism*, when she writes: "In other words, . . ." What follows that clue is another way of saying and understanding what syncretism is. The writer does not, however, set up the other definitions as clearly; it is up to you to find the definitions of *juxtaposition* and *selectivity*.

Our final example of informative writing also includes some amusing expressive writing. Notice how the writer uses baseball statistics (raw information) to tell a story:

1962: A WARM CUP OF COFFEE

Of all of the thousands of players who have been called up late in the season and given a brief chance to show what they can do, probably the most impressive argument was made by a giant named Walter Franklin Bond in September of 1962. . . .

Walt Bond was not destined to be a great player, and destiny in his case was unusually forceful. Bond was 6'7" and fairly mobile for a big guy; his natural position was first base but the [Cleveland] Indians had him playing the outfield. He had hit .320 at Salt Lake City, fourth in the Pacific Coast League, with only eleven homers but 12 triples. The Indians had finished under .500 in '61 and '62, and you might think that a 6'7" guy who could run and hit baseballs out of sight would make an impression on them, but the Indians have never been the kind of organization that would let itself be intimidated by common sense. . . . Bond was assigned to Jacksonville for the 1963 season, and told to work on his grammar or something.

Well, to make a long story short, Walt Bond would be dead of leukemia in five years. He finally got a chance to play, with Houston in 1964, in the worst hitter's park in baseball, and when he seemed in danger of succeeding anyway, they built a park that was even tougher. In 1964 he hit .254 with 20 home runs and 85 RBI—not outstanding numbers under any conditions, but you might note that his teammates Rusty Staub, Jimmie Wynn, Pete Runnels and Joe Morgan hit a combined .215. Of his twenty-seven home runs as an Astro, only nine were hit in Houston. I can't remember what it was, but I vaguely recall that he was involved in some kind of unseemly incident there in '65. Whatever, he hit .316 with Denver in '66, got a brief shot with Minnesota in '67, and died in Detroit on September 14, 1967.

The Bill James Historical Baseball Abstract

The title of this story about Walt Bond is based on a bit of baseball slang. When someone plays in the major leagues for only a short period of time, baseball insiders say he came up "for a cup of coffee." Using this idea, the author turns statistics—essentially raw information—into a story about a baseball player who had only a brief success. He presents a good deal of information, and he does it in a humorous way. Notice how he expresses himself through his voice as a writer, especially in this part:

. . . you might think that a 6'7" guy who could run and hit baseballs out of sight would make an impression on them, but the Indians have never been the kind of organization that would let itself be intimidated by common sense.

. . . Bond was assigned to Jacksonville for the 1963 season, and told to work on his grammar or something.

James is making a joke about the Cleveland team's apparent lack of judgment, and about the fact that the Jacksonville team failed to use Bond and his talents. Although informative writing is often very serious, this passage should help you to realize how difficult it is to classify the kinds of writing, including your own. A writer often has more than one purpose—expressive writing can also be informative, and informative writing can also be expressive. The many examples in this chapter show that writers often use more than one kind of writing in order to reach their audience. Just as you approach reading in different ways, depending on the kind of material and your purpose for reading, so do writers approach writing in different ways.

Writing Assignment ■

Before going on to the assignments to write your own informative essay, look back through this chapter. What did you learn about informative writing that you didn't know before? On the right-hand side of your journal, summarize what you have learned about gathering and arranging information; about reading for transitions; and about finding or providing definitions in informative writing. In small groups, share your journal notes with your classmates.

Assignments in Informative Writing

The following pages guide you through three different informative writing assignments. Here is a brief description of them:

1. The Objective Reporter   This assignment asks you to present information as a reporter must—without letting your personality come between the reader and the facts. You will be asked to rewrite a passage or to describe an event in your own life, presenting "just the facts."

2. Customs and Folkways   This assignment invites you to describe some custom or tradition that is practiced in your family, religion, community, or ethnic group.

3. Writing Oral History   This assignment asks you to interview someone and to present an eyewitness account of the past.

To help decide which assignment interests you most, quickly read what each assignment is about and how you might approach it. Also look over your journal and the informative writing you have already done in this chapter. Perhaps you can develop one of your earlier drafts further, or can adapt it to fit one of the following assignments. If you can't decide which assignment to do, consult with your teacher.

When you have picked an assignment, turn to Chapter 2 for some tips about how to discover your ideas. Then, after you have written your discovery draft, Chapters 4 and 5 and Worksheets 1 through 6 will help you plan and edit your final draft.

Assignment 1.   The Objective Reporter

The book *Bearing the Cross*, by political scientist David Garrow, presents an account of Martin Luther King and the early days of the civil rights movement in the South. Garrow himself did not see the events he describes—he was only two years old when the Montgomery bus boycott began. But from newspapers, interviews with eyewitnesses, and other materials he gathered enough information to write the following descriptions of how King was physically attacked while giving a speech and of the role Rosa Parks played in the bus boycott. Perhaps what is most striking about Garrow's book is his objective, unemotional tone.

Furthermore, by writing about a specific incident involving King, Garrow tells us more about the black leader's commitment to nonviolence than any statement like "Martin Luther King was deeply committed to nonviolence" might. And the story of Parks's resistance captures the spirit of many individuals who "had had the courage to say no."

Write Before Reading   ■

Before you read the following two passages from *Bearing the Cross*, use the
right-hand side of your journal to jot down all that you know about Martin
Luther King's pacifism and about the Montgomery bus boycott. Don't worry if
you blank out or don't know much about King and the boycott; write down
whatever comes to mind.

Late Friday morning, September 28, King addressed the convention's
final session from the stage of the L.R. Hall Auditorium. During his remarks, a
young white man who had been sitting in the sixth row rose suddenly and
approached King. Without warning, the man punched King in the face. A
shocked stillness came over the crowd, which watched in amazement as King
stood his ground and accepted several blows. As one eyewitness described it,
King made no move to strike back or turn away. Instead, he looked at his
assailant and spoke calmly to him. Within seconds, several people pulled the
attacker away. While others led the crowd in song, King and his colleagues
spoke with the assailant at the rear of the stage. Then King returned to the
podium to tell the audience that the man, Roy James, was a twenty-four-year-
old member of the Nazi party from Arlington, Virginia. King said he would not
press charges against him. Birmingham police arrived and insisted that the city
would press charges even if King chose not to. Without delay, James was
hustled before a local court Judge, convicted of assault, and sentenced to thirty
days in jail and a $25 fine. Birmingham's segregationist mayor, Art Hanes,
visited the courtroom to tell James to his face never again to set foot in Birmingham. The entire incident, from assault to sentencing, took barely four
hours. It left most onlookers stunned and impressed by King's lack of fear
when confronted by direct physical violence.

David Garrow, *Bearing the Cross*

THE MONTGOMERY BUS BOYCOTT, 1955–56

Thursday had been busy and tiring for Mrs. Raymond A. Parks. Her job
as a tailor's assistant at the Montgomery Fair department store had left her
neck and shoulder particularly sore, and when she left work at 5:30 P.M. that
December 1, 1955, she went across the street to a drugstore in search of a
heating pad. Mrs. Parks didn't find one, but she purchsaed a few other articles
before recrossing the street to her usual bus stop on Court Square. The buses
were especially crowded this cold, dark evening, and when she boarded one
for her Cleveland Avenue route, only one row of seats—the row immediately
behind the first ten seats that always were reserved for whites only—had any
vacancies. She took an aisle seat, with a black man on her right next to the
window, and two black women in the parallel seat across the way.

As more passengers boarded at each of the two next stops, the blacks moved to the rear, where they stood, and the whites occupied their exclusive seats at the front of the bus. At the third stop, more passengers got on, and one, a white male, was left standing after the final front seat was taken. The bus driver, J. F. Blake, looked back and called out to Mrs. Parks and her three colleagues, "All right you folks, I want those two seats." Montgomery's customary practice of racial preference demanded that all four blacks would have to stand in order to allow one white man to sit, since no black was allowed to sit parallel with a white. No one moved at first. Blake spoke out again: "You all better make it light on yourselves and let me have those seats." At that, the two women across from Mrs. Parks rose and moved to the rear; the man beside her rose also, and she moved her legs to allow him out into the aisle. She remained silent, but shifted to the window side of the seat.

Blake could see that Mrs. Parks had not arisen. "Look, woman. I told you I wanted the seat. Are you going to stand up?" At that, Rosa Lee Mc-Cauley Parks uttered her first word to him: "No." Blake responded. "If you don't stand up, I'm going to have you arrested." Mrs. Parks told him to go right ahead, that she was not going to move. Blake said nothing more, but got off the bus and went to a phone. No one spoke to Mrs. Parks, and some passengers began leaving the bus, not wanting to be inconvenienced by the incident.

Mrs. Parks was neither frightened nor angry. "I was thinking that the only way to let them know I felt I was being mistreated was to do just what I did—resist the order," she later recalled. "I had not thought about it and I had taken no previous resolution until it happened, and then I simply decided that I would not get up. I was tired, but I was usually tired at the end of the day, and I was not feeling well, but then there had been many days when I had not felt well. I had felt for a long time, that if I was ever told to get up so a white person could sit, that I would refuse to do so." The moment had come, and she had had the courage to say no.

Blake returned from the phone, and stood silently in the front of the bus. After a few minutes, a police squad car pulled up, and two officers, F. B. Day and D. W. Mixon, got on the bus. Blake pointed to Mrs. Parks, said he needed the seat, and that "the other ones stood up." The two policemen came toward her, and one, in Mrs. Parks's words, "asked me if the driver hadn't asked me to stand. I said yes. He asked, 'Why didn't you stand up?' I said I didn't think I should have to. I asked him, 'Why do you push us around?' He said, 'I don't know, but the law is the law, and you are under arrest.' So the moment he said I was under arrest, I stood up. One picked up my purse, one picked up my shopping bag, and we got off the bus." They escorted her to the patrol car, and returned to talk to Blake. The driver confirmed that he wanted to press charges under Montgomery's bus segregation ordinance, and the officers took Mrs. Parks first to police headquarters and then to the city jail. By then Mrs.

Parks was tense, and her throat was uncommonly dry. She spied a water fountain, but was quickly told that she could not drink from it—it was for whites only. Her processing complete, Mrs. Parks was allowed to call home and tell her family what had transpired.

David Garrow, Bearing the Cross

Reading Like a Writer   ■

Now that you have read the two passages, compare your notes about what you knew before reading with what you learned. Did your reading confirm what you already knew, or do you need to revise your ideas? On the left-hand side of your journal, write a short passage about these events that incorporates what you already knew and what you learned from your reading.

Guidelines for Assignment 1   ■

1. In small groups, discuss what you think *objectivity* means. Is it possible to be 100 percent objective? Can you point to any examples of true objectivity? In the media? In history? In science? Take notes about the group's discussion, using the right-hand side of your journal.

2. Choose one of the following assignments:

a. Rewrite one of Garrow's passages as though you were an eyewitness who saw the event. Try to describe the scene so that readers can see what happened.

b. Take any passage from a novel or any scene from a film, and rewrite it as though you were a historian recording only the facts.

c. Describe any event from your own life as though you were a historian recording only the facts.

Assignment 2.   Customs and Folkways

Among the things that contribute to the richness of our lives are the religious, ethnic, community, and family customs that we honor. These customs or traditions can range from the most elaborate rituals to the simplest performances—from a marriage ceremony to how one greets a family member after a long absence.

Write Before Reading   ■

Before you read Jan Harold Brunvand's "Customs and Festivals" from *The Study of American Folklore*, use the right-hand side of your journal to jot down all that you know about customs and festivals. Don't worry if you blank out; try to define "customs" and "festivals," and write about the ones you observe in your family, community, or ethnic group.

CUSTOMS AND FESTIVALS

Possibly no other kind of American folklore has been so frequently referred to, yet so vaguely defined, so ill-classified, and so little understood or studied, as folk customs have been. . . .

To begin with, it is clear that customs are closely associated with superstitions. . . . Like superstitions, customs involve both verbal and nonverbal elements that are traditionally applied in specific circumstances. But unlike superstitions, customs as such do not involve faith in the magical results of such applications. Thus, the "customs" that incorporate traditional belief in the supernatural are usually classified as "superstitions."

A **custom** is a traditional *practice*—a mode of individual behavior or a habit of social life—that is transmitted by word of mouth or imitation, then ingrained by social pressure, common usage, and parental or other authority. When customs are associated with holidays they become *calendar customs*, and when such events are celebrated annually by a whole community they become *festivals*.

ballad: a popular romantic or sentimental song

quilting bee: a social gathering that combines work and amusement; in this case, the group meets to sew a quilt

barn raising: a gathering at which people build a barn together

Transmitting folklore is itself customary. Storytelling, ballad-singing, riddle-posing, game-and-prank playing, and the like all depend for their survival on traditional performance and acceptance rather than on official control. Generally folklorists have not separated the customary contexts from folklore texts, except perhaps when studying something like quilting bees or barn raisings rather than quilt patterns or barns themselves, or searching for a "liars' contest" rather than merely for texts of tall tales. But there are more subtle behavioral patterns, integral parts of folklore performance situations, which folklorists are just beginning to study: "framing" devices that initiate and conclude folk transmissions, postural and gestural clues to meaning, audience-response codes, nonverbalized folk beliefs, and the like.

This expanded sense of the term "custom" involves the folklorist in what anthropologists term **ethnography**—the descriptive study of all traditions in a particular group or region. Ethnographic descriptions of different cultures make possible comparative studies, or **ethnology**. . . . **Folklife** refers to the full traditional lore, behavior, and material culture of any folk group, with emphasis on the customary and material categories. . . .

mores: accepted customs that a group sees as essential to its welfare

Not all customs are still living folklore. Those which have become a fixed part of national behavior and are practiced unvaryingly throughout a country (or sometimes several countries) are termed *manners* or *mores*, although their origins may lie in folklore and their sustaining power may still be that of tradition. The domestic manners that characterize Americans include switching the fork from hand to hand while eating, serving certain drinks iced, and maintaining a high degree of informality in social life. Manners may involve different levels of awareness, however: we switch fork hands as a matter of course; but icing drinks is a deliberate act, and social informality may be either studied or "natural."

Mores are defined as traditional modes of behavior that have achieved the status of moral requirements, often being institutionalized in laws. These include such practices as monogamous marriages, the patterns of family naming, and the age when adulthood begins. The attitude of *ethnocentrism* is the assumption that one's own customs, manners, and mores are the "right" ones, and that all others are scaled out in degrees of "wrongness" from this center. Ethnocentrism accounts for feelings among Americans, for example, that may range from intolerance of some other culture's religion (or lack of religion) to mild annoyance occasioned by having to drive on the "wrong" side of the highway in England, or being expected to bow as a greeting in Japan. That culture-contacts may lead to voluntary changes as well as to hostility is demonstrated by the spread of American courtship customs throughout much of the Old World.

National manners and mores, ethnocentrism, acculturation, and related subjects are the concerns of anthropologists, and especially sociologists; folklorists have been concerned mostly with customs that are both traditional and variable, being sustained informally in specific folk groups rather than nationally among the whole population. By the time traditional frontier hospitality evolved into the "Welcome Wagon," and the political barbecue became the "$100-a Plate Dinner," the "folkways" had ceased to have much folkloristic significance, although they still might interest other students of American behavior.

Most true folk customs in the United States are associated with special events, especially those that require "rites of passage"—birth, marriage, and death. They begin at once when a child is born. Boy babies are customarily dressed in blue, and girls in pink, but sometimes only the first child of each sex in a family is so clothed, while later arrivals must make do with hand-me-down infantwear or may appear in other pastel shades. Father is expected to hand out cigars, a custom that may repeat itself after promotions in his occupation as well. (In Mormon-dominated Utah, and perhaps elsewhere from other influences, instead of cigars a new father passes out Tootsie Rolls or bubble-gum cigars.) None of these practices is required by any authority other than local custom, which varies from region to region or even from family to family. Some families have special clothes for the baby's homecoming or christening, or heirloom furniture for its room.

Celebrations of birthday anniversaries may begin as early as the first year in some families, and they may continue through one's entire life. More commonly, however, birthday parties are dropped at about high school age, sometimes to be revived once at the symbolic age of maturity (twenty-one years)

monogamous: married to one person at a time

heirloom: a valued possession passed from one generation to the next and again as an annual celebration in later middle age. Children's birthdays almost invariably are the occasion for spanking—one spank for each year, with extras "to grow on," or "for good measure." Children in some regions maintain a fairly rigid schedule of extra-punishment days before and after the birthday anniversary—"pinch day," "hit day," "kiss day," and so forth. Blowing out birthday-cake candles and wishing are standard customs, sometimes varied by naming the candles for possible marriage partners and assuming that the last candle smoking marks the mate. Birthday gifts at a party may be held over the head of the celebrating child for him or her to guess the donor or to announce the use to which that gift is to be put. For each correct guess the child is granted a wish.

The loss of "baby teeth" is one of the few other non-holiday occasions in a child's life when customs are followed. The most common practice is for the child to sleep with the tooth under its pillow for the "tooth fairy" to buy for a quarter (prices vary). School customs . . . are practiced to some degree in most communities, often being channeled eventually by teachers and principals into well-regulated events. "Dress-up day" or "hillbilly day," under various names, are begun informally by students to vary the routine of regulated school dress, but eventually become sanctioned and controlled by school officials and are placed on the activities calendar. One school custom remains a folk one—the designation of a certain day (often Thursday) as "queer day," when the wearing of a certain color (often green, yellow, or purple) marks the "queers" (homosexuals). Many unsuspecting teachers have been ridiculed behind their backs for unwittingly violating the taboo. The hazing of freshmen, initiation into clubs, and "tapping" for honorary societies are further school occasions for which the establishment has forged ersatz "traditions" to supplant or forestall folk customs, although these seldom catch on as group traditions, and when they do the participants tend to modify them back in the direction of earlier folk behavior.

Courtship and engagement begin a new round of customs that may lead to marriage, the most tradition-regulated personal ceremony in American life, or, more recently, to other arrangements of living together that may have their own folk traditions. Here time has changed but not diminished the role of folklore. Couples formerly were granted the family parlor or porch swing for courting; today they have the automobile. Bundling as a courting custom gave way to "necking" or "petting" in the 1940s and '50s, "making out" and "scoring" later. Ice-cream socials or church "sings" were replaced by drive-ins (both movies and restaurants). Customs of "going Dutch," "blind dates," "double-dating," "study dates," and the like depended on individual finances and desires as well as on local practices. "Going steady" with one partner became a well-entrenched dating pattern surrounded with customary devices for signaling whether one is attached or free (exchanging rings, leaving certain buttons or buckles open, placement of jewelry, etc.). But under the influence of femi-

ersatz: a substitute or a fake; an inferior imitation

bundling: the custom in early New England for an engaged couple to sleep in the same bed fully clothed

eschew: to
avoid, give up

nism by the late 1960s women were less often willing to display signs of "be-longing" to a male, and they were as likely to initiate dates (or eschew them) as to wait to be asked. In some high schools and colleges a so-called "virgin pin" was worn, supposedly indicating by its position or shape whether a girl was or wasn't. Today the decline of a desire to "save one's virginity for marriage" has rendered the "virgin pin" obsolete; instead a lore of aphrodisiacs and folk birth-control methods circulates. Formally engaged couples still often have the time-payment diamond ring to advertise and seal their promises, but custom may decree the exchange of other special gifts as well.

Wedding customs begin with the "shower," often several of them, to emphasize different kinds of needed gifts. Shower parties are customarily for women only, although friends of the bridegroom may occasionally hold a gift "stag party" for him. Certain recreations are reserved exclusively for showers. A favorite is writing down the words of the future bride as she opens gifts. Her remarks are read aloud later as "what she will say to her husband on their wedding night."

Customs of the wedding itself are numerous, and largely regulated by tradition. They include the dress of participants, the seating of guests, the choice of attendants, kissing the bride, throwing rice, passing the bride's shoe around for money, playing pranks on the married couple, and decorating the car. Noisy harassment of brides and bridegrooms is an old custom in the United States. First it was the "shivaree," derived from the Old World word and custom of the "charivari." A crowd of friends and neighbors would awaken a bridal couple with "rough music" and shouting, subjecting them to various indignities, and pestering them until the husband surrendered and set up a treat. The shivaree was also known by such terms as "belling," "warmer," "serenade," "collathump," and "skimmilton." In 1946, a folklore journal reported, a recently married couple in Oregon were awakened and the husband dunked in a rainbarrel, then forced to push his wife around in a wheelbarrow while the celebrants threw firecrackers at him; afterward he was expected to treat the crowd to refreshments. Many Americans can describe similar customs firsthand, and shivarees still occur, but the typical custom today is to decorate and sabotage the honeymoon car. Crepe-paper decorations, signs on the car, additives to the gasoline, a note in the fuel-tank cap ("Help, I'm being kidnapped!") are among the usual tricks. Car inscriptions may include pictures,

ribald: vulgar
but humorous

sayings, ribald rhymes, hearts and arrows (similar to tree carvings), and such formulas as "$1 + 1 = 3$". Sometimes pranks are directed at the newlyweds' home. A favorite is removing the labels from all of their canned goods or tying bells to their bedsprings.

Wedding customs, however rough, are essentially celebrations of a happy time. But customs associated with death are generally fraught with suggestions of fear or superstition. Pouring water out of vases, and stopping the clocks in a house in which death has occurred seem to mask some superstitious fear.

propitiation: an offering to pacify the gods

Draping the furniture in the room in which a corpse lies, or leaving the digging tools by the grave for some days after the burial are marks of respect—or propitiation. Sometimes the disposal of the small personal belongings of the deceased is governed by custom rather than a formal will, and many families commemorate the anniversaries of a beloved's passing by printing annual poems or notices in the classified columns of a newspaper. In some communities the funeral is organized by a traditionally-appointed "arranger": southern and southwestern writers have described family or community "decoration days," "memorial days," or days for "graveyard working" on which people gather at the cemetery for clean-up work, recreation, and to remember those who have passed away. Special foods may be served, and the names of those who died since the last memorial day are read aloud.

Apart from the cycle of life and the "rites of passage," customs tend to cluster around work, recreation, or social events. Family reunions (in Utah, also "missionary reunions"), "Old Home Weeks," and "Homecomings" may be structured around special customs, foods, or entertainments. Communal-labor parties, important to frontier survival, have largely disappeared from American life, except in recent experimental communities or among such religious sects as the Amish, who have deliberately maintained them. But in the past there was a great variety of work parties—quilting bees, apple-peelings, corn-shucking, log-rollings, house-raisings, turkey drives, rabbit drives (followed by a community "rabbit dance") and threshings. Nowadays, although neighbors may willingly "pitch in" to help others in emergencies, these are spontaneous and improvised occasions, usually not traditional ones. One such communal-aid tradition, still fairly common, in small-town neighborhoods, is the so-called "pound party" in which every participant brings a pound of some commodity to help set up housekeeping for a new neighbor or preacher. An urban counterpart is the Harlem "rent party." Certain occupations, such as auctioneering, livestock trading, rodeo work, and the like have rich traditional backgrounds and many continuing folk practices are associated with them.

sects: small factions that split from a larger group

threshings: separating grain from the husk

bear-baiting: a "sport" in which dogs are set upon a chained bear

gander-pulling: riding at full speed, a horseman attempts to pull the greased head off a live gander

Most traditional American frontier amusements were lost or greatly altered in later years. No longer do we enjoy the likes of "bear-baiting" or "gander-pulling" as recreations. Dog fighting and cock-fighting still persist illegally and in secret, while target-shooting matches ("turkey shoots," etc.) have changed their character and survived. Spelling bees, hay rides, taffy pulls, and ice-cream socials survive to some degree. Hunting and fishing are still very popular pursuits, and retain some customary traces, such as marking the forehead of the hunter with the blood of his first kill, or having the game divided among the participants of the hunt by a blindfolded outsider. Traditions have also developed in modern sports and children's games: choosing sides by odd or even fingers, choosing the server in tennis by spinning the racket, rallying for the serve in ping pong, deciding the order of play in baseball by placing hand over hand on the bat, tossing a coin for the kick-off in football.

Calendar customs in the United States cluster around a very few annual events, unlike those in Europe that are linked to many more occasions. (Large collections of British folklore have been devoted to descriptions of nothing but such customs.) American tradition has retained few Old World celebrations and has originated even fewer native ones. In chronological summary, the common American calendar customs may be listed as follows: *St. Patrick's Day*, wearing green; *April Fool's Day*, playing pranks; *Easter*, dyeing eggs and wearing new clothes; *May Day*, giving "May baskets"; *Independence Day*, shooting fireworks and giving patriotic speeches; *Halloween*, going "begging"; *Christmas*, caroling and hanging mistletoe; *New Year's Eve*, attending a "watch party" at which there is much noisemaking and general congratulations at the stroke of midnight. Other holidays on the American calendar—whether religious, patriotic, or folk in origin—tend to have only sporadic or commercially stereotyped customs associated with them. *Valentine's Day* card-exchanging is a good example, for without the elementary schools' and the merchants' emphasis of it, the custom would probably long since have died out. *Ground Hog Day* can hardly be thought of as an occasion for folk celebration, since practically the only observance of it nowadays is in newspaper feature articles. *Mother's Day* and *Father's Day* are officially established occasions only for further gift-giving, but another such holiday, *Labor Day*, has become the traditional time in some regions for "closing the summer cottage" or ending the season with one last beach party.

The most typical and original American holiday is certainly Thanksgiving—a combination of the traditional European peasant harvest festival with the first New England settlers' day of giving thanks to God. Really, the Pilgrims' "first Thanksgiving" so often depicted had more of the former character than the latter, while the special meal we eat on Thanksgiving Day nowadays is more Victorian than Colonial in its choice of foods and modes of preparation. The televised professional football games of today's holiday had their counterparts in the games and contests of early New England holidays.

There is little more to distinguish calendar customs from true **folk festivals**, perhaps, than the degree of community involvement in them and the elaboration of celebrations. Some of the most interesting American festivals are immigrant-group seasonal traditions uniquely developed in the United States. The commercialized Mardi Gras of New Orleans, for example, is much more elaborate and sophisticated than most Old World carnival days or than the traditional celebrations in some parts of rural Louisiana, where a party of masked riders travels from farm to farm singing and begging for food. The

penitente:
repenting,
performing
penance

processions of the *penitente* brotherhood (carrying Christ's cross and receiving His whippings on their own backs), which originated in Spain centuries ago, differ markedly in the American Spanish Southwest, where they have evolved along new lines, even absorbing some Indian elements. The gradual change in the nature of Czech and Slovak harvest festivals as they were revived and sustained in the United States is typical of other such efforts at retention of Old World celebrations. Here, because the participants were no longer farmers, the spontaneous community ritual of Europe became a well-organized public drama with clearly defined actors and spectators. Whether there are any purely American festivals is uncertain, but probably the best case could be made for the rodeo. All others seem to have clear foreign prototypes: the county fair with harvest festivals, the circus with its ancient Roman ancestor, the family reunion with tribal and clan gatherings.

prototypes: an original that serves as a model

One unusual American celebration, probably derived from German festivals, is the "New Year's Shoot," as it is called in North Carolina, or the "New Year's Sermon" of Missouri. A party of riders travels from house to house, beginning at midnight of New Year's Eve, pausing at each one for the leader or "preacher" to deliver a set speech. Afterward, firearms are discharged and the party is invited into the house for a treat. The custom has elements in it common to English "mumming," which is still found in vigorous tradition in Nova Scotia, and resembles the customs of "belsnickles and shanghais" followed in the late nineteenth century in Virginia. The procedure is also very much like the country Mardi Gras of Cajun Louisiana, and has a dim parallel perhaps in the traditional Southern holiday greeting "Christmas gift!"

mumming: wearing a disguise to appear in a (usually silent) play

The observance of Passover by East European Jews in the United States is one of the few imported festivals that has been systematically compared to its original form. The changes are characteristic of America—the traditional "search for leaven," formerly conducted with a candle and a quill, is now performed with a flashlight and brush; shopping for new clothing replaces the "visit to the tailor"; the ritual cleansing of dishes and utensils is rendered unnecessary by ownership of a special set of them for exclusive holiday use; and the careful handwork in the baking of matzoh has been automated out of existence by the invention of the matzoh machine. New quasi-customs have appeared in the United States—the "Third Seder" (Passover meal) held outside the family circle, individual brand-preferences among the various commercially prepared Passover foods, new games played with the traditional old-country food (nuts), and songs sung in English (including the black spiritual "Go Down, Moses") after the Seder.

quill: a large feather from a bird's wing

matzoh: unleavened bread eaten at Passover
quasi-: almost, somewhat

A further transplanting of holiday celebrations is exhibited in the Americanized Christmas customs that took root in Japan as early as the middle of the nineteenth century and flourished there, especially since the Allied Occupation following World War II. So pervasive is the celebration now that it is even marked on calendars issued by Shinto and Buddhist organizations, and there have been proposals either to make Christmas a new national holiday or to designate December 25 as "International Goodwill Day." Japanese merchants display Christmas decorations; families put up Christmas trees, or printed pictures of them; Christmas carols are played, parties held, and gifts exchanged. Lacking a fireplace chimney on which to attach their Christmas stockings, many

Shinto: Japanese religion that reveres nature spirits and ancestors

Japanese children find presents placed near their pillows in the morning. Some, however, fasten their stockings on the pipe of the bathroom stove on Christmas Eve. . . .

Jan Harold Brunvand, *The Study of American Folklore*

Reading Like a Writer ■

Now that you have read Brunvand's description of customs and festivals, compare the journal entry you wrote before reading this essay with what you learned. Did your reading confirm what you already knew, or do you need to revise your ideas about customs?

Guidelines for Assignment 2 ■

In this writing assignment, you will write about some aspect of what you know about your own religious, ethnic, community, or family customs.

1. In small groups, discuss and list examples of customs and festivals, and, if you can, describe their significance or history. One way you might approach this assignment is to ask people in your group what kinds of customs or festivals they tend to observe on a regular basis. How many different religious, ethnic, and community folkways can you identify in your class alone? How might a family evolve its own traditions that sets it apart from other families?

Pay special attention to Brunvand's discussion of *ethnocentrism* on page 148. Can you think of some other examples of this attitude? Take notes about the discussion in your journal on the right-hand side.

2. Choose one of the four categories—religious, ethnic, community, or family—that you might be interested in writing about. How you define "community" is up to you; a community might be the town or the neighborhood you grew up in, a group of friends, people in a club or on a sports team to which you belong, or any other group. When you begin writing, make sure that the category you've chosen is clear to your reader.

3. You might want to concentrate on one particular custom, or one particular incident; you might want to trace the history of a tradition, or even discuss why you still participate in the custom, or why you have chosen not to participate. Or, write about your experiences with ethnocentrism. Perhaps you have found yourself in a community or culture that you have had to learn about; perhaps your own community or culture sometimes needs explaining to people who are unfamiliar with your customs.

Assignment 3.   Writing Oral History

When we study the past, we usually study the written or recorded words of people long gone. We may rummage among dusty documents, or old books; we may play scratchy records, or view old films. In many cases, we can only study the words of people who historians thought were prominent in the public eye and who were caught up in important events. Of course, the letters and diaries of both important and ordinary people exist, but often ordinary folk are neglected by those who write history.

Today however, a new way to study history is evolving—the oral history. While anyone can be the subject of this new approach, the primary use of the oral history is to allow ordinary people to speak for themselves, and thus to contribute their voices to the record. Tim Wells, who wrote *444 Days*, an oral history of the hostages held in Iran from 1979 to 1981, introduced his book this way:

> When [the hostages] were finally released in January of 1981, the hostages returned to a whirlwind of publicity that was followed by relative silence. As a consequence, popular perceptions about the treatment of the hostages are based almost entirely on journalistic accounts that have done as much to distort as to reveal the actual conditions of their captivity. As a group, the hostages feel that much of what has been written about them in the popular press is neither accurate nor truthful, and many resent the way they have been treated by the news media. One hostage explained, "It didn't take me long to learn that the media have no soul. All they wanted were the most sensational aspects of the story. That led to a lot of exaggerated commentary when we were released." This oral history is an attempt to redress that grievance. In order to obtain accurate first-person accounts of the captivity, I have spent the past 2 [and a half] years talking with the former hostages. In the process I traveled over twenty thousand miles and gathered in excess of five thousand pages of interview transcript.
>
> Tim Wells, *444 Days*

As we can see from Wells's comments, an oral history provides alternative interpretations of events, telling things that otherwise might not be recorded. This allows us to view history not as an impersonal catalog of events, but as living testimony of what happened. Consider: How have the events of our times affected you and those around you? "History" does not have to mean momentous, world-changing events; it includes the collective experiences of us all.

Wells began his project with prepared interview questions and a tape recorder. An interview is the basis of any oral history. The difference between an interview and an oral history, however, is that the history is woven together to make a continuous narrative which does not include the interviewer's questions.

After transcribing hours of taped interviews, for Wells the hardest part was to select, arrange, and edit his material. And that is the essence of this assignment: Once you have done the "research" and gathered the content, you must decide how to arrange your material, editing as you go. You have already had some practice writing about another person when you wrote a biography of a classmate. This assignment is different because you will put yourself in the place of the person you interview, and then you will write in the first person "I." Thus, although your main purpose is to inform, you may also find that the techniques you learned in Chapter 6 for writing expressive prose will be helpful.

For further examples of an oral history, let us look at one man's story from *444 Days* and at a student's history of his father.

Write Before Reading

Before you read the following passage, use the right-hand side of your journal to jot down all that you know about the Iran hostage crisis. Don't worry if you blank out; instead, write about what it might be like to be a hostage.

BILL BELK, COMMUNICATIONS OFFICER

On Christmas day, I was tied to a straight chair because of my escape. I was still in solitary, and I was very tightly bound hand and foot with nylon rope. My ankles were tied to the legs of the chair and my wrists were tied to the back of the chair. I couldn't move an inch. There wasn't a bit of slack in that rope.

One of the guards brought in a little twig that he called a Christmas tree. Even in the situation I was in, they brought in this evergreen branch with two or three Christmas decorations on it, and set it in the corner for me. They also brought around some sweet potato pie with marshmallows all over the top of it, and some hot tea. They untied my hands long enough to let me eat, and then tied me right back up. I thought it was rather ironic that they would do this, since I was being punished for trying to escape. And Christmas isn't a Moslem holiday to begin with. It just isn't their thing at all. I was sitting there tied to my chair, thinking, "What a hell of a place to be for Christmas. I should be at home with my family. What the hell am I doing here?"

Another thing that was really a kick in the teeth during this time was that I remember hearing Joe Subic in the room next to me. He was busy talking to the guards about getting Christmas cards to all of his relatives and friends. I was wondering why the guards were being so nice to him, and how in the hell he could get Christmas cards written. I could hear him talking, and I could also hear that he had a typewriter in there. He was actually typing. That really shocked me. I figured there must have been some sort of capitulation or something. Then later on I learned that Subic had allowed himself to be used for propaganda purposes, and that in return he was given special treatment.

They kept me tied up like that for several days. The only time they untied me was to let me go to the bathroom or to let me eat—and with the exception of that Christmas pie it was strictly a bread and water diet. They'd give me a couple of minutes to eat, then it was back to the ropes. After a couple days of this I was going nuts. Day after day would go by with me tied to that chair. You can't imagine what it's like when you have absolutely nothing to do but sit there blindfolded and wait for somebody to come in and blow your head off. Some things get beyond words. I don't quite know how to explain what that misery was like. I was sore, I was tired, I was angry, and I was bored. I'd think about anything and everything just to keep my mind occupied. I planned a swimming pool for my back yard, and I'd think about my wife. I'd wonder what she was doing. I'd also think about my father, who had been dead for seven years.

There's also a bit of irony in this, because I'd think about an old friend by the name of Danny White. I knew Danny back when I was an airman in the air force. For a while they made me a turnkey and put me down in the stockade. Can you believe that? I used to be a prison guard. I was the bad guy down there in the jail, turning the key on all the other bad guys.

After a while, they brought in my friend Danny White. He had gone AWOL and had been given thirty days. He tried to escape and made it over the wall, but the MPs found Danny and brought him back. He was thrown into solitary confinement and put on a bread and water diet. This was 1955, and back then military justice could be pretty harsh. They did things then that they wouldn't do now. Danny was put in a very small cell, and his bed was nothing but a steel frame that slanted out from the wall. He was given one blanket and a pot to go to the bathroom in. That was it. The walls were bare and he didn't have anything to read. He couldn't go anywhere, and he couldn't do anything. All he had to eat was bread and water. He wasn't even allowed to sleep well, because every thirty minutes someone would go in and make sure that he was awake. I felt sorry for Danny, and thought it was a cruel punishment. I really did. But when I was on duty I had to go in there and wake Danny up. I was told to. I was just a flunky turnkey, and the sergeant made me go in and do it. Every thirty minutes I'd go into the cell and say, "Get up, Danny! Get up!" He was supposed to stand up on his feet whenever someone went in there. He had to go through thirty days of total and complete isolation with absolutely nothing to do, and frequent harassment. It's a wonder he didn't lose his mind.

Well, the irony is that twenty-five years later I was the prisoner who was suffering harassment on a bread and water diet with absolutely nothing to do. I was the prisoner who had tried to escape. I'd sit there blindfolded and tied to the chair, and I couldn't help but wonder, "Is it going to be thirty days before I'm released from this torture? Is it going to be thirty days before they untie me and take this godforsaken blindfold off?" I'd think about old Danny White and would regret that I hadn't let him sleep, regardless of what that sergeant had said. You know, I could've just gone in there and told him to get up without really bothering him. I can't imagine how Danny put up with that for thirty days. During the time I was tied to the chair, I realized what a terrible thing that was. At least I could sleep.

Tim Wells, 444 Days

Reading Like a Writer ■

Now that you have read Bill Belk's account of his experiences, think about your knowledge of the hostage crisis. How did what you know influence your response to Belk's narrative? If you couldn't remember much about the crisis, how did *not* having information influence your response? Compare this first-person (*I*) narrative approach with David Garrow's objective accounts of Martin Luther King and the civil rights movement. Think about how the two different approaches affected you. On the left-hand side of your journal, write a paragraph about which approach affected you more, and why.

A student introduced this oral history of his father with a short biographical paragraph:

> Lawrence Stephen Crowley was born in the Boston City Hospital on August 21, 1937. He was sent to the Kennedy Home for Boys at the age of four. He was moved to a state home in Hopedale, Massachusetts, and at the age of six, was sent to yet another state home run by Mr. and Mrs. Dolher of Oxford, where he was brought up with other orphaned boys. Mr. Crowley still resides in Oxford where he now owns a construction company. He is happily married to Mary Lou Armstrong and has two children, Catheline (16) and Larry Jr. (19). He says:

> I don't remember much about my mother or the things that had happened before I was given up to the state. No one had really revealed any information about my parents to me when I was growing up and I really don't care to know. There is a reason for everything, and I'm sure my parents had theirs, or they wouldn't have given me up. That is all in the past. I can't remember it, and I'm not going to try to.

> Most of the kids in the state homes weren't there because they didn't have parents, but because their parents couldn't handle them. They were problem kids, and half of them had nothing else to do but cause trouble—I suppose most of them are in jail now or something like that. We weren't all bad, but we sure weren't angels.

> In the Dolher home there were maybe 10 to 15 kids in the family, some coming, some going. We used to sleep three to a bed and take our baths every Saturday night. There wasn't much privacy.

We were divided into "Big Kids" and "Little Kids." Everyone had to suffer being a Little Kid before becoming a Big Kid. All of us had our own responsibilities. The big kids would have to do the hard labor like till the fields, paint the barn and pick the crops. The little kids had their responsibilities too, like gather the berries and feed the animals. The big kids always ate first and the little kids got the short end of everything, but every little kid knew he would be a big kid someday and be able to pick on somebody smaller. The big kids always tormented the little kids. I can remember once when I was a little kid, the big kids tied me to a tree in a pasture with a red handkerchief around my eyes. They brought old Max, our bull, down from the hill, and they led the bull around the tree. That was enough to scare me, but they then put him in front of me. I could imagine his sharp horns waving in front of my face. Then they jabbed me in the stomach, pretending it was the bull. I don't think I was ever so scared in my life.

There was another time I was pretty scared when I was a big kid—about 16 or so. A bunch of us were just riding around and someone suggested that we go to the abandoned Greek Church. We all had thought the church was haunted the whole time we were growing up. When we finally got to the church, we roamed around for a while, and from out of nowhere, something jumped out of the darkness at us. We scattered like rats, screaming our heads off. The thing chased us down the stairs to the basement where we found bodies all covered with blood. I ran outside and locked myself in the car and wouldn't let anyone in. But the whole thing was a setup. Some of the others in the home had already been there and were pretending to be dead. They had poured ketchup all over themselves. This kid John played the madman. He was kind of nuts anyway. That was a good time.

There were a lot of times that were good, and a lot of times that could have been better. People cared about you in the home, but you had to help yourself to get anywhere. I always tried to make my bad times seem just a little better than they really were. I guess I can attribute my success in my life to the hard work and discipline I learned when I was growing up in the home.

After leaving the home, I went to school in Boston at the Wentworth Institute of Technology for two years. Things for me weren't easy, trying to go to college and paying for it at the same time, but I see it now as a way to build character. I think that is an experience that every college student should have. I bet a student would appreciate college a little more if he or she had to work at the same time.

Larry Crowley, student

Larry said that he had never heard the story about the bull and the haunted church before. However, once he had asked his father to be the subject for his oral history, his father opened up and told him a number of things about his childhood.

Guidelines for Assignment 3   ■

1. Pick a person who you think would be suited for an oral history. Most likely, a person older than twenty-five would be best, because she or he will have more experiences to share than younger people will. Someone a generation or two older than yourself would be best. Anyone who has gone through a remarkable personal experience (serious illness, losing a loved one, getting divorced, etc.)—and is willing to talk about it—might be a possibility.

Think of the changes in the past twenty or thirty years that this person might be able to tell you about: the Viet Nam war, student unrest in the 1960s, the feminist movement, inflation, civil rights. A person who moved to the United States and who remembers his or her native country well might be another good choice.

2. Decide what questions you might ask this person, and discuss them in class, in small groups. Keep the following in mind.

a. Get all the vital statistics: birth date, place of birth, early childhood, education, work history, marital status, children, and so on. Some of this material might be useful as an introduction, as in the example you just read.

b. Ask questions that may help you focus your oral history—questions that may bring out a main idea or overall theme. You might ask the person such questions as: What one event changed your life the most? What important historical or social events did you live through that affected your life? What difference did these events make? (Be prepared to drop this line of questioning if the interview goes in an interesting direction that you didn't expect. Be ready to ask follow-up questions, just as you would in a conversation with a friend.)

3. When conducting the interview, use a tape recorder if at all possible.

4. When you transcribe the taped interview, copy it *exactly as it is* on the tape, using only one side of the paper. Skip lines in copying; you may want to rearrange the material later, and you will need the space.

5. Read the interview material several times to help you decide how to arrange it. What main idea or theme do you see in the person's life? To bring that out, which material should you cut or shorten? Which should you emphasize? You don't have to tell about the person's life chronologically, from birth to the present. Just because you asked the questions in a particular order doesn't mean that you have to arrange the person's responses in that same way. Think of your readers: Is there an especially good quotation that will lead them into your oral history or that will sum it up effectively?

chapter 8

Writing to Persuade

So far, we have discussed and drafted expressive writing and informative writing. In this chapter we will focus on the purpose behind persuasive writing. Again, remember that *persuasive writing* is only a convenient label which lets us group certain kinds of writing that have common features. In fact, to some degree *all* writing is essentially persuasive, since the very least thing that a writer wants is to get another person to pay attention, to agree to enter the writer's world. Even if your main purpose is to express or to inform, you also want to persuade readers to pay attention.

What Is Persuasive Writing?

Persuasive writing can range from writing that urges readers to take some direct action (to vote in a certain way, for example) to writing that simply asks readers to stop and think about something (such as air pollution or drug abuse). Some common types of persuasive writing are advertisements, political speeches, sermons, and editorials.

Persuasive writers must be especially aware of their audience. A writer whose purpose is to persuade someone to join the army, for example—or to give up cigarettes, to get married, to change banks, to aid the homeless, to support laws against drunk driving, and so on—must carefully assess how words may affect a reader. Is the language too aggressive? Too wishy-washy? Too smug or pompous? Does the writer use enough convincing examples to support his or her point of view? Is the writer willing to acknowledge that others might have a different viewpoint? These are some of the issues we consider when we talk about **rhetoric**: the art of using language in a way that changes how people think or feel, or that persuades them to go out and do something. Persuasive writers, then, must keep coming back to the role the audience plays in shaping what the writer writes.

Reading Assignment   ■

1. Bring an example of persuasive writing to class, and share it with your classmates. Discuss whether the examples are purely persuasive, or whether they also contain elements of expressive or informative writing. Did anyone find an example that is *only* persuasive?

2. People often use the word *argument* when they talk about persuasive writing. Because that word has many negative meanings (such as "fight" or "controversy"), we often forget its more neutral meanings (such as "proposal" or "point"). In class, discuss your reaction to the word *argument*.

Writing Assignment   ■

The first assignment in Chapter 7 asked you to write a short essay in your journal in which you provided information or an explanation about something that happened to you. Now, on the left-hand side of your journal, rewrite that essay so that it presents a persuasive argument to explain *why* the event happened as it did. Convince your readers that you know the reason that the event happened.

Reading Persuasive Writing

Persuasive writing asks that you pay attention to it. You may have to reread it several times. Your first reading gives you a general idea of the essay's point and an outline of the writer's argument. But you may not be able to summarize the argument, yet. This can be frustrating. Shouldn't you know what a piece of writing is about after you read it? Since the answer is often *no* (and your own experience tells you that this is true), perhaps you need to think again about what happens when you read.

*Re*reading is a much more important step than reading for the first time. When you read for the first time, you have no idea what to expect. But when you reread, you can *anticipate* what is coming next; you can rely on your memory, which allows you to make better sense of a piece of writing the second, third, or fourth time around.

How much you reread depends on your purpose for reading. You wouldn't reread a newspaper if all you wanted was an idea of the day's events. On the other hand, when you read a textbook and lecture notes to prepare for an essay exam, you might reread often, in order to concentrate on the main ideas. And if you were preparing for an objective test, chances are you would reread in order to memorize dates, names, and important facts.

You should reread the selections in this chapter for two reasons: to fully grasp the ideas and arguments of the writer, and to learn how different writers use language to persuade their readers. Let's begin with a piece of student writing. In the following introduction to a longer essay, the writer wants to persuade us that there are not enough female role models on television:

> Strong and good looking, he comes in to save the day. He is reliable, unselfish, helpful, and committed to protecting the innocent. He is our superhero. The only thing wrong with this definition of the American hero is that the hero is rarely a heroine. If he can leap from tall buildings with a single bound, why can't she?
>
> Our heroes are presented as role models, men worth imitating; yet a woman daydreams about a knight in shining armor who will save her, not about being that knight. Thinking like this is a result of the kind of heroes women see most: cartoon superheroes and the heroes of television. The superheroes we grew up with were all men. Superman, Spiderman, Batman and Robin fought crime in the streets. Of course, we saw Batgirl and Supergirl, but they tagged around in the background. Why don't we have Superwoman and Batwoman? Our television heroes are mainly men, such as Don Johnson of "Miami Vice," Spenser of "Spenser for Hire," and MacGyver of "MacGyver." But the question is, why are there so many more male heros than heroines in everything?
>
> Kim Collins, student

Part of this writer's persuasive strategy is to name specific television shows and cartoons. Active readers will test Kim's assertions by reflecting on their own memories of television characters. They then might believe Kim, or agree with her—not because *she* says so, but because their own memories and experiences say so. A reader who does not agree with Kim will have to come up with examples that prove the opposite of her argument. Either way, the active reader must work at making the passage mean something.

Write Before Reading ■

Before you read the following passage, use the right-hand side of your journal to jot down what you know about public child care, and what your feelings about it are. Try to keep a distinction between what you know and what you feel about public child care.

> It is time the U.S. government recognized the fact that it makes economic as well as humanitarian sense to invest in the health and well-being of small children. Only then is a nation able to make the most of its chief asset, people. Neglecting children triggers direct costs: welfare charges, hospital charges, and court and imprisonment charges. In recent years we have become penny-wise

and dollar-foolish, saving a few dollars on food subsidies for pregnant poor women and then spending $40,000 to $100,000 of public money to care for each underweight preemie that is born to many of these same women. But besides incurring these direct costs, by neglecting our children we are compromising the educational standards and future productivity of our nation. After all, America faces an even bigger challenge in this sphere than Western Europe does. Because our divorce rate is enormously high, our family structure is much weaker than that typical of many Western European nations, and still, we continue to do so much less for our children. If our government cares about America's children or about the long-term economic health of the country, massive changes need to be made in our child care policies.

Sylvia Ann Hewlett, *A Lesser Life*

preemie:
premature baby

Write After Reading ■

Now that you have read the passage, compare your notes about what you knew about child care with what you learned. Did your knowledge—or the lack of knowledge—make you more receptive or less receptive to this writer's argument? Now look at your notes about your feelings about child care. Did your feelings and opinions make you more receptive or less receptive to this argument? Reread the passage, keeping the answers to these questions in mind.

On the left-hand side of your journal, write a response to the argument Hewlett makes. Then, look over your response. Is it based mainly on your feelings and opinions, or is based mainly on facts and information? Can you say why?

In arguing the case for public child care, Hewlett cannot depend on her readers to use their own knowledge and experiences to test what she is saying. Unlike Kim, who knew that her readers would know about TV programs, Hewlett knows that most readers simply do not have statistics and facts about child care and government expenses in their heads. Instead, her main strategy is to persuade us that she is an authority on the subject. Once we believe in *Hewlett,* we might believe in her *ideas.*

Hewlett has chosen not to appeal to our emotions in building her argument, but that does not prevent us from responding emotionally. After all, the subject of children tends to evoke very strong feelings. As readers of persuasive writing, we must be able to recognize when we do respond in an emotional way, so that we can determine if that influences how we read.

In the next passage, the writer does rely on readers' emotions to help make his point, but he does it gently:

Fifty miles down a dirt road in Wyoming one time, the old bus suffered two flat tires, which was one flat tire too many. We sat there for an hour wondering what to do about it before a rancher came along in his pickup truck. "Looks like you boys need some help," he said. He took us to a gas station on the highway, waited until the flats were fixed, drove us back to the bus, and helped us jack up the wheels and change the tires. By then it was getting dark. He said, "Nothing to do but take you boys home with me, I guess." His wife cooked us elk steaks for dinner, tucked us under warm quilts for the night, and sent us off full of flapjacks and sausage the next morning. Her husband followed us to the highway to make sure we didn't have any more flat tires. I don't know what he planned to do with those twenty-four hours, but he ended up giving most of them to some stranded strangers.

To read the front pages, you might conclude that Americans are mostly out for themselves, venal, grasping, and mean-spirited. The front pages have room for only defense contractors who cheat and politicians with their hands in the till. But you can't travel the back roads very long without discovering a multitude of gentle people doing good for others with no expectation of gain or recognition. The everyday kindness of the back roads more than makes up for the acts of greed in the headlines. Some people out there spend their whole lives selflessly. You could call them heroes.

Charles Kuralt, *On the Road*

venal: open to bribery or corruption
till: the drawer in a cash register that holds money

The passage begins in a roundabout way, with an anecdote about a flat tire and the generosity of strangers, and then it moves into a general discussion of how Americans have lost faith in one another. Finally, Kuralt reaches his persuasive point: that good people are still to be found. Notice how different this approach is from Hewlett's use of statistics. One approach is not necessarily better than the other, however. Each writer must decide on a persuasive strategy that fits the material and that will be effective in convincing the audience.

Kuralt's passage illustrates that our purposes for writing often overlap. The passage is expressive in that Kuralt relates a story from his own experience; but the purpose of that story is to support the argument that America is full of unpublicized heroes. By combining expressive writing with persuasive writing, Kuralt hopes that his audience will be more receptive to his point.

In the next paragraph, another writer asks us to consider *his* definition of a hero:

vista: a distant view or comprehensive awareness

My hero is Man the Discoverer. The world we now view from the literate West—the vistas of time, the land and the seas, the heavenly bodies and our own bodies, the plants and animals, history and human societies past and present—had to be opened for us by countless Columbuses. In the deep recesses of the past, they remain anonymous. As we come closer to the present they emerge into the light of history, a cast of characters as varied as human nature. Discoveries become episodes of biography, unpredictable as the new worlds the discoverers opened to us.

Daniel Boorstin, The Discoverers

Boorstin defines "hero" in a more abstract way than Kuralt does: his hero is "Man the Discoverer," not the everyday sort of person whom Kuralt admires. Note that *we,* the readers, have to stop and supply our own examples of "countless Columbuses." Like much persuasive writing, this passage requires us to read carefully, and to read again.

Reading and Writing Assignment

Stop for a moment to consider the four examples of persuasive writing that you have read so far. Which writers want you actually to do something in response to their writing? Which writers simply want you to think about the issues they raise? Reread the four passages, and on the right-hand side of your journal, jot down notes about each writer's persuasive intention. Did he or she want you to think, or to act? Say why you think so.

Write Before Reading

Before reading the next passage, jot down notes on the right-hand side of your journal concerning your travel experiences, both good and bad.

> There are those whom we instantly recognize as clinging to the traditional virtues of travel, the people who endure a kind of alienation and panic in foreign parts for the after-taste of having sampled new scenes. On the whole travel at its best is rather comfortless, but travel is never easy: you get very tired, you get lost, you get your feet wet, you get little cooperation, and—if it is to have any value at all—you go alone. Homesickness is part of this kind of travel. In these circumstances, it is possible to make interesting discoveries about oneself and one's surroundings. Travel has less to do with distance than with insight; it is, very often, a way of seeing.
>
> Paul Theroux, Sunrise with Seamonsters

Write After Reading

Compare your notes about travel experiences with what Theroux says. Does he describe what travel has been like for you? On the left-hand side of your journal, write a response to the last point he makes: "Travel has less to do with distance than with insight; it is, very often, a way of seeing."

Theroux wants to persuade us that his opinion of travel, based on personal experience, is valid. You may get the feeling from this passage that Theroux has traveled a good deal. If so, you may be willing to accept him as an authority because you recognize that he has had extensive experience with his subject.

Write Before Reading

Before you read the next passage, use the right-hand side of your journal to jot down your ideas about what makes a good parent.

> It is apparently very necessary to distinguish between parenthood and parentage. Parenthood is an art; parentage is the consequence of a mere biological act. The biological ability to produce conception and to give birth to a child has nothing whatever to do with the ability to care for that child as it required to be cared for. That ability, like every other, must be learned. It is highly desirable that parentage be not undertaken until the art of parenthood has been learned. Is this a counsel of perfection? As things stand now, perhaps it is, but it need not always be so. Parentage is often irresponsible. Parenthood is responsible. Parentage at best is irresponsibly responsible for the birth of a child. Parenthood is responsible for the development of a human being—not simply a child, but a human being. I do not think it is an overstatement to say that parenthood is the most important occupation in the world. There is no occupation for which the individual should be better prepared than this, for what can be more important to the individual, his family, his community, his society, his nation, and the world of humanity than the making of a good human being? And the making of a good human being is largely the work of good parents. And it is work—hard work—not to be irresponsibly undertaken or perfunctorily performed. Yet parenthood, perhaps like politics, is the only profession for which preparation is considered unnecessary.
>
> Ashley Montagu, *The American Way of Life*

Although Montagu does not provide specific examples to illustrate his points, that does not prevent an active reader from providing examples. Notice Montagu's tone: He seems impatient and slightly angry with irresponsible parents. How does his tone affect how you respond?

Write After Reading

1. Now that you have read the passage, compare Montagu's argument with your own notes about what makes a good parent. On the left-hand side of your journal, write a response to Montagu's concepts of parenting. What do you find persuasive—or *not* persuasive—about his argument?

2.   After you write your response, imagine how some other audiences might respond to Montagu's argument. On the right-hand side of your journal, identify the audiences, and say what you think their response would be.

Our final example of persuasive writing is very different from what we have read so far:

> Mr. Isenberg, who is eighty-nine years old, finds a boarding arrangement a mixed blessing. He does not have to make his own bed, buy furniture, or clean the apartment. However, his landlady, whom he describes as a "witch," does not allow him to turn on lights or use the electricity to shave. He is forced to live as a "street person." At 6:00 A.M. Mr. Isenberg eats breakfast at the local Donut Shop. By 8:30 he is at the Jewish Center, where he showers and shaves. He eats lunch at the JC Nutritive Program and spends the rest of the day playing cards. By 4:30 P.M. he is at home and has eaten the soup his daughter brings each week. He walks around the neighborhood until 8:00, when it is time to go to sleep. A retired painter, Mr. Isenberg goes to the Painters' Union to play cards on Saturday and Jewish holidays. On Sunday the Jewish Center is open again, and he spends the day there. He pays his landlady $50 a month, plus one dollar for the use of the refrigerator and another dollar for electricity. She pays $95 a month and sleeps in the living room; he has the bedroom. They quarrel often.
>
> Doris Francis, *Will You Still Need Me, Will You Still Feed Me, When I'm 84?*

This passage doesn't seem to have a persuasive purpose. You cannot point to any one phrase or sentence and say, "Here is the author's main point." However, if the passage arouses our sympathy for Mr. Isenberg—(and it does, doesn't it?)—it has succeeded in being persuasive. The writer wants us to think about the predicament of retired persons who may not have enough money to live decently. The passage simply describes one person's day-to-day life, and we readers fill in the blanks and develop the meaning. In this case, we are persuaded that the elderly deserve better treatment.

The next section examines how introductions can influence the way readers anticipate what is coming in a piece of writing, and how conclusions can help readers reflect on what they have read.

Reading Introductions and Conclusions

It sounds obvious, but as readers we expect introductions to introduce, and conclusions to conclude. As writers, we must take care that our introductions and conclusions provide such cues for our readers.

Readers are able to recognize beginnings and endings first by how the writing is arranged. An essay, for example, has a title and begins on the first page; the last page and paragraphs signal the conclusion. Readers can even point to specific words and phrases in an essay that introduce ("In the following passage . . ."; "When I was in grade school . . .") and conclude ("In summary . . ."; "Finally . . .").

Besides such obvious cues, however, readers respond to other factors in identifying introductions and conclusions. Readers say, "It *feels* like a beginning," or "I could *sense* that the writer was wrapping up." Such comments indicate that each piece of writing has its own structure and meaning, and that readers will find them even when they are not as obvious as the examples just given.

Introductions

Following are several examples of introductions. Each one plainly points to the writer's subject:

> The word "comfortable" did not originally refer to enjoyment or contentment.
>
> Witold Rybczynski, *Home*

> Margarine caught on quickly in both Europe and the United States, where patents began pouring out in 1871, and large-scale production was underway by 1880.
>
> Harold McGee, *On Food and Cooking*

> America is infinite and various. The infinity shows up on our odometer. As for variety, we have found that on the road at lunchtime we can choose from all kinds of—hamburgers.
>
> Charles Kuralt, *On the Road*

> Of all of the thousands of players who have been called up late in the season and given a brief chance to show what they can do, probably the most impressive argument was made by a giant named Walter Franklin Bond in September of 1962.
>
> Bill James, *The Bill James Historical Baseball Abstract*

Introductions are often called **leads**, or **lead-ins**, by journalists, and from the above examples we can see why. Each of them actually leads us into the writer's subject and sets limits on it. We expect that Rybczynski is going to tell us what *comfortable* originally meant; that McGee will discuss the popularity and history of margarine; that Kuralt will describe the variety of hamburgers available in the United States; and that James will tell us something about Walt Bond's one great season. (Note that James's lead is the only one that implies a value judgment. He wants to persuade us that Bond had the most impressive single season—which careful readers will understand from the cue "probably.")

Here is the lead to a passage that we read in Chapter 7:

> Piaget identified three major areas related to question answering which could explain a reader's inability to consider several items of information at the same time. . . .
>
> Betty C. Holmes, "The Effect of Prior Knowledge on the Question
> Answering of Good and Poor Readers"

After reading this one sentence, we can anticipate that the writer will tell us what those three major areas are.

The next two leads point to comparisons the writer will make between city and country people. In the first lead, he begins with city people; in the second, he begins with country people:

> City people try to buy time as a rule, when they can, whereas country people are prepared to kill time, although both try to cherish in their mind's eye the notion of a better life ahead. . . .

> Country people tend to consider that they have a corner on righteousness and to distrust most manifestations of cleverness, while people in the city are leery of righteousness but ascribe to themselves all manner of cleverness.
>
> Edward Hoagland, "The Ridge-Slope Fox and the Knife-Thrower"

Many writers find that introductions are the hardest part to write. If you have trouble with the introduction for a short essay, imagine having to write one for a whole book! Here is the introductory sentence to a 600-page history of British colonization of Australia:

> In 1787, the twenty-eighth year of the reign of King George III, the British Government sent a fleet to colonize Australia.
>
> Robert Hughes, *The Fatal Shore*

Of all the choices Hughes could have made to introduce his book, he chose to write a simple chronological lead. He then continues:

reconnaissance: a survey to examine a region's terrain
enigmatic: puzzling, mysterious

> Never had a colony been founded so far from its parent state, or in such ignorance of the land it occupied. There had been no reconnaissance. In 1770 Captain James Cook had made landfall on the unexplored east coast of this utterly enigmatic continent, stopped for a short while at a place named Botany Bay and gone north again. Since then, no ship had called: not a word, not an observation, for seventeen years, each one of which was exactly like the thousands that had preceded it, locked in its historical immensity of blue heat, bush, sandstone and the measured booming of glassy Pacific rollers.

From this introduction we might also anticipate that the book is not going to be a dry history for specialists, because the language is designed to appeal to a variety of readers. It's even poetic: ". . . locked in its historical immensity of blue heat, bush, sandstone and the measured booming of glassy Pacific rollers."

Here is another example of an introduction that is anything but dry. It leads off with two anecdotes (short, humorous stories):

A writer looking for a funny ending to his interview with Bob Hope asked the comedian recently if he thought there was still sex after 65. "You bet," said Hope, "and awfully good, too. [Pause for a beat of exquisite timing.] Especially the one in the fall."

geriatric: having to do with the aged

The image of geriatric lovemaking seems always good for a laugh. A few years ago, Dr. Mary Calderone, executive director of SIECUS, the Sex Information and Education Council of the U.S., and one of the nation's leading authorities on sex education, was answering questions from an audience of Chicago high-schoolers. When one daring teenager asked, "How old are you, are you married, and are you still doing it?" the students broke into giggles. Dr. Calderone was characteristically forthright. When the laughter died down, she said, "The answer to the first part of that question is 64, and the answer to the other two is yes." Then she added, "Young people do not have a monopoly on sexuality. It is with you all your life."

Norman M. Lobsenz, "Sex and the Senior Citizen"

The writer hopes that this introduction will draw readers in; by getting us to share a joke, he makes us more receptive to his argument. And we can easily anticipate the point of his article: that one's sex life need not end after a certain age.

Here is another introduction that begins with an anecdote:

Recently the television news magazine "Sixty Minutes" featured a story about a number of adults who had developed cancer in their lymph nodes following radiation treatments in early childhood. A mother who was interviewed on the program said that her (now adult) child had been given extensive X-ray treatments early in his life for what was described by the family physician as a "funny sounding" cry. When she was pressed by the "Sixty Minutes" interviewer to explain why she had allowed her child to undergo heavy doses of radiation for a relatively minor matter, the mother protested, "You never questioned a doctor in those days. The pediatrician was God!"

"God," in other words, was somebody not to be questioned. Ordinarily, though, we regard questions and answers as important means of exchanging information between people. The talk that occurs between a physician and patient would seem to offer a particularly important opportunity for an exchange of information, for here its presence or absence can have life and death consequences. From a practical perspective, patients appear to be the best sources of information on certain medical questions; certainly, they are the doctors' sole sources of information regarding their subjective experiences of health and illness. So, we can understand how physicians might be predisposed to questioning their patients.

Candace West, *Routine Complications: Troubles with Talk between Doctors and Patients*

Besides drawing readers in, this anecdote cues us to the author's attitude about communication between doctors and patients. She believes that they don't talk enough.

The next introduction gives readers a short survey of what the author plans to cover:

> No discussion of language in the USA could hope to be complete unless it pays careful attention to the languages spoken by this country's first inhabitants. The fact that languages (and *not* a single language, with many dialects) are at issue here must be emphasized from the outset. For there are by present estimate, over 200 distinct Indian language traditions currently attested within the Indian tribes and communities of the fifty states. These languages have long been a significant (even if frequently overlooked) component of the nation's cultural resources. They are certainly not "limited" in their descriptive power, nor are they "primitive" in their potential for expressiveness. The structural details of Indian languages reflect profound appreciation for the physical world and its natural order. European colonists depended on this understanding as a means for their own survival on numerous occasions during the contact period. Reflexes of that dependency, and of the various forms of interaction which subsequently came to replace it, have become commonly attested in American English usage. Words of Indian-specific cultural items (*teepee, wampum, kachina*), foodstuffs (*succotash, maize*), place names and geographical terms (*Tallahassee, Mississippi*), along with phrases ranging from the most esoteric (*Gitchee Gumee, Nokomis,* and other items from Longfellow's poetry) to the most trivial of purposes (*kemo sabe* of Lone Ranger and Tonto fame) are all familiar vocabulary to most of the nation's citizenry.
>
> William L. Leap, "American Indian Languages"

In the rest of his essay, the author then develops most of the ideas in this introductory paragraph. Just as with West's lead-in, Leap gives us a strong impression of his position about the significance of Indian languages. We expect him to demonstrate their significance further, probably by giving additional examples.

A very common strategy for introducing a topic is to ask a question:

> Happy or unhappy, families are all mysterious. We have only to imagine how differently we would be described—and will be, after our deaths—by each of the family members who believe they know us. The only question is, Why are some mysteries more important than others?
>
> Gloria Steinem, *Outrageous Acts and Everyday Rebellions*

If you look back at assignment 3 at the end of Chapter 6, you will find a longer version of this passage. Notice that the author doesn't even answer the questions she poses here. Nor might we expect an answer. Instead, the question itself prompts readers to think about why some mysteries are more important than others—that is, to think about the ideas the author is about to explore. The question itself is all the introduction we need.

Stop for a moment, and glance over the introductions that we have examined. Notice that the earlier examples were very short, and that most of the last ones were longer. Depending on how complex a topic is, the writer may have to provide a good deal of information in the introduction. Consider what your readers are likely to know about your topic, and use your introduction to prepare them for the points you will cover in your essay.

Reading and Writing Assignment   ■

Read the introductions to the passages in the assignments at the ends of Chapters 6, 7, and 8. On the right-hand side of your journal, make notes about the various strategies the writers use to introduce their topics. On the left-hand side, summarize what you have learned about introductions that you didn't know before.

Conclusions

The following examples of conclusions may seem a little strange, because you will not know what came before them in the essay. If you examine them closely, however, you probably can guess what each essay was about, and what points the authors made. A good conclusion should wrap the subject up for your readers, so that they'll feel you have covered the material you introduced at the beginning of the essay.

Our first example makes it clear that the essay was about the historical King Wenceslas and the Christmas carol that an English minister wrote about him:

Yuletide: Christmastime
repertoire: the pieces of music that a player can perform
erudite: learned

The rest is history. "Good King Wenceslas" was an instant hit, and generations of happy carolers have since made it a classic of the Yuletide repertoire. It is perhaps John Mason Neale's most lasting contribution—a development that the erudite cleric could hardly have anticipated. And as for Good King Wenceslas himself, although he cannot lay claim to the indispensability of a Santa Claus, it can nonetheless be said that there are those for whom Christmas would not be the same without him.

Barry Hoberman, "Wenceslas of Bohemia"

The sentence "The rest is history" provides a transition from the body of the essay to the conclusion. It gives readers a feeling of finality. The rest of this concluding paragraph serves the same function as "and they lived happily ever after."

The next writer finds a tidy way to end an article about the now-extinct Tasmanian tiger of Australia:

> A recent expedition produced sightings of many possums, six wallabies, three Tasmanian devils, one boobook owl and one spiny anteater. The expedition also produced a few squirmy moments when the old four-wheel-drive Daihatsu wouldn't start on a remote bush track. "Two hundred meters further on there'll be a big tiger," grunted Miss Richards as she pushed the vehicle, "and by the time we get this thing down there it'll be gone."
> Needless to say, it was.
> "Australians Have a Devil of a Time Tracking (Extinct) Tasmanian Tiger"

In this case, the very last sentence—"Needless to say, it was"—provides the feeling of finality. We can assume that the article told of many fruitless efforts to track down a Tasmanian tiger.

Following is the first sentence of a concluding paragraph. It leads into a final summing-up of the specific points that the author made in the body of the essay:

> From this perspective it is clear that the pleasure derived from preschool play is controlled by different motives than simple sucking on a pacifier.
> Lev Vygotsky, "The Role of Play in Development"

Finally, let us look at a conclusion that sums up an article and leaves readers with something further to think about. This last sentence ends an article about the place of Black English in American society:

> . . . As black people go moving on up toward separation and cultural nationalism, the question of the moment is not to which dialect, but which culture, not whose vocabulary but whose values, not *I am* vs. *I be*, but WHO DO I BE?
> Geneva Smitherman, "English in Blackface, or Who Do I Be?"

By ending with a question, Smitherman asks readers to think further about language as a symbol of cultural identity. She asks them to think further about her essay as a whole.

Reading and Writing Assignment

Read the conclusions to the passages in the assignments at the ends of Chapters 6, 7, and 8. On the right-hand side of your journal, make notes about the various strategies the writers use to end their essays. On the left-hand side, summarize what you have learned about conclusions that you didn't know before.

How to Draft Persuasive Writing

By now you should have a good idea of what persuasive writing is. You have read some selections of persuasive prose, and you have written some persuasive writing yourself. Let's build on what you have done so far by reading some more examples of persuasive writing, by discussing the writing situation and audience, and by doing a few more assignments that are a bit more complicated.

As readers, we are generally interested in writing that is somehow *provocative*—that is, writing that causes us to take action or to feel emotion. Remember: We might look at *all* writing as persuasive. To be provocative, however, a writer must be willing to give readers plenty to think about. Here is an example of provocative writing:

> TV and the movies have spoiled the most intimate moments of our lives. They have given us conventions which dominate our expectations in instants whose intensity would ordinarily make them spontaneous and unique. We have conventions of grief, which we learned from the Kennedys, and ordained gestures for victory by which we imitate the athletes we see on the tube, who in turn have learned the same things from other jocks they saw on TV.
>
> Scott Turow, *Presumed Innocent*

This writer argues that TV and movies have somehow dulled our ability to feel things. He asks us to examine our own emotions and to compare them with what we have seen on TV or in films. We must reread this passage a few times, and must actively call on our own memories. For example, after something happened, did you ever exclaim, "It was just like in the movies!"? Or, when you picture an ideal date, do you think of a romantic dinner that you saw some couple having on a soap opera? Is your idea of wealth and luxury based on "Lifestyles of the Rich and Famous"? Have you ever been out with friends having a good time and felt like you were in a soft-drink commercial? These are the kinds of questions the passage asks readers to consider.

Successful persuasive writing must move beyond simply stating one's opinion. It must, as we said, give readers something to think about. Too many writers think that simply by saying something they make it true. But an *assertion* (that is, a statement of opinion, or a conclusion, or an observation) must be supported by facts or details. Often, all we need are details that our own experiences and observations bear out. But to be persuasive, a writer must provide answers to questions like "How?" or "Why?"

Facts, examples, explanations, analyses, and anecdotes all help to support a writer's assertions. Such things provide the *how* and the *why* that readers need if they are to understand and be persuaded. Consider the following statements:

Our society is built on a paper foundation. . . . No American who wishes to hold a place of any significant responsibility can avoid the necessity of written communication.

Why should any reader believe this? All we have to go on is an assertion, a simple statement of opinion. But look what happens to the passage when the author's examples are put back in. Now it is much more convincing:

Our society is built on a paper foundation. Every large building in a great metropolis existed first in hundreds of pages of closely written specifications. Every modern bridge, every highway, has emerged from the mind of man with the assistance of the written word. Millions of typewriters clatter from morning to night, creating the correspondence, the reports, the records upon which commerce, industry, and government depend for essential information. Forests fall to convey to modern man the news of this country and of the world. Constantly letters flow across the land, carrying messages of love and pain, business and leisure, to millions of readers. Even in the armed forces, thousands of messages are received and transmitted daily at any large base. It is said in the Navy that "communications cannot win a war, but they sure as hell can lose it." No American who wishes to hold a place of any significant responsibility can avoid the necessity of written communication.

Donald R. Tuttle, "Composition"

In the next passage, the writer makes his point in the first sentence, and then he quickly supports it:

Within the past thirty years, Americans have become increasingly more mobile, increasingly more addicted to moving around. According to a recent study, an American family changes its residence on the average of once every five years. Approximately forty million Americans change their address every year. The number of Americans living in mobile homes has also grown dramatically.

Russell Lynes, "The Movers"

This writer doesn't expect readers to believe him just because he says so. By quickly citing some statistics, he is much more convincing. (Of course, readers should always be cautious of how writers use statistics. For the moment, however, we'll trust our writers.)

When you write a persuasive essay, keep in mind that your own opinions, based on your own experiences, may have to be balanced by the experiences and wisdom of others. One person's experiences are very limited compared with all of humanity's. Always consider whether you can support your points better by drawing on other people's experiences. A trip to the library or an interview with a knowledgeable person might be helpful in supporting your own point of view.

The writer of the next passage draws on readers' general experiences in making some observations about young children:

> A very young child tends to gratify her desires immediately; normally the interval between a desire and its fulfillment is extremely short. No one has met a child under three years old who wants to do something a few days in the future. However, at the preschool age, a great many unrealizable tendencies and desires emerge.
>
> Lev Vygotsky, "The Role of Play in Development"

Although Vygotsky may have other experts in developmental psychology in mind, or even well-read individuals who spend a good deal of time with children, he doesn't use statistics, as Lynes did. Instead, he appeals to our personal experience: "No one has met a child under three years old. . . ."

Our next writer also appeals to readers' experiences to support his own observations:

> . . . like many other people, I suppress a desire to travel in my own city. I think we do this because we don't want to know too much. And we don't want to be exposed. As everyone knows, it is wrong to be too conspicuously curious—much better to leave this for foreign places.
>
> Paul Theroux, *Sunrise with Seamonsters*

In this case the writer generalizes, saying that "many other people" do not travel in their own cities. He bases this on his own feelings, which he believes he shares with others: "we don't want to know too much." Note how he appeals to his audience: "As everyone knows. . . ."

The next writer takes the opposite approach by admitting that his point of view may be different from other people's:

> I am aware that the other participants in this story would tell parts of it in other ways, sometimes because their memory of what happened differs from mine and, perhaps in even more cases, because no two people ever see the same events in exactly the same light.
>
> James Watson, *The Double Helix*

Watson, who discovered the structure of DNA along with Francis Crick, acknowledges that others may remember these events differently than he does. In a way, this makes readers more receptive to his point of view, because he portrays himself as someone who, after all, is only human.

The author of the next passage points to a common misconception about slang:

> Many people think they know instinctively when they encounter slang, and their response is usually negative. These same people may be surprised, however, to discover what slang has been. Nice started out as a slang word,

and it now occupies a front position in a long and respected list of nice but meaningless words. A number of other words, as H. L. Mencken points out in his famous discussion of slang, started out as slang and end up filling vacuums in our existing vocabulary. Among others, Mencken mentions rodeo, racketeer, and hold up.

Anne Nichols, "Slang"

By noting that there is a difference of opinion about slang, and summing up the opposite position, Nichols is able to argue her point more effectively, through a few good examples. In effect, she says that if people who dislike slang can accept *nice* and *rodeo* as standard American English, then their reason for disliking slang in the first place is awfully shaky. She wins the argument by showing that her opponents are "illogical."

Logic is sound and adequate critical thinking: getting from A to B without any wrong turns. In writing, to be logical is to take an assertion and develop it further through facts, explanations, or personal experiences so that readers can understand (and perhaps believe) the point.

This isn't always easy—especially when real-life models don't seem very logical. Television programs, for example, seem to teach us that every problem can be solved—in an hour or in a half-hour. Often, the solutions themselves aren't logical or believable. The same is true of commercials, which often make a very illogical appeal: If we buy Smilebrite toothpaste or Luther jeans, we will be popular, happy, and loved. Logically, we know that there is no connection between a particular brand of toothpaste and happiness. But advertisers know that we are not always logical, and they aim their persuasive appeals at people's emotional needs. Careful readers are not so easily swayed, and careful writers support their appeals with logic.

Reading and Writing Assignment ∎

We hear a lot of heated discussion these days about "our rights" under the American Constitution and its Bill of Rights. Such discussions often center around the tension that exists between society (or the local community) at large and individuals. But how many Americans know what the Constitution and its Bill of Rights really say? To argue about our constitutional rights without knowing exactly what the Constitution says isn't very, well, *logical.*

1. Go to the library, and study the Bill of Rights (the first ten amendments of the U.S. Constitution). In small groups in class, discuss what you learned. On the right-hand side of your journal, make notes about the group's discussion; remember to list any examples that the group discusses.

2. Select one right that is guaranteed by the Bill of Rights. On the left-hand side of your journal, write a page or so about (a) how society might be harmed if people *exercised* that right, or (b) how society might be harmed if people *did not have* that right.

Among the more common examples of persuasive writing are reviews of books, records, films, concerts, or museum exhibits. In everyday conversation, you might discuss the latest record or film and express your opinion briefly. It's easier to just say, "It was great!" (or "It was terrible!") than to analyze *why* you think so. Furthermore, very few friends would tolerate a long-winded critique in which you take over the entire conversation. But written reviews go far beyond simply announcing one's likes or dislikes. The following assignments will give you a chance to practice your persuasive skills in writing about music or films.

Writing Assignments

1. On the left-hand side of your journal, describe what kind of music you like, and explain why you like it. Assume that your audience (a) is someone who does *not* like that kind of music or (b) is someone who doesn't know anything about it. You might want to read some music reviews before you begin, to get an idea of how others write reviews. Remember to use specific examples to support your opinions.

2. Develop assignment 1 into an essay that you support by means of recorded examples of your favorite music. The challenge here is to pick only two or three songs or pieces, or parts of songs—say four or five minutes total—that illustrate your points about the music. Remember to let your essay do most of the work; the recordings are only to support your claims. (Simply writing, "Oh, listen to the second cut—you'll understand" will not do.)

3. Choose a favorite movie or one that you have seen recently. On the left-hand side of your journal, write a page or so persuading a particular audience either to see the movie or not to see it. (You define the audience—children, teenagers, parents, teachers, etc.—and explain why they should or should not see this movie, giving specific examples to defend your position.) The following suggestions will help you prepare to write this persuasive journal entry.

a. On the right-hand side of your journal, answer questions like these: Are the movie's plot and characters believable or unbelievable? Are you drawn into the film's world, or do you feel distanced in some way? Can you relate to the characters' predicament? Is there a message? Is the movie primarily serious, or is it a comedy? Can you think of any other movies like this one? What makes it so special to you?

b. Read some film reviews to discover what kinds of information they have in common. For example, most reviews include the film's name; its director and leading actors; the type of film (science fiction, romantic comedy, thriller, etc.); a brief summary of the plot that does not give away the film's ending; and some opinion about the film's appeal or success. On the right-hand side of your journal, list the information you will use in writing your review.

Persuasive writing does not always make judgments about what is good or bad about something. A writer can also be persuasive in exploring relationships between events or between people in order to understand them better. One student, for example, wrote a paper in which she explored how her religious training as a child had contributed to the kind of person she had become. She did not have to judge the training as good or bad in order to write a successful paper.

Writing Assignment   ■

Before going on to the assignments to write your own persuasive essay, look back through this chapter. What did you learn about persuasive writing that you didn't know before? On the right-hand side of your journal, summarize what you have learned about reading persuasive writing; about introductions and conclusions; and about supporting your opinions in persuasive writing. In small groups, share your journal notes with your classmates.

Assignments in Persuasive Writing

The following pages guide you through three different persuasive writing assignments. Here is a brief description of them:

1.   The Language of Clothes   This assignment asks you to argue that clothing has hidden meanings—or does not.

2.   What We Talk about When We Talk about Love   This assignment invites you to define what *you* mean when you talk about love, and to describe how you learned about love in the first place.

3.   Independence   This assignment asks you to present an argument about how to deal with the changes that we go through as we grow up and become independent.

To help you decide which assignment interests you most, quickly read what each assignment is about and how you might approach it. Also look over your journal and the persuasive writing you have already done in this chapter. Perhaps you can develop one of your earlier drafts further, or can adapt it to fit one of the following assignments. If you can't decide which assignment to do, consult with your teacher.

When you have picked an assignment, turn to Chapter 2 for some tips about how to discover your ideas. Then, after you have written your discovery draft, Chapters 4 and 5 and Worksheets 1 through 6 will help you plan and edit your final draft.

Assignment 1.   The Language of Clothes

In the following passage, Alison Lurie compares clothing to language. She says that clothing can "speak" to us in the same way that words can, since clothes can symbolize, or stand for, many things about ourselves.

> For thousands of years human beings have communicated with one another first in the language of dress. Long before I am near enough to talk to you on the street, in a meeting, or at a party, you announce your sex, age and class to me through what you are wearing—and very possibly give important information (or misinformation) as to your occupation, origin, personality, opinions, tastes, sexual desires and current mood. I may not be able to put what I observe into words, but I register the information unconsciously; and you simultaneously do the same for me. By the time we meet and converse we have already spoken to each other in an older and more universal tongue.
> . . . if clothing is a language, it must have a vocabulary and a grammar like other languages. Of course, as with human speech, there is not a single language of dress, but many: some (like Dutch and German) closely related

and other (like Basque) almost unique. And within every language of clothes
there are many different dialects and accents, some almost unintelligible to
members of the mainstream culture. Moreover, as with speech, each individual
has his own stock of words and employs personal variations of tone and meaning. . . .

The vocabulary of dress includes not only items of clothing, but also hair
styles, accessories, jewelry, make-up and body decoration. Theoretically at
least this vocabulary is as large as or larger than that of any spoken tongue,
since it includes every garment, hair style, and type of body decoration ever
invented. In practice, of course, the sartorial resources of an individual may be
very restricted. Those of a sharecropper, for instance, may be limited to five or
ten "words" from which it is possible to create only a few "sentences" almost
bare of decoration and expressing only the most basic concepts. A so-called
fashion leader, on the other hand, may have several hundred "words" at his or
her disposal, and thus be able to form thousands of different "sentences" that
will express a wide range of meanings. Just as the average English-speaking
person knows many more words than he or she will ever use in conversation,
so all of us are able to understand the meaning of styles we will never wear.

To choose clothes, either in a store or at home, is to define and describe
ourselves. Occasionally, of course, practical considerations enter into these
choices: considerations of comfort, durability, availability and price. Especially
in the case of persons of limited wardrobe, an article may be worn because it is
warm or rainproof or handy to cover up a wet bathing suit—in the same way
that persons of limited vocabulary use the phrase "you know" or adjectives
such as "great" or "fantastic." Yet, just as with spoken language, such choices
usually give us some information, even if it is only equivalent to the statement
"I don't give a damn what I look like today." And there are limits even here. In
this culture, like many others, certain garments are taboo for certain persons.
Most men, however cold or wet they might be, would not put on a woman's
dress, just as they would not use words and phrases such as "simply mar-
velous," which in this culture are considered specifically feminine.

Alison Lurie, *The Language of Clothes*

Guidelines for Assignment 1 ■

1. On the left-hand side of your journal, write a response to this passage. Do
you agree with Lurie's theory or not? Do you think clothes and language have
anything in common? Can you give some examples? (In the rest of her book,
Lurie explores the meaning of clothes in relation to youth and age, color and
pattern, fashion, and such things as time, place, status, and sex.)

2. In small groups, try to work out your own version of the language of
clothes, and list some examples. Take notes about the group's discussion on the
right-hand side of your journal.

3. Write a persuasive essay in response to Lurie's argument. There are several ways to respond to Lurie's theory, and you must decide which way suits your purpose. For example, if you agree with her, you might want to support her case further by relating your own experiences with wearing clothes that send certain messages, or by reporting on what you have observed about other people's clothing. Or, you might want to explore how or why clothes communicate.

Perhaps you disagree with Lurie, feeling that in today's world "anything goes." But does it, really? This argument might be harder to support, but you may want to pursue it and see where it leads. Maybe you can write an essay *limiting* how far Lurie goes with her argument.

Here are some other ideas you might want to consider:

a. If you want to expand the comparison of clothing to language, consider how one or two of the following might be related to clothing: archaic words, foreign words, slang, vulgar language, clichés, "The King's English," and conventional speech. (If you aren't sure of what these terms mean, look them up in a dictionary or grammar book before beginning. For example, archaic words are those which people don't use much anymore, like *forsooth* and *nay*. Can you think of any kinds of clothing that are so old-fashioned or out of date that people's heads would turn if you wore them? Hoop skirts or full-length capes might fit this description.)

b. You might want to gather information from others before writing your essay. You could, for example, show people an advertisement or a picture from a magazine and ask them how they might respond to the person based on his or her clothing alone. Or, ask them what they consider to be "well dressed" or "properly dressed" or "badly dressed."

c. Explain why you dress the way you do. Imagine a reader such as a parent, or some person in authority, or someone from another country who is trying to read clothing "messages" in the United States.

d. You might take Lurie's approach and argue that there is a language of cars, sports, food, or hairstyles.

4. Use Lurie's passage as you explore your subject in a draft by drawing comparisons between what she says and your own argument. Assume that your reader is familiar with the passage, and refer directly to it. You may need to give a two- or three-sentence summary of the passage; be sure to include the author and title.

5. After you write a discovery draft, reread Lurie's passage. Based on your rereading, make notes for revision in the margins of your draft.

Assignment 2. What We Talk about When We Talk about Love

The title of this assignment is taken from a short story by Raymond Carver. In the story, as two married couples sit around a kitchen table talking one afternoon, they discover that they are not talking about the same thing at all when they talk about love.

In fact, disagreements about what love is are not so unusual in real life. We all come to loving (love for a child, a parent, a sibling, a friend, a lover, and so on) with different attitudes and different expectations about how we ought to act—and about how the loved one is supposed to act toward us.

In this assignment, you are invited to think about what *you* mean when you talk about love, and how you learned about love in the first place.

Write Before Reading   ■

Before you read the following passage, write an entry on the left-hand side of your journal in which you discuss how you formed your ideas about love. You may have been influenced by a parent or someone else or by books, movies, songs, and so on. Then, on the right-hand side, directly opposite your entry, list some people you love or have loved whom you might write about.

When love is constant and enduring, it persists despite changes in the friend's traits, even changes in those traits that first awoke the love and that were its central focus. This kind of constancy is assured only at a very general level: it is directed to the same person . . . and the attachment remains at roughly the same level of devotion. If Louis's love for Ella when he is twenty is radically different from his attitude at sixty, has his love been constant? Presumably, constancy can be preserved by defining the object and functional roles of his attitude in a sufficiently general manner. But such generality is unlikely to reassure those who wonder if they still love, when little they desire or do has remained the same.

When Louis and Ella are concerned about the continuity of their loves, they are not only interested in constancy, though perhaps some of their concerns could be rephrased in that way. What might concern Ella is whether it is she who influences or affects the character of Louis's love and whether his delight in her ramifies to affect other things about him. When Ella does not want Louis to love her as Don Juan might have loved Elvira, her concern for his fidelity might be a way of expressing her concern for whether his delight focuses on her rather than on his dazzling gifts as a lover. She wants his speeches, his charming attentions, and his deftly winning ways to be not only directed *at* and *to* her, but to take their tenor and form from his delighted recognition of what is central to her. It is not enough that he gets the color of her eyes right, when he gets to that part of the serenade describing their enchantment. Nor is Ella's worry laid to rest by being assured of his fidelity,

ramifies: branches out
Don Juan: legendary Spanish lover
Elvira: wife of Don Juan
deftly: skillfully
tenor: the general meaning

connoisseur: a person with knowledgeable taste

conducing: contributing, leading

permeable: capable of being penetrated; here, a free flow of ideas, changes, etc., between the lover and the friend

obtuse: slow to perceive, dull; here, not open to change

Scarlatti: Italian classical composer

Schubert: Austrian classical composer

Orwell: author of *1984* and *Animal Farm*, as well as a distinguished journalist

assured that Louis is no Don Juan, ranging over variables for his joys as a connoisseur of the subtle and interesting differences between women and their ever so wonderful effects on him. For whatever good such assurance might do her, Ella could be convinced that if she were to die, or if they were to have an irreconcilable falling out, Louis would feel lost, mourn, and only gradually be healed enough to love someone else. But both she and her successor Gloria might be aggrieved that Louis always brings the same love, a love that is contained within *his* biography, to be given as a gift. Presumably Gloria does not want to inherit Louis's love for Ella: she wants Louis to love her in a wholly different way, defined by the two of them. This is a complex and compounded hope: that Louis's love will be formed by his perceiving—his accurately perceiving—the gradual changes in her, and in his responses being appropriately formed by those changes. If Ella and Gloria love Louis, they want the changes they effect in him to be consonant and suitable to him as well as to them, conducing to his flourishing as well as theirs. It is because they want their love to conduce to his flourishing that it is important that they see him accurately and that their interactive responses to him be appropriate.

There is a kind of love—and for some it may be the only kind that qualifies as true love—that is historical precisely because it does not (oh so wonderfully) rigidly designate its object. The details of such love change with every change in the lover and the friend. Such a love might be called *dynamically permeable*. It is permeable in that the lover is changed by loving and changed by truthful perception of the friend. Permeability rejects being obtuse to change as an easy way of assuring constancy. It is dynamic in that every change generates new changes, both in the lover and in interactions with the friend. Having been transformed by loving, the lover perceives the friend in a new way and loves in a new way. Dynamism rejects the regionalization of love as an easy way of assuring constancy: the changes produced by such love tend to ramify through a person's character, without being limited to the areas that first directly were the focus of the lover's attention.

To see how this works out, let's gossip a bit about Ella, Louis, and Gloria. Louis's love for Ella began with his enchantment at her crisp way of playing Scarlatti, the unsentimental lyricism of her interpretation of Schubert, her appreciation of Orwell's journalism. After a while, he found that he was enchanted by traits he'd never noticed or admired in anyone else: the sequence of her moods, the particular way she had of sitting still, head bent when she listened to music. He came to love those traits in her, or her in those traits—he could hardly tell which. He came to appreciate such traits in others because her having them had delighted him. And he changed too, not necessarily in imitation of her, but because of her. An acute observer could discern changes in Louis that had their origins and explanation in his love of Ella, changes that were deeper than those that arose from his desire to please her. Some of these changes might conflict with, and threaten, other long-standing traits. If Louis's interest in Ella brings an interest in medieval music, it brings him into new company as well. The ramified consequences of his new interests are likely to interfere with his Friday night jam sessions with his old friends in the hard rock group. Either his responses to Ella ramify, and he acquires a new taste in companions, or he attempts to regionalize the changes that Ella effects on him. Both alternatives have significant consequences on them, and on him. If his dynamic interactions do not ramify, there will be conflicts between his pre-Ella and his post-Ella self. But if they do ramify, his psychological continuity is loosened by his being formed and reformed by each new friendship (Of course, such problems are often solved by Louis and Ella sharing important parts of their lives, partners in common enterprises. Sharing their lives and activities assures their both being formed by a common world as well as by each other.) If Louis and Ella are wise, they are careful to avoid the extremes of both regionalization and ramification. Fortunately, this is not wholly a matter of insight and foresight: a person's previous traits resist transformation. If Louis truly interacts with Ella, he cannot become a person formed by and designed to suit her fantasies.

We shall return to the difficulties of regionalization and ramification, the difficulties of abstract constancy and hypersensitivity. For the moment, let us suppose that in this idyllic fairy tale, Louis came to realize that he would continue to love Ella even if she were to lose those traits that first drew him to her and that were still the focus of his joy in her. Even if someone else played Scarlatti more brilliantly, Schubert more discerningly, and had even more trenchant views on the relation between Orwell and Brecht, he would not transfer his love. . . . Nor does it mean that the character of his devotion would remain unchanged by whatever changes might occur in her. He'd be lunatic to love her at sixty in just exactly the same way as he had at twenty; and he'd be cruel to love her way of playing Scarlatti if her hands had been mangled in an accident. Nor can his love be analyzed by a set of counterfactuals. If she became Rampal's accompanist, he would. . . . If her mother moved next door, he would. . . . If she became paralyzed, he would. . . . If she declared herself impassioned of a punk-rock-schlock electronic guitar player, he would. . . . If Glorious Gloria, the Paragon of his Dreams, invited him to join her in a trip to Acapulco, he would. . . . If this kind of love could be analyzed in a set of counterfactuals, that set would have to be indefinitely large. For there are an indefinite number of changes that will occur and that will affect Louis if he loves Ella.

Amélie Rorty, "The Historicity of Psychological Attitudes:
Love Is Not Love Which Alters Not When It Alteration Finds"

trenchant:
insightful
Brecht: German
playwright and
poet

**counter-
factuals:**
contrary
to fact or reality
Rampal: a flutist
schlock:
merchandise of
inferior quality

Guidelines for Assignment 2   ■

1. On the right-hand side of your journal, write a summary of what is most significant about this passage. On the left-hand side, directly opposite, write a response to the passage. Think about the second part of the title, too: "Love Is Not Love Which Alters Not When It Alteration Finds." This refers to a sonnet by Shakespeare, which begins as follows:

> Let me not to the marriage of true minds
> Admit impediments. Love is not love
> Which alters when it alteration finds,
> Or bends with the remover to remove:
> O, no! it is an ever-fixed mark.

Rorty has added one important word to Shakespeare's line *(not)*. Continuing on the left-hand side of your journal, compare what Rorty has to say with what Shakespeare says about love.

2. In small groups, discuss what you think Rorty believes about love. Turn to the journal entry you wrote before reading—about what has most influenced your ideas and expectations about love—and share your thoughts with your group. Then, discuss how you might use Rorty's ideas in writing about your own experiences with love. Do you agree with what she says? Make notes about the group's discussion on the right-hand side of your journal.

3. Pick an event from your life that illustrates why you have the expectations and beliefs about love that you do. Think about what actually happened—the reality of the experience versus the expectations you had about love before this event happened. Did you or the loved one change during the course of the relationship? Was the change positive or negative? (Before picking a topic, re-read your journal for ideas. You may already have a draft about an event in your life that fits this assignment.)

4. Consider your response to Rorty's passage and to the group's discussion. As you explore your topic in a draft, compare your attitudes toward love with Rorty's. Refer to the passage specifically in your own writing. You also might want to refer to Shakespeare's sonnet.

Assignment 3.   Independence

This assignment asks you to write about your experiences moving from dependence to independence, and to present an argument for dealing with the changes that we go through as we grow up.

Write Before Reading ■

Before you read the following passages, use the left-hand side of your journal to describe some of your experiences in becoming independent.

In childhood, disturbances caused by emotions can be soothed by actions from parents. When a child is sad, he is picked up and comforted. When he has nightmares, he goes and sleeps with Mom or Dad. Disturbing emotions that a child has can be taken care of by simple actions or explanations from parents.

In adolescence, parents lose their power to comfort or explain away fears, because emotions are more demanding and powerful. When he is unhappy, the adolescent himself must understand the emotions behind this unhappiness before he can be happy again. For example, if I feel crushed because a good friend has gone off to spend the weekend with another friend, I have to work this out myself so that I cease to feel abandoned and lonely. I may go out and see another friend. This shows me that I am capable of having other friends also; that I can survive without my good friend just as she can survive without me.

Also, as the adolescent grows more independent his values begin to differ sharply. Often now, I feel that I must not talk about some of my problems with my parents, because they would think of a totally different solution than one that would be appropriate for me. This would only confuse me. I must figure out for myself what I want out of the situation that presents the problem. No one can do this for me, certainly not my parents.

When I was about twelve, I was very afraid of death. I didn't see the point in living if I was going to die. I used to cry and cry for my parents' attention, but they couldn't take away this fear from me; they were helpless. The strength they had had in dissolving my childhood fears was gone. I had to come to an understanding of death on my own. Even though I knew they couldn't help, I think I kept on crying in order to prove to them and to myself that they were unable to stop my crying, that they were helpless this time and it was my problem. This loss of their power was disturbing to both my parents and me. I felt anxious; a lonely, sick feeling would come easily. I'm sure they also felt very frustrated, and for a while just did not know how to help me. This loss of power has been beneficial, in that it has forced me to search for my understanding of me and of life, independent of my parents.

rash: hasty or
bold
subjective:
personal; guided
by one's own
opinion

Now I will make a rash and subjective statement, and say that parents of adolescents must be as clever and perceptive as possible. It is their responsibility to decide whether the child is mature enough to carry through with what he wants to do, that is, whether or not to let him do things like going out alone, staying out late, and traveling alone. If they let him do anything without questioning, he could easily feel abandoned and that nobody gives a damn. From there, he could feel that growing up is too much for him to handle, that it is just not worth all the trouble. On the other hand, if parents don't let the adolescent be on his own enough, he may feel that they are not allowing him to grow up. He is not only trapped into coming home at 10:30, but he is also trapped into not being able to explore his limits and feelings about himself. He is using someone else's limits, and he is afraid he will start feeling someone else's feelings also. Parents should try and understand this stress, and assess the amount of the child's knowledge of himself. Parents should support, by being willing listeners and not trying to measure the adolescent in their own values. This is something which I think should happen more than it does.

Tina de Varon, "Growing Up"

cognitive: having to do with how knowledge is acquired

motoric: having to do with the movement of muscles

It seems to me that independence is achieved when the child (or adult) is able to see himself as generally successful in achieving goals. The goal may be cognitive, or motoric, or interpersonal—what matters is not so much the content of the goal as the nature of the resolution. . . . As children grow older, the nature of the crises and goals changes, but the important question seems to be whether the parent has the patience to allow the child to solve the problem for himself. It seems to me that we underrate the independence motive in children. When they try to dress themselves, comb their hair, color a picture, clean their room, finish a puzzle, they are not only mimicking adult behavior, identifying with suitable people, improving specific skills—they are also, in numerous and diverse ways, teaching themselves that they have skills and that they can cope (more or less) all by themselves. The child who is confident in his abilities and who explores the world and his skills from the basis of a secure parental affection is less likely to use dependent behavior as a means of punishing, exploiting, and manipulating. That child will be slower to use dependent behavior in order to master tasks because he will try to perform the tasks himself before asking for help. And that child will enjoy affection but he will not need it in continuous doses in order to reassure himself that he exists and is estimable. Does a child do things in order to be rewarded, praised, or even punished (at least that's some sort of attention), or does he do it for himself and then share the pleasure of accomplishment with someone else?

Children, like adults are never entirely independent. There are always critically important persons whose love and esteem are essential. There are narrow margins for success and failure here because a parent rewarding dependence is seen as loving whereas his consistent training for independence can be perceived as rejection. For example, when a child comes home and says, "Somebody hit me!" the mother who responds with "Oh, my poor dear" fosters dependence, and the mother who says "Who hit first?" may be fostering guilt, and the mother who says "What happened?" and hasn't taken sides may be fostering independence. In different proportions, an emphasis of the "What happened?" response with only a bit of the other two is likely to result in a child who leans on himself first and who looks for objective criteria to assess life's happenings.

Judith Bardwick, *Psychology of Women: A Study of Bio-Cultural Conflicts*

Guidelines for Assignment 3   ■

1. On the right-hand side of your journal, write a summary of what is most significant about each of these passages. On the left-hand side of your journal, directly opposite your summary, write a response to each of the passages.

2. In small groups, discuss what the two writers believe about independence and growing up. Do you agree or disagree with their points of view? We often think of college as a movement *toward* new experiences, new friends, and so on, but that is only half the picture; it is also a movement *away from* family and hometown friends. What impact does this movement have on a person's experiences with dependence and independence? Make notes about the group's discussion on the right-hand side of your journal.

3. Choose an event from your life to write about that illustrates how you came to terms with your increasing independence as a person. (Reread your journal entries for ideas.) Based on this event, argue for a way to help children and young people become independent.

4. Consider the responses you wrote to these two passages. As you explore your topic in a draft, compare your own attitudes toward growing up with the attitudes of de Varon and Bardwick. When you refer to these passages, assume that your reader is familiar with them but might need a two- or three-sentence summary of their contents. Be sure to include the author and title.

5. After you write a discovery draft, reread the two passages. Based on your rereading, make notes for revision in the margins of your draft.

part *four* ■

Editing Your Writing

Keeping Track of Your Errors
Recognizing Parts of Sentences
Recognizing Types of Sentences
Fine-Tuning Your Sentences

Introduction: Strategies for Editing

How should a writer go about studying grammar? Some people think grammar shouldn't be taught at all, while others think students benefit the most from repetitive, constant drills. The truth probably lies somewhere in the middle of these two positions. Of course, an individual's needs and past experiences with grammar study should be taken into account.

The phrase "studying grammar" is a bit misleading, because it implies that you ought to sit down and study a grammar book in the same way that you study biology or history. Instead, the best way to "study" grammar is to begin with a piece of your own writing. With the help of a teacher, classmate, tutor, or friend, identify the kinds of mistakes you make. Then concentrate on discovering why you make them in the first place. Finally, learn how to avoid or correct the particular kinds of mistakes you make often.

There are not as many rules for a writer to follow as you might think—or even as you might like. In a way, avoiding sentence-level problems (that is, problems with grammar) is less about learning rules than about learning *patterns* of language. Such patterns can change, depending on the knowledge of the audience, the formality of the situation, the complexity of the information, and the unique aspects of each sentence.

Keep in mind that studying the language of grammar doesn't make a writer an expert in *using* grammar. Grammarians have their own technical language, as do specialists in any other field. (For example, computer specialists toss about such words as *modem, interface,* and *floppy disk.*) Technical language can be confusing to nonspecialists. It certainly isn't easy to remember the difference between a predicate nominative and a predicate adjective while you are writing. Nor do you have to. Although some technical language is used in the following discussion of grammar, its purpose is to explain patterns of language so that you can use them in your writing.

Wherever possible, the technical language of grammar will include a short description and then an example of the thing itself. Thus, a *gerund* will first be defined (a noun formed from a verb plus *-ing*); then it will be described (an *-ing* noun); and then an example will be given (*meeting*). This way, you can choose the best way to understand and remember the concept or pattern.

It is not our purpose here to discuss all aspects of grammar errors. Instead, we'll focus on the most common mistakes and copying errors that writers often make. (Copying errors result when you transfer ideas from your mind to the paper, or from an earlier draft.) We're only interested in the kinds of errors that bother most readers a good deal—errors that prevent good communication between writers and readers. We will focus especially on the following errors:

— Sentence fragments, run-on sentences, and comma splices
— The lack of *-ed* on verbs in the past tense
— The lack of *-s* on the plurals of nouns
— Problems with singular verbs and possessives in the third person (*he, she, it*)
— Agreement problems between subjects and verbs and between pronouns and nouns
— The lack of apostrophes or unnecessary ones

Each of these errors will be defined and explained in the following chapters. You may have to read these chapters differently than the rest of this book. You'll find many more definitions and examples on these pages than elsewhere. It may be helpful for you to stop, reread, and review material. Convenient stopping places are marked with the heading "Reread and Review."

The following chapters are designed to help you edit your own writing by discovering which kinds of errors you make most often. The basic rules are outlined here to guide you. But you must begin with your own writing. Don't learn a rule ahead of time just because you think you might make a mistake. Chapter 9 will tell you how to use a "grammar log" to discover the areas you need help with. As usual, consult with your teacher when questions arise.

Writing Assignments ■

1. On the left-hand side of your journal, write a short definition of *grammar,* and state how it is different from other aspects of writing. On the right-hand side, give a few examples to show what you mean.

2. Interview someone who has an office job, and find out what his or her ideas of "correct" grammar are. How does this person define "correct" grammar? Report your findings to the class.

chapter 9 ∎

Keeping Track of Your Errors

This chapter will show you how to keep track of your sentence-level errors in a **grammar log**, which is a written record of errors that you make often. Such information will help you discover your own grammatical trouble spots. More important, it will allow you to diagnose your grammar problems (identify the causes of the particular errors you make).

Diagnosing Your Writing Problems

Figure 1 (page 196) shows what a grammar log looks like. Notice that this one is divided into sentence-level errors (grammar problems) and punctuation errors. In the chapters that follow, we'll cover the two kinds of problems separately.

The point of the grammar log is to record what your "personal grammar" is, so that you can compare it with "written grammar" (edited American English). By comparing the two, you will discover where your personal grammar goes astray (if it does). Then you can learn to spot your errors and correct them before you prepare a final paper for your readers.

Although you can make entries in your grammar log at any time, it's good to form the habit of doing so at two points: (1) whenever you find errors in your drafts, and (2) when your teacher returns a paper with comments on it. After all, if an error escaped your notice during drafting or on a final paper, it is probably something that you need to focus on.

How to Use Your Grammar Log

With your teacher's help, try to find the pattern to the problems and errors you have recorded in your grammar log. For example, suppose you learn that you often write sentence fragments. That is, your "sentences" lack either a subject or a verb, like the last example in Figure 1 (*Who* was "Braiding her hair"?). Perhaps you find that most of your fragments begin with the *-ing* form of a verb, as

195

Figure 1   A grammar log with separate sections for grammar problems and for punctuation problems

Personal Grammar	Written Grammar	Reasons for Differences
the colleges policy	the college's policy	I don't see why I need the apostrophe.
I skip classes yesterday.	I skipped classes yesterday.	I don't always say *-ed*.
Tom and me were sorry.	Tom and I were sorry.	When there's more than one subject, I write *me* instead of *I*.

Personal Punctuation	Written Punctuation	Reasons for Differences
I know the bus driver saw me coming as I ran for the bus he didn't wait.	I know the bus driver saw me coming as I ran for the bus, but he didn't wait.	I have trouble finding clauses.
Cheryl sat in front of the mirror. Braiding her hair.	Cheryl sat in front of the mirror, braiding her hair.	I forget that *-ing* is not always a verb.

in "Walking along the river" (or "Braiding her hair"). If so, you should review Chapter 10, "Recognizing Parts of Sentences." There you will learn that the *-ing* form of a verb can also function as a noun or as an adjective; it is not always a verb. The following chapters will explain such details of grammar. For now, the real point is to give an example of how to use your grammar log. In this case, when you edit your next rough draft, you can underline all *-ing* words. Once you have done that, you can check each one to be sure that it is used in a complete sentence. Thus, you can avoid writing sentence fragments by paying special attention to the pattern that makes you write them—the *-ing* pattern.

Look again at the third example in Figure 1. The writer knows that she would never say, "Me was sorry." But when the subject of a sentence means "me *plus* someone else," she forgets to call herself "I." Having discovered this from her grammar log, she can underline all such double subjects in her drafts, and then she can check each one to be sure that she didn't repeat her mistake again.

Figure 2   An example of a spelling log

Misspelling	Correct Spelling	Reasons for Confusion	Tips for Remembering
seperate	separate	It doesn't sound like an *a*.	There is *a rat* in *separate*.
alot	a lot	It sounds like one word.	I wouldn't write *alittle*.
writting	writing	I didn't know that double consonants affect pronunciation; that's why some words have them and others don't.	*writing* rhymes with *biting*; *writting* rhymes with *fitting*

How to Use Your Spelling Log

The methods described here for keeping your grammar log can also be applied to any problems you may have with spelling. Figure 2 shows an example of a spelling log, which works the same way as a grammar log does. In this example, a student has collected some of his misspellings, and, with the teacher's help, he has figured out why he misspells those particular words. Notice the column on the far right; here he records tips for remembering the correct spellings of words that give him trouble. Chapter 12 covers some typical spelling problems and gives tips for remembering how to avoid them.

Your grammar log and spelling log will make you aware of your personal writing problems so that you can think about what causes them. Don't get discouraged if you find yourself repeating the same errors or if it's difficult to figure out why you make them. Most writers do have particular problems with grammar, punctuation, or spelling, and usually such problems have been built up over a lifetime—they take on the force of habit. Changing any habit takes time. A good way to start is by becoming aware of your writing habits.

Assignments   ■

1. Study Figures 1 and 2, and use them to guide you in setting up a grammar log and a spelling log.

a. You might want to divide your grammar log into two sections, so that grammar problems and punctuation problems each start on a separate page.

b. If you put your logs toward the back of your journal, you can find them easily whenever you want to make a new entry, or whenever you want to check something you recorded earlier.

c. If your journal is a loose-leaf binder, you can add pages to your logs wherever you need them. If your journal is not a loose-leaf binder, you still can put your logs toward the end. But remember to leave enough pages between the logs so that you can add notes whenever you discover new writing or spelling problems that need attention.

2. Look over your journal entries, your drafts, and any papers that your teacher has returned. Do they reveal any grammar or spelling problems that come up often? If so, record them in your logs, following the examples in Figures 1 and 2. If you can't figure out the causes or patterns of your errors, consult with your teacher.

chapter 10

Recognizing Parts of Sentences

Some grammarians believe that we are born with a basic knowledge of grammar and of how sentences work. How else could we understand all the millions of sentences that we hear, or speak, or read, or write in a lifetime? Even when a sentence or a paragraph has no punctuation or other cues, we can usually figure out the sense of it. For example, read the following paragraph:

> the first thing arnie noticed was a hat the hat was of fresh white canvas as if just bought by someone unused to the strong sun of the gulf coast it went floating as if with nothing under it just above the stacked products at the top of the high display shelves something in the hats stop and go motion now turning toward a shelf now moving on seemed on the first instant to touch a nerve of familiarity

Chances are that once you started to read, you had to slow down in order to see where parts began and ended (perhaps you even silently added the missing punctuation and capital letters). One reason you can read this paragraph at all is that words tend to group together in small "chunks" of meaning when we read—something like this:

> the first thing   arnie noticed   was a hat
> the hat   was of fresh white canvas   as if
> just bought   by someone   unused to
> the strong sun   of the Gulf Coast

> it went floating   as if with nothing under it
> just above the stacked products   at the top
> of the high display shelves

> something in the hat's   stop-and-go motion
> now turning toward a shelf   now moving on
> seemed on the first instant   to touch a nerve
> of familiarity

In fact, when you read, you probably don't even read every single word on the page. You probably read in chunks. Instead of paying attention to every word, you pay attention to what the words mean *in combination with each other*. That's normal. Now read the paragraph as the author wrote it:

> The first thing Arnie noticed was a hat. The hat was of fresh white canvas, as if just bought by someone unused to the strong sun of the Gulf Coast; it went floating as if with nothing under it, just above the stacked products at the top of the high display shelves. Something in the hat's stop-and-go motion, now turning toward a shelf, now moving on, seemed on the first instant to touch a nerve of familiarity.
>
> Elizabeth Spencer, *The Salt Line*

Finally, here is the same paragraph, but this time it has errors in punctuation that can be as tricky as no punctuation at all:

> The first thing Arnie noticed was a hat. The hat was of fresh white canvas. As if just bought by someone unused to the strong sun of the Gulf Coast it went floating as if with nothing under it. Just above the stacked products at the top of the high display shelves. Something in the hat's stop-and-go motion now turning toward a shelf. Now moving on, seemed on the first instant to touch a nerve of familiarity.

Even with this misleading punctuation, you can reconstruct the sense of the passage because you know something about sentences. You may have made a few false starts. But by moving ahead and then moving backward—by *re*reading—you could better understand what you read.

You may be asking: If I'm supposed to know so much about sentences, why do I get so many red marks on my papers? Well, most people make errors in writing, and there's a reason that we make the errors that we do. We develop certain "blind spots" and cannot see what we do wrong. The same kind of thing happens when we look at an optical illusion—a picture that is drawn in such a way that it plays tricks with our eyes. In Figure 1, for example, do you see an old woman or a young woman? When you first look at Figure 1, you may see the picture one way; then, when you look again, more closely, you may see it the other way. Or, you may have difficulty seeing the picture more than one way (if so, ask someone to help you see the *two women* in this picture). Even when you can see both pictures in an optical illusion, your eyes may not switch between the two easily. One picture may dominate the other.

So it is for many of us with grammar, too. Some writers find it difficult to correct their sentence-level errors because they can't proofread well. A writer who learned a rule incorrectly or who understood a sentence pattern incorrectly may not be able to erase that wrong idea from memory. Or a writer's spoken

Figure 1   How old is this woman?

language may influence his or her written language (a mispronounced word is very likely to be written as a misspelled word). Or maybe a writer never learned a particular rule in the first place.

The point is that it probably won't help much to sit down and memorize rules about grammar; first you must figure out *why* an error slipped past you. You need to train yourself to see your writing in a new way. Just as you have to study Figure 1 to see beneath the "surface"—to see the woman behind the woman—you can look deeper into your own writing. Beneath the surface, you may find that what you're actually saying is different from what you mean to say.

◇ *Reread and Review*

Editing Your Writing

A writer may search for and correct sentence-level errors during any stage of the writing process. Whether you are brainstorming, drafting, or revising, you certainly should correct any grammar or spelling errors that catch your eye. That way, you won't carry errors forward to the next stage of writing.

But editing is really the final stage of writing in which you focus on every word and every sentence, looking for errors that might distract your readers from the message you want them to get. During editing, you focus less on *what* you said than on *how* you said it. Did you make mistakes that will make your writing less effective?

The rest of this chapter is divided into short sections that describe the basic parts of sentences and some common errors that writers make with them. Remember to "reread and review" after each section.

What Is a Sentence?

Sometimes it is easier to say what *isn't* a sentence than to say what *is*. Read the following groups of words, and try to identify the *one* sentence in each group. If you have trouble, first check off the examples that you are pretty sure are *not* sentences; then see what you have left.

for the child to sing sweetly
the child's sweet song
the sweetly singing child
the child singing sweetly
the child is singing sweetly
that the child is singing sweetly
if the child is singing sweetly
whenever the child is singing sweetly

for the woman to smile knowingly
the woman's knowing smile
the knowingly smiling woman
the woman smiling knowingly
the woman was smiling knowingly
that the woman was smiling knowingly
because the woman was smiling knowingly
so that the woman was smiling knowingly

for the bomb to explode suddenly
the bomb's sudden explosion
the suddenly exploding bomb
the bomb exploding suddenly
the bomb exploded suddenly
that the bomb exploded suddenly
when the bomb exploded suddenly
unless the bomb exploded suddenly

for the student to be genuinely astonished
the student's genuine astonishment
the genuinely astonished student
the student being genuinely astonished
the student was genuinely astonished
that the student was genuinely astonished
since the student was genuinely astonished
although the student was genuinely astonished

Sarah D'Eloia, "The Uses—and Limits—of Grammar"

Writing Assignment ■

On the right-hand side of your journal, describe how you found the sentence in each group of words. Then, on the left-hand side, jot down a definition of *sentence*.

The sentence has been defined in a number of ways by grammarians. Here are three possible definitions:

1. A sentence begins with a capital letter and ends with a period.

2. A sentence is a group of words that expresses a complete thought or idea.

3. A sentence includes a subject, a verb, and sometimes an object.

Even though the above groups of words were not punctuated as sentences (as in definition 1), you probably could find most of the sentences anyway. And, since some of the examples you eliminated probably *did* express a complete thought, perhaps definition 2 isn't very helpful, either. But look again at definition 3. All the sentences you found *did* have a subject (or noun) and a verb. Some of the nonsentences seem to have subjects and verbs, too, but they also have additional words such as *that* and *since*, which seem to cancel them out. So definition 3 seems most useful: A **sentence** includes a subject, a verb, and sometimes an object. The next few sections will explain these matters further.

◊ *Reread and Review*

Subjects and Predicates

Grammarians divide sentences into two parts: (1) all the things that go with the subject and (2) all the things that go with the predicate. Read the following two sentences:

> A more sophisticated radar imaging system was tested. Archaeologists discovered the long-hidden remnants of an elaborate network of canals.
>
> (Wilford)

Separated into subject and predicate, the parts of these sentences look like this:

Subject	Predicate
A more sophisticated radar imaging system	was tested.
Archaeologists	discovered the long-hidden remnants of an elaborate network of canals.

The concept of subject and predicate can be confusing because, as the above examples show, each one can include more than just single words.

The **subject** *means the same thing as* the main noun in a sentence—and more. In the sentence "The young but determined student passed all of her exams," the subject is *student*. But grammarians would include some additional words in identifying the subject. In this sentence, "young but determined" are words that describe the student, and so they are seen as part of the subject "chunk."

The **predicate** *means the same thing as* the main verb in a sentence—and more. In the sentence "The young but determined student passed all of her exams," the verb is *passed*. Again, grammarians would include some additional words in identifying the predicate; "all of her exams" are words that add information to the verb, and so they are seen as part of the predicate "chunk." Like most words that follow a verb, "all of her exams" is called the **object** of the sentence; that is, the noun that follows the verb receives the action of the verb.

◊ *Reread and Review*

The Forms and Functions of Words

You may have trouble finding subjects and predicates because words in a sentence may *look like* one thing but may *function like* something else.

Grammarians have labels for every kind of word in a sentence, classifying them as nouns, pronouns, adjectives, verbs, adverbs, prepositions, conjunctions, or interjections. Such labels are known as the "parts of speech," and we'll look at them more closely later. The important point now, however, is that sometimes we can't label a word unless we know how it functions in a sentence. It is more useful now to classify words by their *form* (what they look like, and what changes they go through) and by their *function* (how they work in a sentence).

For example, the verb *try* can be changed into the following forms: *tries, tried, trying*. And the noun *lion* can be changed into *lions, lion's,* and *lions'*. Notice that *try* functions as a verb in each of the following sentences, even though its form changes:

He tries to win the lottery every week.

He tried to win the lottery last week.

He is always trying to win the lottery.

However, in the next sentence, *try* does not function as a verb but as a noun:

He gave winning the lottery a good try.

A great deal of the power and flexibility of English as a language comes from the fact that words can so easily change their function. With just a few different letters, one word can function as a noun, or a verb, or some other part of speech. This flexibility, however, also makes English a difficult language to learn. And it can make grammar difficult, too. But it will help if you identify and classify a word first by how it looks; then by how it functions; and sometimes both by how it looks and by how it functions.

Let's look at the verb *to swim* for another example of the difference between a word's form and function. In this case, the *to* is part of the **infinitive** form, the form of the verb that contains no time—no past, present, or future:

Verb forms
I <u>swim</u> every day during the summer.

I <u>swam</u> last night in the moonlight.

I <u>have swum</u> across the lake before.

Nouns
<u>Swimming</u> is fun.

<u>To swim</u> is fun.
Let's go for a <u>swim</u>.

Adjectives
<u>Swimming</u> quickly, I reached the raft first.

The boy is "<u>swum out</u>." (slang)

Adverb
We get along <u>swimmingly</u>. (That is, we get along well.)

When you eliminated the nonsentences from the groups of words earlier, you probably did so because you realized that words which looked like verbs were not really functioning as verbs. Thus, the nonsentences did not really have verbs. Here are some more examples of how words that look like verbs sometimes function as something else and sometimes have different meanings:

Verbs
We <u>light</u> the lamps at dusk.

A piece of newspaper in the fireplace <u>will light</u> immediately.
He <u>lit</u> a cigar.

Nouns
The <u>light</u> was so bright it blinded us.

The <u>lighting</u> was so poor in the room that I couldn't read.

Adjectives

He wore a <u>light</u> green jacket.

Her <u>light</u> skin burns easily in the sun.

A <u>light</u> rain fell.

<u>Lighting</u> the candles, she smiled.

Adverb

He tapped the door <u>lightly</u>.

Finally, here are some sentences that further illustrate how slippery English can be because words can take different forms and functions:

"We <u>sang</u> that <u>song</u> last time," she said.

"Your action <u>surprises</u> me. It is a <u>surprising</u> thing, and you really didn't have <u>to surprise</u> me," he said in a <u>surprised</u> tone of voice. He held the gift-wrapped <u>surprise</u> in front of him, and, <u>surprisingly</u>, did not drop it.

The professor did not mean <u>to bore</u> the class; however, his lecture was very <u>boring</u>, and the whole class was <u>bored</u>. Students told others that the prof was a <u>bore</u> because he spoke so <u>boringly</u>.

<u>Interestingly</u> enough, the teacher hoped <u>to interest</u> her students in biology, and her explanations were so <u>interesting</u> that the whole class was <u>interested</u>, because they began to develop an <u>interest</u> in biology.

"Oh <u>rot</u>!" Waldo exclaimed. "I hate <u>rotten</u> fruit, and clearly the waiter has served me a fruit cocktail that has been left <u>to rot</u>."

At this point, don't worry about trying to label every word in a sentence. If you recognize that words can change their forms and functions in a sentence, you have learned an important lesson. Knowing this will help you to control punctuation and to turn sentence fragments into complete sentences when you edit.

◇ *Reread and Review*

The Subject, or Main Noun

The **subject** of a sentence can usually be described as the doer of the action that is implied by the verb. The subject can be a single noun; a noun clause (a group of words that functions as a noun); or a pronoun (a word that substitutes for a noun, like *they* or *she*).

A **noun** can be described in the following ways:

— A word or clause that *names* a person, place, or thing
— A word that can often be found by other words that signal it (like *a, an, the, this, that*, and so on)
— A word that can often be found by *parts* of words that signal it, like *-ion, -ment, -ance, -al, -y, -ure, -er, -ness, -hood* (nat*ion*, astonish*ment*, and so on)
— A word that can be made plural, or that has a plural sense (computer*s*, pencil*s*, mice, team, and so on)
— A word that can change case (the dog has a collar = the dog's collar)
— A word or clause that can occupy subject positions in a sentence
— A word or clause that can occupy object positions in a sentence (direct object of a verb or the object of a preposition)

In summary, a noun can be a single word, or more than one word, or even the infinitive form of a verb:

1. Single words: *dog, student, jealousy, swimming* (Note that this last noun is formed from a verb + *-ing*. Such a noun is called a **gerund**.)

2. Groups of words (a clause), which often follow *that: that the bird outgrew its cage, that he ran home*

3. Infinitives (the *to* form of a verb): *to dance, to relax*

In the following passage, all the underlined words are nouns:

Without <u>enforcement</u> from the executive <u>branch</u>, in this <u>case</u> in the <u>form</u> of a <u>ruling</u> from the <u>Interstate Commerce Commission</u> ordering <u>compliance</u>, the Supreme Court <u>ruling</u> would be meaningless. (Williams)

◇ *Reread and Review*

The Verb

A **verb** can be described in the following ways:

— A word that has a special form (*to* + *verb*) called the *infinitive*; the infinitive can *never* function as a verb, but only as a noun, an adjective, or an adverb (*to live, to rain*)
— A word that shows action or a state of being
— A word that can often be found by *parts* of words that signal it, like *-ify, -ate, -ize*, and so on (clar*ify*, levit*ate*, econom*ize*)
— Most verbs have *-s* and *-ing* forms

— Most verbs use *-ed* to indicate the past tense; some verbs show the past tense differently and are called irregular (*bring = brought; break = broke* or *broken*)

Like nouns, verbs can also be a single word or more than one word:

1. Single words: *burns, burned, cry, is, seem*

2. Groups of words (with other verbs that indicate time or some other relation): *had burned, is crying, should have known*

3. With prepositions (words that usually connect nouns or pronouns to other words in a sentence): *put up with*

◇ *Reread and Review*

The Passive Voice

Finding the subject and the predicate of a sentence can get a little complicated when a writer is faced with the passive voice. The **passive voice** can sometimes hide the true subject and verb because it reverses their usual order in a sentence.

For example, in the sentence "I did it" the order is subject + predicate, and it is clear who is doing what. (This verb pattern is called the **active voice** because the pattern is subject + predicate.) In the passive version, "It was done by me," the order has been reversed to predicate + subject. Notice that the passive voice of the verb changes the subject, from *I* to *by me*. Because of the reversed order, the subject, or doer of the action, might be hard to find. Here are a few more examples of active voice and passive voice:

Active voice

Morton Thiokol manufactured defective "O" rings that caused the Challenger to blow up.

Miriam left the oven on overnight.

He decided to fire the employees with the least seniority.

Passive voice

The defective "O" rings that caused the Challenger to blow up were manufactured by Morton Thiokol.

The oven was left on overnight by Miriam.

The employees with the least seniority were fired by him.

The passive voice can weaken writing when it adds unnecessary padding to sentences. Notice that the examples of passive voice all use more words than the examples of active voice do. Many readers object to the passive voice because it seems that the writer hides behind it or uses it to avoid responsibility. For example, when we remove the subject—the real doer of the action—in the following sentences, notice that things "just seem to happen"; no one is held responsible:

> The oven was left on overnight.

> A decision was made to fire the employees with the least seniority.

Sometimes, however, the passive voice may be more accurate and more effective. For example, in reporting about a scientific experiment, the active voice would emphasize the doer of the action:

> The lab technician left the petri dishes in the refrigerator at 55 degrees for 24 hours.

In this case, the procedure of the experiment is much more significant than the person who performed it, and the passive voice would emphasize that:

> The petri dishes were left in the refrigerator at 55 degrees for 24 hours.

◇ *Reread and Review*

Reading and Editing Assignment ■

Look over any draft or any journal entry, and underline the subject and predicate of each sentence (including any two- or three-word verbs). Circle parts of sentences that *look like* they contain verbs but really are functioning as something else (nouns, adjectives, adverbs).

If you used any passive verbs, rewrite the sentences with active verbs—unless you have a good reason for using the passive voice.

Exchange your draft or journal entry with a classmate, and check each other's work.

Phrases and Clauses

Because we read in chunks rather than word by word, one way to increase our reading speed is to practice grouping parts of sentences together. Groups of words tend to fall into units called phrases and clauses. Look at the following examples, and try to see what the difference is:

Phrases	*Clauses*
toward the teacher	who was a teacher
many dancers	that he was a dancer
running to work	before he ran a mile
leaving early	when he left
an early train	because she was ill
a cross look	although she came early
the windy street	if Wanda went fishing
to dance divinely	which caught on a nail

A **phrase** is a group of two or more words that forms a unit and expresses a meaning. Common types are **prepositional phrases** (*toward* the teacher); **infinitive phrases** (*to dance* divinely); and **verbal**, or **participial**, **phrases** (*running* to work). A phrase is never a sentence, even though it may contain a word formed from a verb. The following phrases are not sentences because they do not have subjects:

Driving crazily down the street
Living close to the ocean
Exhausted by final exams
Made angry by the noise

A **clause**, on the other hand, does contain a subject and a predicate. Therefore, all sentences are clauses, because a sentence also has a subject and a predicate. However, not all clauses are sentences. Look at the following examples:

Who hit my brand-new car
Which left a trail of crumbs
That caused the landslide

Even though these clauses do contain a subject and a predicate, that does not mean they *function* as complete sentences. Instead, a clause may function as a noun, an adjective, or an adverb in a sentence. If so, the clause will contain "signal words" to tell you so. In these examples, the words *who, which,* and *that* signal that the clauses are not functioning as complete sentences. If you find such signal words, the clause is *not* a sentence.

A clause that has a subject and a predicate is called the **main clause** (or the **independent clause**). But if a clause has a signal word plus a subject and a predicate, it is a **dependent clause** (or **subordinate clause**).

◊ *Reread and Review*

The Noun Clause

In discussing the subject of a sentence, we have already mentioned the following characteristics of a **noun clause**:

— A noun clause can occupy subject positions in a sentence.
— A noun clause can occupy object positions in a sentence (direct object of a verb or the object of a preposition).
— A noun clause usually begins with *that: that the bird outgrew its cage; that he ran home*.
— A noun clause can be an infinitive (the *to* form of a verb, as in *to listen*).

Following are some examples of noun clauses signaled by *that*. Such clauses cannot stand alone as sentences and therefore, are dependent on the main clause (subordinate to the main clause):

That I couldn't ever go into the bedroom with him again, simply saying it wasn't right

That all of these dimensions may be operating

That the city would press charges even if King chose not to

Here are the same noun clauses as they appear in complete sentences. Notice how they depend on their main clauses to be meaningful:

The first time my boyfriend and I spent time in my bedroom, talking and nothing else, my mother said that I couldn't ever go into the bedroom with him again, simply saying it wasn't right. (Miss Manners)

The poor readers' responses to text implicit questions reveal that all of these dimensions may be operating. (Holmes)

Birmingham police arrived and insisted that the city would press charges even if King chose not to. (Garrow)

Next, here are a few examples of infinitives as noun clauses. Again, they cannot stand alone as sentences, and so they are dependent (subordinate) clauses:

To choose clothes . . . To define and describe ourselves

To move

To buy time . . . To kill time

And here are the same infinitives as noun clauses within complete sentences:

> To choose clothes, either in a store or at home, is to define and describe ourselves.   (Lurie)

> To move is as natural to the American as maintaining roots is to the European.   (Lynes)

> City people try to buy time as a rule, when they can, whereas country people are prepared to kill time, although both try to cherish in their mind's eye the notion of a better life ahead.   (Hoagland)

◇ *Reread and Review*

Reading and Editing Assignment   ■

Look once again at the draft or journal entry in which you circled parts of sentences that seem to contain verbs but might really be functioning as something else. Now you know that such sentence parts are phrases and clauses. Put a check mark where you think you may have written a noun clause. If you have *not* used any noun clauses, put a check mark where you think you could combine two or three short sentences to make a noun clause.

Exchange your draft or journal entry with a classmate, and check each other's work.

Modifiers

So far, we have talked about phrases and clauses and have shown that they can be nouns, adjectives, or adverbs. Now we will look closely at adjectives and adverbs, which are both **modifiers**: single words or groups of words that add details to nouns and verbs.

Sometimes called *qualifiers* or *limiters*, modifiers answer questions like Where? Which? When? Why? How? How much? Under what conditions? Basically, adjectives modify nouns and pronouns, while adverbs modify verbs. But let's look more closely at modifiers.

An **adjective** can be described in the following ways:

— An adjective gives further information about nouns and pronouns; it answers such questions as *Which? What kind? How many?*
— An adjective can be tested by its position in a sentence, as follows (put adjectives in the blank slots):

> The _____ NOUN is very _____ .

Only an adjective will fit into both slots. Notice that adjectives usually come before a noun or pronoun.

— An adjective often ends in the following letters: *-ous, -y, -ful, -ic, -ate, -ish, -ary, -ive, -able*
— An adjective of one syllable takes *-er* to form the comparative (sweet*er*) and *-est* to form the superlative (sweet*est*). If it is more than one syllable, add *more* to form the comparative (*more* difficult), and add *most* to form the superlative (*most* difficult).
— An adjective can be made from verbs by adding *-ed* (called the past participle) or *-ing* (called the present participle).
— An adjective may be one word, or it may be a string of words; it can always be cut from a sentence without affecting the main clause.

An **adverb** can be described in the following ways:

— A word, phrase, or clause that gives information about time, place, frequency, cause, or manner about verbs; an adverb answers such questions as *How? Where? When? Why? To what extent?*
— Adverbs are the most movable of all words, phrases, and clauses in a sentence.
— Adverbs often end in the following letters (but not always): *-ly, -ward, -like, -wise.*
— You can turn most adjectives into adverbs with the ending *-ly.*
— Adverb clauses are signaled by such words as *although, when, after, before,* and so on.
— An adverb can always be cut from a sentence without affecting the main clause.

Here are some examples of single-word adjectives and adverbs:

Adjectives	*Adverbs*
good	well
beautiful	beautifully
exact	exactly
helpless	helplessly
quick	quickly
definite	definitely
angry	angrily

Note: A small group of words can serve both as adjectives and as adverbs: *early, fast, late, high, hard, long, low, deep, near.*

Here are some examples of adjectives formed from verbs, by adding the endings *-ed* or *-en*:

detailed writing	inexperienced driver
written work	ironed clothing
spoken word	broken line

Note: Adverbs can be formed with *-ed* as well, and usually come in phrases like "in a deranged manner" and "in a relaxed manner."

Here are some examples of adjectives formed from verbs, by adding *-ing*:

closing time	speaking voice
singing birds	relaxing exercise

◇ *Reread and Review*

Adjectives and Adverbs in Action

Now that we've looked at the various kinds of adjectives and adverbs and how they are formed, let's look back at some of the passages you have already read. Pay close attention to how the writers use adjectives and adverbs to add details and information to their basic sentences.

For example, in the following passages the underlined adjectives were all formed from verbs.

What could have changed this elegant, Lincolnesque student voted "Best Dressed" by his classmates to the gaunt, unshaven man I remember? Why did he leave a young son and a first wife of the "proper" class and religion, marry a much less educated woman of the "wrong" religion, and raise a second family in a house near an abandoned airstrip? . . .   (Steinem)

The other day I was walking through Lincoln and saw an encampment of gypsies on a patch of waste ground—the caravans, the wrecked cars, the junked machines, the rubbish; and children wandering through the cityscape in metal. The little area had a "foreign" look to me.   (Theroux)

At the same time it is not uncommon to forget . . . the answer to an exam question about material studied just a few hours before.   (Feldman)

The 1957 edition of the Standard College Dictionary defines slang in part as "Language, words, or phrases of a vigorous, colorful, facetious, or taboo nature, invented for specific occasions or uses, or derived from the unconventional use of the standard vocabulary."   (Nichols)

Constantly letters flow across the land, carrying messages of love and pain, business and leisure, to millions of readers.   (Tuttle)

Somebody once observed to the eminent philosopher Wittgenstein how stupid medieval Europeans living before the time of Copernicus must have been that they could have looked at the sky and thought that the sun was circling the earth.   (Burke)

The following examples of adjective clauses are signaled by *relative pronouns* ("relative" because they relate to, and refer to, the nouns that precede them). Before studying the examples, keep these points in mind:

— When referring to persons in the subject position in a sentence, use *who*.
— When referring to persons in the object position in a sentence, use *whom*. (We'll discuss *who/whom* in Chapter 12.)
— When referring to inanimate objects and animals, use *which, that,* and sometimes *where*. (Although some people do use *who* with animals, it is not generally accepted to do so.)

Linda, who had a right to be angry, screamed.

He annoyed Dennis, whom he called a fool.

The hose that was left in the sun rotted.

I fed the kitten that I found.

Next, here are some examples of adverb clauses that are signaled by adverbs:

After he stopped laughing, he got to work.

Although she was sleepy, Nancy kept studying.

We didn't swim because the tide was high.

Now read the following sentence, in which the subject and the predicate of the main clause are underlined:

My companion James Fenton, however, whose idea the venture was, enigmatic, balding, an ex-correspondent of the war in Vietnam and Cambodia, a jungle in himself, was a wise old man in these matters.   (O'Hanlon)

All the other words in this sentence modify or in some way describe the subject (My companion James Fenton). We might map the sentence like this:

My companion James Fenton,
            however,
                        whose idea the venture was,

enigmatic,
balding,
an ex-correspondent of the war in Vietnam and Cambodia,
a jungle in himself,

was a wise old man in these matters.

In the following examples of adjective and adverb clauses (underlined), notice that the clauses cannot stand alone as sentences. They are dependent, or subordinate, clauses:

A so-called fashion leader, on the other hand, may have several hundred "words" at his or her disposal, and thus be able to form thousands of different "sentences" that will express a wide range of meanings.   (Lurie)

On my way to the Whim I slowly walked toward the Clare Bridge, staring up at the gothic pinnacles of the King's College Chapel that stood out sharply against the spring sky.   (Watson)

In order to achieve this overall view we develop explanatory theories which will give structure to natural phenomena: we classify nature into a coherent system which appears to do what we say it does.   (Burke)

A shocked stillness came over the crowd, which watched in amazement as King stood his ground and accepted several blows.   (Garrow)

No American who wishes to hold a place of any significant responsibility can avoid the necessity of written communication.   (Tuttle)

Without defending your mother, who certainly should keep her word and not treat your friends rudely, Miss Manners feels sorry for her.   (Miss Manners)

Although he continued to use the toy, its keyboard soon became a maze of missing letters and, for those that were saved from the vacuum cleaner, taped-on buttons.   (Petroski)

City people try to buy time as a rule, when they can, whereas country people are prepared to kill time, although both try to cherish in their mind's eye the notion of a better life ahead.   (Hoagland)

I think we do this because we don't want to know too much. (Theroux)

It is my belief that if needs that could not be realized immediately did not develop during the school years, there would be no play, because play seems to be invented at the point when the child begins to experience unrealizable tendencies.   (Vygotsky)

That "knowledge" structured everything they did and thought, <u>because it told them the truth.</u>   (Burke)

At the time I didn't know anything about policies in other countries, and <u>after thinking about Helen's situation for a while,</u> I decided it must be some sort of special deal.   (Hewlett)

In 1947 CORE had organized the "Journey of Reconciliation" <u>after the Supreme Court ruled that segregated seating on interstate buses and trains was unconstitutional.</u>   (Williams)

<u>While any number of questions can be raised about the authenticity of contemporary expression which some Indian groups have given to traditional culture,</u> questions have never been raised about the legitimacy of cultural details conveyed through, or accompanied by, Indian language terms.   (Leap)

Finally, here are some examples of infinitives that function as modifiers:

My mother came in and very rudely started telling us <u>to leave.</u>   (Miss Manners)

Juxtaposition is the failure on the part of the child <u>to consider</u> the relationship of two events or ideas placed next to each other in a passage. (Holmes)

The leave-taking was so random I trusted the United States Army <u>to relocate</u> me satisfactorily.   (King)

I suppress a desire <u>to travel</u> in my own city.   (Theroux)

As one eyewitness described it, King made no move <u>to strike back or turn away.</u>   (Garrow)

They wanted to modernize their industry, improve roads and waterways, and develop communications, but they were ideologically opposed to a strong central government with the means and authority <u>to carry out</u> the program.   (Rosengarten)

◊ *Reread and Review*

Reading and Editing Assignment ■

Look once more at your draft or journal entry, and mark where you have used single-word modifiers. If you do not find many, perhaps you can see places where you could add some.

Next, look again at your circled clauses and phrases. Reread those sentences, thinking of them now as modifiers. If you have not used many modifying phrases and clauses, do you see any places where you might combine two or three short sentences to make some? Don't worry if you cannot say for sure whether a clause is functioning as an adjective or an adverb.

Exchange your draft or journal entry with a classmate, and check each other's work.

chapter **11**   ■

Recognizing Types of Sentences

In this chapter, we'll classify sentences according to patterns that you already know, but perhaps have never examined in a systematic way.

Types of Sentences

We can classify sentences into four main types: *simple, compound, complex,* and *compound-complex.* Remember to reread and review each of the following sections about sentence types.

The Simple Sentence

A **simple sentence** has only one main clause, including a subject and a predicate. In the following examples of simple sentences, the subjects are in italic type; the verbs are in bold type:

The *cowhand* **rounded up** the stubborn steers.

Martha calmly **spoke**.

I **will not put up with** that kind of treatment.

Michela and *Freda* **played** tennis last summer.

Freda **played** tennis and **went** to aerobics class during the fall semester.

We can divide the parts of these simple sentences into subjects and predicates as follows:

Subject	Predicate
The *cowhand*	**rounded up** most of the stubborn steers.
Martha	calmly **spoke**.
I	**will not put up with** that kind of treatment.

219

Each of these first three examples of simple sentences has only one subject and one verb. Now examine the next two sentences:

Subject	*Predicate*
Michela and *Freda*	**played** tennis last summer.
Freda	**played** tennis and **went** to aerobics class during the fall semester.

The first of these sentences has two subjects (*Michela* and *Freda*) plus one verb (*played*); the second sentence has one subject (*Freda*) and two verbs (*played* and *went*). *These are still simple sentences,* but the first one has a compound subject, and the second one has a compound predicate.

◇ *Reread and Review*

The Compound Sentence

A **compound sentence** has two main clauses, each with a subject and a predicate. Compound sentences are two or more simple sentences joined together. Here are some examples of compound sentences:

The *cowhand* **rounded up** most of the stubborn steers, but *he* **lost** three of them.

Martha calmly **spoke**, and the whole *class* **listened**.

I **will not put up with** that kind of treatment, and the *boss* **knows** it.

Michela **played** tennis last summer, but *she* **decided** not to this year.

Freda **played** tennis all last summer, and this year *she* **has taken up** racquetball.

We can divide the parts of these compound sentences into subjects and predicates as follows:

Subject	*Predicate*
The *cowhand* but *he*	**rounded up** most of the stubborn steers, **lost** three of them.
Martha and the whole *class*	calmly **spoke**, **listened**.
I and the *boss*	**will not put up with** that kind of treatment, **knows** it.

| *Michela* | **played** tennis last summer, |
| but *she* | **decided** not to this year. |

| *Freda* | **played** tennis all last summer, |
| and this year *she* | **has taken up** racquetball. |

A compound sentence has *two* or more clauses, each with a subject and a verb. The clauses are combined into one sentence to show that their content is related or parallel in some way.

◇ *Reread and Review*

Reading and Editing Assignment ■

Even though your draft or journal entry is getting very marked up by now, let's continue to work with it. This time, locate and mark each of your simple or compound sentences. You'll find them easily because you have already marked subjects and verbs to identify clauses. Remember, however, that not all clauses are sentences. (Review the discussion of dependent clauses in Chapter 10.)

If you do not find many compound sentences in your writing, do you see places where you could combine two or more closely related simple sentences to make one compound sentence?

Exchange your draft or journal entry with a classmate, and check each other's work.

The Complex Sentence

A **complex sentence** has one or more main clauses and one or more dependent clauses (discussed in Chapter 10). Here are some examples of complex sentences:

Though the *cowhand* **rounded up** most of the stubborn steers, *he* **lost** three of them.

Martha calmly **spoke** while the whole *class* **listened**.

The *boss* **knows** that *I* **will not put up with** that kind of treatment.

Although *she* **played** tennis last summer, *Michela* **decided** not to this year.

Since *Freda* **played** tennis all last summer, this year *she* **has taken up** racquetball.

We can divide the parts of these complex sentences into main clauses (underlined) and dependent clauses. Note that the signal words are part of the dependent clause, and they make that clause subordinate to the main clause:

Though the *cowhand* **rounded up** most of the stubborn steers, *he* **lost** three of them.

Martha calmly **spoke** while the whole *class* **listened**.

The *boss* **knows** that *I* **will not put up with** that kind of treatment.

Although *she* **played** tennis and racquetball last summer, *Michela* **decided** not to this year.

Since *Freda* **played** tennis all last summer, this year she **has taken up** racquetball.

The Compound-Complex Sentence

A **compound-complex sentence** can be any combination of two or more main clauses and one or more dependent clause. In the following examples, the main clauses are underlined:

Though the *cowhand* **rounded up** most of the stubborn steers, *he* **lost** three of them, and *he* **looked** for them all night.

Martha calmly **spoke** while the whole *class* **listened**; *she* **felt** good.

Sentences can be as complicated and as long as the writer wants them to be. The important thing is to write effectively for your audience, which always includes paying attention to grammar. Notice that even these compound-complex sentences can be longer; yet they are effective, and they are grammatically solid:

Though the cowhand rounded up most of the stubborn steers and the wild horses, he lost three of the horses, and he looked for them all night.

Martha calmly spoke while the whole class listened; she felt good and almost jumped for joy.

◇ *Reread and Review*

Reading and Editing Assignment   ■

Now locate and mark places in your draft or journal entry where you have used complex sentences or compound-complex sentences. Look for the dependent clauses that you marked earlier. These will lead you to complex sentences. If you do not find many, do you see places where you might combine closely related sentences into a complex sentence?

Exchange your draft or journal entry with a classmate, and check each other's work.

How to Punctuate Sentences

Punctuation is a characteristic of written English, not of spoken English. We don't "speak" commas or semicolons; rather, we might pause for shorter or longer periods between the main parts of sentences.

A writer, however, needs to employ all the punctuation marks of written English in order to write clearly understood sentences. Although incorrect punctuation does not always interfere with our reader's understanding, it at least can be distracting. Furthermore, *correct* punctuation steers the reader to the writer's exact meaning; it keeps the reader on track.

To help you steer your readers, the following sections present general guidelines for punctuating sentences. There will always be exceptions to the rules—especially rules about writing. But to "break" a rule, you first have to understand what the rule is for.

Punctuating the Simple Sentence

The most basic rule for punctuating a simple sentence is: *Do not overpunctuate*. Unless a sentence has modifiers that must be set off with commas, do not separate the subject from the verb.

Not: Michela and Freda, played tennis last summer.

But: Michela and Freda played tennis last summer.

Punctuating the Compound Sentence

Join the two main clauses of a compound sentence together with a comma (,) plus a conjunction (that is, connecting words like *and, but, or, not*). You also can join the clauses with a semicolon (;) alone. This rule is summarized here:

_____,	and	_____
_____,	but	_____
_____,	or	_____
_____,	nor	_____
_____;	_____	

Following are some examples of correctly punctuated compound sentences:

They craved a literary and a technical culture worthy of their status, **but** they imported their books, tools, and simple machines from people hostile to their ideals. They wanted to modernize their industry, improve roads and waterways, and develop communications, **but** they were ideologically opposed to a strong central government with the means and authority to carry out the program.   (Rosengarten)

Nature is disordered, powerful and chaotic**, and** through fear of the chaos we impose system on it.   (Burke)

Many people think they know instinctively when they encounter slang**, and** their response is usually negative.   (Nichols)

For example, when a child comes home and says, "Somebody hit me!" the mother who responds with "Oh, my poor dear" fosters dependence**, and** the mother who says "Who hit first?" may be fostering guilt**, and** the mother who says "What happened?" and hasn't taken sides may be fostering independence.   (Bardwick)

In England a man stands for Parliament; in America he runs for the Senate.   (Lynes)

The past, I thought, had served its full uses and could bury its own dead; bridges were for burning; "good-bye" meant exactly what it said.   (King)

Travel has less to do with distance than with insight; it is, very often, a way of seeing.   (Theroux)

A very young child tends to gratify her desires immediately; normally the interval between a desire and its fulfillment is extremely short.   (Vygotsky)

When writing a compound sentence, remember: *Always use a comma plus a conjunction, OR a semicolon alone.* It's usually not accepted in edited American English to join the clauses of a compound sentence with a conjunction *and* a semicolon (; and), because that is considered overpunctuating. Use a conjunction with a comma, or a semicolon alone.

Note: Another, more specialized way to punctuate a compound sentence is with a semicolon and an adverb (usually called a *conjunctive adverb*):

$$\text{_____; therefore, _____}$$
$$\text{_____; however, _____}$$
$$\text{_____; yet _____}$$
$$\text{_____; so _____}$$

◇ *Reread and Review*

Mispunctuating Compound Sentences

Compound sentences sometimes are mispunctuated in two ways:

Comma Splice (Comma Fault)
Freda played tennis all last summer, this year she has taken up racquetball.

Run-on Sentence
Freda played tennis all last summer this year she has taken up racquetball.

In the first example of a mispunctuated sentence, the two clauses are joined by a comma only; the conjunction is missing. This is called a **comma splice**, or **comma fault**. In the second mispunctuated sentence, the two clauses run into each other without any punctuation at all. This is called a **run-on sentence**. (Note that a run-on sentence is not one that "runs on" for too long; it is a sentence that is mispunctuated. There is no rule about how long a sentence can be. Some writers have made sentences as long as a few pages.)

A writer is most likely to make a comma splice when the second clause of a compound sentence begins with a pronoun (*he, she, it, we, you, they*). Here are correctly punctuated examples:

> Imagination is a new psychological process for the child; **it** is not present in the consciousness of the very young child, is totally absent in animals, and represents a specifically human form of conscious activity. (Vygotsky)

> Black communication is highly verbal and highly stylized; **it** is a performance before a black audience who become both observers and participants in the speech. (Smitherman)

> Country people do not behave as if they think life is short; **they** live on the principle that it is long, and savor variations of the kind best appreciated if most days are the same. (Hoagland)

> They have great authority in the scientific and general communities, **and they** are seen as somehow more rigorous and precise than other sciences. (Raup)

If you are having trouble with the rules about punctuating compound sentences, don't feel too frustrated. Many writers have difficulties with compound sentences, but that doesn't keep them from writing them. Nor should you avoid compound sentences by writing only simple sentences. After all, you can't expect to become an expert on punctuation in one lesson.

◇ *Reread and Review*

Punctuating the Complex Sentence

When we discussed punctuating the simple sentence, we said that the basic rule is not to separate the subject from the verb. This is also true for complex sentences.

When considering the dependent clause of a complex sentence, you will do fairly well with these guidelines: *Separate an introductory dependent clause from the rest of the sentence with a comma. In most cases, do not separate an ending dependent clause from the rest of the sentence with a comma, unless the ending clause is exceptionally long.*

Following are some examples of correctly punctuated complex sentences that begin with dependent clauses. Notice the comma between the dependent clause and the main clause:

> Although the child may remember most of the information read, he or she may not be able to select the particular facts which answer the question.   (Holmes)

> Although the latter approach might be more objective, it would fail to convey the spirit of an adventure characterized both by youthful arrogance and by the belief that the truth, once found, would be simple as well as pretty.   (Watson)

> After contently poring over The Times, I wandered into the lab to see Francis, unquestionably early, flipping the cardboard base pairs about an imaginary line.   (Watson)

> While others led the crowd in song, King and his colleagues spoke with the assailant at the rear of the stage.   (Garrow)

The following complex sentences end with dependent clauses, and no commas separate them from the main clauses:

> Although the child may remember most of the information read, he or she may not be able to select the particular facts which answer the question.   (Holmes)

> We think of progress as "covering ground" and we admire the man who "makes it under his own steam."   (Lynes)

> No one has met a child under three years old who wants to do something a few days in the future.   (Vygotsky)

> Your mother is behaving the way she is because she has not thought the problem through.   (Miss Manners)

> That child will be slower to use dependent behavior in order to master tasks because he will try to perform the tasks himself before asking for help.   (Bardwick)

The following complex sentence ends with an exceptionally long dependent clause, and so it is punctuated with a comma:

The social sciences could be added at the "soft" end, although many of the sciences higher on the pecking order do not even recognize fields like economics and sociology as sciences.   (Raup)

One final note: If you review the previous section about compound sentences, you will see that the semicolon (;) is used only to separate *main* clauses. In a complex sentence, do not separate a dependent clause from a main clause with a semicolon:

Incorrect	*Correct*
Your mother is behaving the way she is; because she has not thought the problem through. (Miss Manners)	Your mother is behaving the way she is because she has not thought the problem through. (Miss Manners)

As with most rules about English grammar, there are exceptions to the guidelines given here. Sometimes, if a sentence is long and involved, it is helpful to use both commas and semicolons, as in this example:

There is no record, oral or written, of the precise date at which a rainbow was first noticed; and even now, in the middle of the twentieth century, it is not possible to boast that the formation of the bow is understood in all details. The theory of the rainbow evidently arose in man's sense of wonder; and now, thousands of years later, it has become enmeshed with the intricacies of advanced mathematics.

Carl Boyer, *The Rainbow: From Myth to Mathematics*

◇ *Reread and Review*

The Sentence Fragment

A **sentence fragment** is not really a "sentence" at all, because it is missing either the subject or the verb. One main cause of sentence fragments is that writers use a word that looks like a verb but doesn't really function like one. (See the discussion of clauses in Chapter 10.) Another cause of fragments is that writers simply end a sentence too soon.

We might make a distinction between two types of sentence fragments. A **broken sentence** (which is not found in formal writing) reflects a thought that has been interrupted in some illogical way. A **minor sentence** (which *is* found in formal writing) is a phrase or clause that has been separated from the main clause. Here are examples:

Broken Sentence
Seeing the various European countries without drinking ages trusting their

youth to be intelligent and responsible about drinking; is not the U.S. saying that they do not trust their youth?

Minor Sentence
Europeans have no minimum drinking age. Trusting their youth to be intelligent and responsible about drinking.

The broken sentence really doesn't make much sense, and there's no simple way to fix it. The writer will have to start over. The minor sentence, however, can be fixed easily. Here are two ways to do it:

Trusting their youth to be intelligent and responsible about drinking, Europeans have no minimum drinking age.

Europeans have no minimum drinking age because they trust their youth to be intelligent and responsible about drinking.

The minor sentence above illustrates a common error: By mispunctuating and putting a period after *age*, the writer detached the dependent clause from the main clause. When checking your sentences, look closely at places where you have capitalized a signal word to begin a sentence (words like *after, who, which, before*). Does a main clause follow immediately? Can you attach that dependent clause to a sentence which comes immediately before or after it?

Here is another example of a detached dependent clause that makes a minor sentence (underlined):

After burning my hand in the kitchen, I decided to take a break from playing the galloping gourmet. I acquired a new skill. One which produced less scorching results. I learned how to unwrap a TV dinner.

And here is the passage as it should be punctuated:

After burning my hand in the kitchen, I decided to take a break from playing the galloping gourmet. I acquired a new skill, one which produced less scorching results. I learned how to unwrap a TV dinner.

Barbara Lesane, student

Minor sentences do show up in informal American English, especially in advertising. But it takes a skilled writer to use such fragments successfully, because they require the reader to supply what's missing. Also, unless a piece of writing contains very few or no errors, readers cannot tell whether sentence fragments are intentional or are a lapse on the part of the writer. If you are unsure about your own use of sentence fragments, discuss your draft with your teacher or with any thoughtful reader.

◇ *Reread and Review*

Reading and Editing Assignment ■

Now check the punctuation in your draft or journal entry. If you already have marked your compound, complex, and compound-complex sentences, you can easily correct any mispunctuation. Look for sentence fragments, comma splices, and run-on sentences.

Exchange your draft or journal entry with a classmate, and check each other's punctuation.

If you made any punctuation changes, you might want to add some notes to your grammar log, under the "Reasons" column.

Additional Punctuation Notes

Patient experiences difficulty swallowing tires easily.

Yes, anyone might experience difficulty swallowing tires. Perhaps this is what the writer means:

Patient experiences difficulty swallowing; tires easily.

Although this example is extreme, too little or too much punctuation can sometimes cause real problems for readers. For example, when the Republicans met in 1984 to draft the party platform for the coming election, a single comma was debated by the subcommittee on the issue of tax increases. The draft that started all the trouble read:

[Republicans] oppose any attempts to increase taxes which would harm the recovery and reverse the trend to restoring control of the economy to individual Americans.

This meant that the Republicans did not oppose *all* tax increases—just *harmful* taxes. As some members of the committee pointed out, however, Ronald Reagan had pledged not to raise any taxes for whatever reason. After some discussion, the committee inserted a comma:

[Republicans] oppose any attempts to increase taxes, which would harm the recovery and reverse the trend to restoring control of the economy to individual Americans.

As reported in *Time*, August 27, 1984

Now the statement means that Republicans oppose *all* taxes. It may be hard to believe that one comma can change the meaning of an entire sentence, but let's look at another example:

No American can avoid the necessity of written communication.

If you wanted to add the clause "who wishes to hold a place of any significant responsibility," how would you punctuate the sentence? Would you set off that clause with commas?

> No American, who wishes to hold a place of any significant responsibility, can avoid the necessity of written communication.

Or would you insert the clause without commas?

> No American who wishes to hold a place of any significant responsibility can avoid the necessity of written communication.   (Tuttle)

The sentence that uses the commas says that no *American*—no matter what she or he does—can avoid writing. But the sentence without the commas says that only Americans *who hold responsible jobs* must worry about writing. The sentences say two different things.

In all the examples above, the sentences *without* the commas have a more limited, or more restricted, meaning. The dependent clauses are not separated from the main clauses because they *define* the main clauses. Such a clause is called a **restrictive clause**, or a **defining clause**.

On the other hand, the sentences *with* the commas simply contain extra, added information. Their dependent clauses are separated from the main clauses because they are plain modifiers.

Here are a few more examples of sentences with a restrictive, or defining, clause:

> In order to achieve this overall view we develop explanatory theories which will give structure to natural phenomena: we classify nature into a coherent system which appears to do what we say it does.   (Burke)

> Somebody once observed to the eminent philosopher Wittgenstein how stupid medieval Europeans living before the time of Copernicus must have been that they could have looked at the sky and thought that the sun was circling the earth.   (Burke)

> Most of us have memory abilities that lie somewhere between the two unusual extremes presented above.   (Feldman)

Some grammarians insist that only the signal word *that* should be used when writing defining or restrictive clauses, but these examples show that not everyone does this.

Next, here are some sentences with **nonrestrictive clauses**; they are set off by commas because they simply modify the main clauses by presenting additional information:

A shocked stillness came over the crowd, <u>which watched in amazement as King stood his ground and accepted several blows.</u>   (Garrow)

Constantly letters flow across the land, <u>carrying messages of love and pain, business and leisure,</u> to millions of readers.   (Tuttle)

Without defending your mother, <u>who certainly should keep her word and not treat your friends rudely,</u> Miss Manners feels sorry for her.   (Miss Manners)

Remember: no commas = restrictive clause; commas = nonrestrictive clause.

Now, let's turn to the issue of using (or not using) punctuation to create special effects in writing. Read the following passage, and add punctuation wherever you think it is needed:

the night max wore his wolf suit and made mischief of one kind and another his mother called him wild thing and max said ill eat you up so he was sent to bed without eating anything that very night in maxs room a forest grew and grew and grew until his ceiling hung with vines and the walls became the world all around and an ocean tumbled by with a private boat for max and he sailed off through night and day and in and out of weeks and almost over a year to where the wild things are

Now compare the punctuation in the following original passage to the passage as you punctuated it. Very likely, the author has used *less* punctuation than you did:

The night Max wore his wolf suit and made mischief of one kind and another his mother called him "Wild Thing!" and Max said "I'LL EAT YOU UP!" so he was sent to bed without eating anything. That very night in Max's room a forest grew and grew—and grew until his ceiling hung with vines and the walls became the world all around and an ocean tumbled by with a private boat for Max and he sailed off through night and day and in and out of weeks and almost over a year to where the wild things are.

Maurice Sendak, *Where the Wild Things Are*

In this example the writer violated the normal patterns of punctuation in order to create an effect; perhaps he wanted to imitate the breathless quality of a young child telling a story. Have you ever noticed how children use *and* over and over again to connect ideas? They talk or write as though everything happens all at once. That's the effect Sendak may be trying to capture in writing, and he does it by punctuating in an unusual way.

Finally, remember that correct punctuation—as baffling as it may seem—is a mixture of common sense and a few general rules. As with all aspects of writing, you should consider your audience and your purpose: What kind of punctuation do readers expect in a piece of writing?

◇ *Reread and Review*

Reading and Editing Assignment   ■

Look over your draft or journal entry one last time to examine your punctuation practices. Keeping the above discussion in mind, should you add or remove any punctuation to improve the sense or effect of your sentences?

Exchange your draft or journal entry with a classmate, and check each other's work.

If you made any changes in punctuation, you might want to add some notes to your grammar log, under the "Reasons" column.

chapter 12

■

Fine-Tuning Your Sentences

During drafting and revising, a writer concentrates on the content of a paper—on getting the ideas and examples into an effective organization that fits the writer's purpose and audience. While focusing on content, however, it is easy to lose track of how the individual parts of sentences fit together. That's a good reason to view editing as a separate, final stage of the writing process. During editing, you shift your focus from the content of the paper in order to concentrate on the details of each sentence and word.

This chapter looks closely at some important details that you should examine during editing. Remember to reread and review each section of the discussion.

Making Subject and Verb Agree

Your editing so far has ensured that your sentences *are* sentences, and that their clauses are grammatically solid. Now you should focus on **subject-verb agreement**. A basic principle of English sentences is that subjects and verbs must *agree*, or share in, the same number. In other words, singular subjects need singular verbs, and plural subjects need plural verbs. In the following examples, the subjects are in italic type, and the verbs are shown in boldface:

> *Singular subjects and verbs*
>
> After all, *America* **faces** an even bigger challenge in this sphere than *Western Europe* **does**. Because our divorce *rate* **is** enormously high, our family *structure* **is** much weaker than that typical of many Western European nations. . . . (Hewlett)

> *Plural subjects and verbs*
>
> The fact that *languages* . . . **are** at issue here must be emphasized from the outset. . . . The structural *details* of Indian languages **reflect** profound appreciation for the physical world and its natural order. (Leap)

Both singular and plural subjects and verbs

Basically it **suggests** toughness and independence, but many subtle *variations* of this message **are** possible, depending among other things on the color and shape of the hat and its trimmings. . . . Plain leather *hatbands* . . . **suggest** the simple approach to life and physical energy of the beef cattle to which the leather once belonged; expensive hand-tooled *bands and decorations* of silver and feathers **imply** a high-flying life style and an extensive bank account.   (Lurie)

One reason why writers make errors in subject-verb agreement is simple: If you cannot identify the subject and the verb, then it is difficult to make them agree. In addition, if a writer does not pronounce the final -*s* on some verbs, she or he also might not write it. For example, read the following sentence out loud:

Rather, the *definition* **suggests** the breadth of slang, a breadth not always acknowledged or understood.   (Nichols)

Because of the *st* at the end of *suggests*, the final -*s*, which marks a singular verb, gets lost. Most people don't stress it, and so they might not hear it. If people don't stress the final -*s* on a number of verbs, that -*s* may not show up where it is needed in writing.

In speaking, a small number of people do not make distinctions between singular and plural when using the verbs *to be* and *to have*. In casual conversations, we might hear "They *was* going" or "They *has* enough" instead of "They *were* going" or "They *have* enough." Again, our hearing might affect our writing. But remember that speech is much less formal than writing. Most readers do expect "They *were* going" or "They *have* enough" in formal writing situations.

Errors in subject-verb agreement also can occur when a phrase or a clause comes between the subject and the verb of a sentence. Here are a few examples:

Incorrect	*Correct*
Current anthropological and sociological *studies* on aging **supports** a policy of age-segregated housing for the elderly.	Current anthropological and sociological *studies* on aging **support** a policy of age-segregated housing for the elderly. (Francis)
Mr. Isenberg, who is eighty-nine years old, **find** a boarding arrangement a mixed blessing.	*Mr. Isenberg*, who is eighty-nine years old, **finds** a boarding arrangement a mixed blessing. (Francis)

In these examples, a writer might get tripped up by the phrase "on aging" or by the clause "who is eighty-nine years old," because they come between the subject and the verb. Even so, the subject and verb should agree, as in the right-hand column.

In the next example, a singular phrase (underlined) comes between the plural subject and the verb of the sentence:

Incorrect

The various *fields* of science **has** a well-defined pecking order.

Correct

The various *fields* of science **have** a well-defined pecking order.   (Raup)

The same kind of problem arises when a plural phrase (underlined) comes between a singular subject and its verb:

Incorrect

An examination of prize-winning picture books **reveal** that women are greatly underrepresented.

Correct

An examination of prize-winning picture books **reveals** that women are greatly underrepresented. (Wertzman)

Problems sometimes arise because *it* and *there* look like the subject when they appear at the beginning of a sentence. But the true subject will be found on the other side of the verb in sentences beginning with *it* or *there*:

Incorrect

There **is** always critically important *persons* whose love and esteem are essential. There **is** narrow *margins* for success and failure here because a parent rewarding dependence is seen as loving whereas his consistent training for independence can be perceived as rejection.

Correct

There **are** always critically important *persons* whose love and esteem are essential. There **are** narrow *margins* for success and failure here because a parent rewarding dependence is seen as loving whereas his consistent training for independence can be perceived as rejection.   (Bardwick)

Soon the whole place was clapping along to "Get off My Back, Woman," and there **was** even a few timid *shouts and whistles.*

Soon the whole place was clapping along to "Get off My Back, Woman," and there **were** even a few timid *shouts and whistles.*   (Lee)

In the next example the true subject is again on the other side of the verb, and again the verb must agree with it (not with the phrase that begins the sentence):

Incorrect

At the other end of the spectrum **is** *fields* like ecology, paleontology, and behavioral biology.

Correct

At the other end of the spectrum **are** *fields* like ecology, paleontology, and behavioral biology.   (Raup)

Be especially alert when editing a sentence with a **collective noun**, a noun that looks singular but may have a plural meaning. Some common examples are *people, committee, group, class, team*, and so on. Collective nouns usually need a singular verb but sometimes need a plural verb (The *public* **has/have** a right to know). Nouns relating to government are usually treated as singular (The *committee* **meets** on Wednesdays). So are those relating to athletics (The *team* **is** ready) and to business (The *corporation* **seeks** new customers). In these cases, the writer wants to stress that the group acts together as single unit, and so the verb is singular. But if a writer wants to stress that the individuals in the group are acting separately, then the verb would be plural (The *audience* **are taking** their seats).

A list of common collective nouns follows:

army	family
audience	group
board	staff
class	team
community	party
corporation	public
crowd	university

◇ *Reread and Review*

Reading and Editing Assignment   ■

You have already located the subjects and predicates in your draft or journal entry in earlier editing assignments. Now, check them to see that each subject and verb agrees in number.

Exchange your draft with a classmate, and check each other's work.

If you made any corrections in subject-verb agreement, you might want to add some notes to your grammar log, under the "Reasons" column.

Making Pronouns and Antecedents Agree

Another type of agreement error occurs when a writer loses track of the noun that a pronoun refers to, making an error in **pronoun-antecedent agreement**. (An *antecedent* is the original noun that the pronoun refers to; *ante* is a Latin word meaning "before.") Just as subjects and verbs must agree in number, a singular noun needs a singular pronoun, and a plural noun needs a plural pronoun.

Read the following sentence:

Whenever a *secretary* needed help, **they** could go to Ms. Rodriguez.

Notice that *secretary* is a singular noun, but the writer uses a plural pronoun (*they*) to refer to the one secretary. We might guess that the writer started out thinking of "any secretary of the group in the office," but by the end of the sentence the writer was thinking of "secretaries" (*them*, instead of *her* or *him*). We might guess the same about the next example:

As long as *consumers* will buy unsafe bikes, the biking industry will supply **it**.

This writer started out with a plural noun (*consumers*) but ended up thinking about a single person and a single bike (*it*, instead of *them*).

Words like *everyone, everybody, anyone*, and *no one* often lead to problems in pronoun-antecedent agreement:

Anyone can buy a ticket to the concert—if **they** have enough money.

Everyone got **their** shoes thoroughly soaked.

Anyone and *everyone* are singular, but because we use them in general statements, they seem to include more than one person. The same kind of thing happens when speakers and writers use the plural pronoun *they* on purpose, because they want to avoid sexist language (discussed in Chapter 3). But there are other ways to avoid sexism without making errors in pronoun-antecedent agreement.

◇ *Reread and Review*

Reading and Editing Assignment ■

Check your draft or journal entry to see that each pronoun agrees with its antecedent in number.

Exchange your draft with a classmate, and check each other's work.

If you made any corrections in pronouns, you might want to add some notes to your grammar log, under the "Reasons" column.

Pronoun Case

Just as we may find the traces of a thousand-year-old leaf pressed between layers of rock, we can find traces of the older forms of our language in modern English. These "fossils" of language can give us trouble with grammar, especially when it comes to pronouns.

Case refers to the relationship between a pronoun and the verb. Is *X* doing the action (*subject case*), or having the action done to it (*object case*)? Case also shows the relationship that we call possession (*possessive case*), which we will discuss in detail later.

We don't have to worry about case when using nouns, since they stay the same whether they are the subject or the object of a sentence. But with pronouns, we use different forms for each case:

Subject Case	Object Case	Possessive Case
I	me	my/mine
who	whom	whose
he	him	his
she	her	her

Remember that the subject case is usually the subject of the sentence; the object case often ends in an *m*.

We usually get the case right with singular pronouns in the subject case: *I* went to the party.

When we use a compound subject, however, we often run into a problem: *Me* and Paul went to the party; *Her* and Johanna live close by. In these two examples the writer has used the object case for pronouns that are the subjects of their sentences: *I* (and Paul) went to the party; *She* (and Johanna) live close by. If you divide the compound subject into each of its parts, you see that the pronouns are the subjects, and you will use the subject case.

◇ *Reread and Review*

Reading and Editing Assignment ■

Check the pronouns in your draft or journal entry to see that you have used the correct case for each one.

Exchange your draft with a classmate, and check each other's work.

If you made any corrections in pronoun case, you might want to add some notes to your grammar log, under the "Reasons" column.

Recognizing the Uses of Final -*s*

The Sign of Singular Verbs

Earlier in the chapter we discussed how to make the subject and the verb agree in number. Now let's look at the most important signal we use to distinguish a singular verb from a plural verb: final -*s*.

In the present tense, the *third-person singular* form of the verb (that is, the verb we use with *he, she,* or *it*) does something unexpected: It ends with *-s:*

Singular	Plural
I giggle	we giggle
you giggle	you giggle
he, she, it giggles	they giggle

This rule for third-person singular verbs in the present tense is exactly the opposite of the rule for nouns (which we'll discuss in the next section). That is, the *-s* on a verb indicates the singular, but on a noun it indicates the plural.

There are three different ways to pronounce the final *-s* on a verb, depending on which letters the verb ends with. Read the following groups of verbs out loud, from top to bottom:

Group 1	Group 2	Group 3
cut cuts	call calls	buzz buzzes
hop hops	flee flees	pass passes
lock locks	rob robs	budge budges
cough coughs	try tries	push pushes

The words in group 1 end with a strong *s* sound; those in group 2 sound more like a *z*; and the words in group 3 end with *ez*. However, not all speakers pronounce the final *-s* in three different ways. A person may pronounce it in some situations but not in others. (Don't worry about the exact sounds of these plural endings; even if you don't pronounce them all yourself, you recognize them when others do.) Some speakers may not pronounce the final *-s* at all. If so, that final *-s* may not get written.

◇ Reread and Review

The Sign of Plural Nouns

Another use of the final *-s* is to indicate the *plural* form of a noun. (This is just the opposite of the rule for verbs, where it indicates the singular.) And, like the pronunciation of verbs, the final *-s* on nouns has three different sounds, depending on which letters the noun ends with. Read the following groups of nouns out loud, from top to bottom:

Group 1	Group 2	Group 3
duck ducks	dog dogs	horse horses
back backs	bag bags	badge badges
tent tents	toy toys	kiss kisses
lamp lamps	town towns	page pages

Again, group 1 ends with a strong *s* sound; group 2 sounds more like *z*; and group 3 ends with *ez*.

Some English words that have been borrowed from other languages have unusual forms in the plural, because they don't end in -*s*:

Singular	*Plural*
datum	data
phenomenon	phenomena
criterion	criteria

In addition, some nouns have two forms for the plural. *Syllabus*, for example, can be pluralized either as *syllabi* or as *syllabuses; appendix* can be either *appendices* or *appendixes*. Your dictionary shows how to form the plural of such unusual nouns, which also can lead to problems with subject-verb agreement:

Incorrect	*Correct*
The *data* **is** incorrect.	The *data* **are** incorrect.
Several startling *phenomena* **was** observed.	Several startling *phenomena* **were** observed.

◇ *Reread and Review*

Reading and Editing Assignment ∎

Check your draft or journal entry to see that you have used correct forms for verbs and nouns that end with a final -*s*.

Exchange your draft with a classmate, and check each other's work.

If you made any corrections in the final -*s* of verbs or nouns, you might want to add some notes to your grammar log, under the "Reasons" column.

The Sign of the Possessive

The **apostrophe mark** (') has several uses in English. It takes the place of one or two letters when we make a **contraction** by joining two words (to contract means "to make smaller"). A word like *don't* is *do not* run together, and the apostrophe mark takes the place of the second *o; there's* is a contraction for *there is*; and *I'll* is a contraction for *I will*.

We also use the apostrophe to indicate the plural of a letter or a number: "I got three *C's* on my lab reports"; "His *1's* look like *7's*."

When it appears with the letter *s*, the apostrophe mark has another, very important use: It indicates that a noun has a *possessive* quality, as in the singular *girl's* and the plural *girls'*. (Note where the mark goes in relation to the *s*: singular = *'s* ; plural = *s'*.) Another way we indicate this possessive quality is with *of*, as in "the notebook *of* the girl," "the milk *of* the cow," and so on.

We have just looked at the use of *-s* to form the plural of nouns. In writing, the apostrophe mark indicates the difference between a plural noun and a possessive one. When we speak, however, we cannot always distinguish among the plural, the singular possessive, and the plural possessive. For example, read the following words out loud:

students	*(plural)*
student's	*(singular possessive)*
students'	*(plural possessive)*

These words—and others that form their plurals with *-s* and that have possessive forms—are all pronounced exactly the same. As a result, we can't hear the difference between a plural noun and a possessive noun. In addition, as we mentioned earlier, some people do not pronounce the final *-s* on words when they speak.

In writing, however, we can see and interpret the different meanings of *s*, *'s*, and *s'*. The apostrophe sign, then, is only part of *written* grammar, which is why we sometimes forget to add it to a possessive noun. We can't indicate it in any way when we speak, and so we may forget it when we write.

Another complication in using the apostrophe is that we also have separate pronouns to indicate the possessive. Here are the singular possessive pronouns:

my computer
this computer *of mine*
your radio
that radio *of yours*
his watch
her sneakers
its whiskers

And here are the plural possessive pronouns:

our apartment
that apartment *of ours*
your television
that television *of yours*
their car
that car *of theirs*

Notice that *your* and *of yours* can be either singular or plural. Also notice that no apostrophe is needed with pronouns, even when they end with -*s*. We only use this mark with nouns, not with pronouns. We don't need to write "that book of your's" because *yours* already indicates possession.

An especially tricky pronoun is *it*, because the possessive form is *its* (no apostrophe with pronouns). Remember that *it's* is the contraction for *it is*. The rule for *its* and other pronouns is just the opposite of the rule for nouns. Nouns need the apostrophe to indicate possession, and pronouns do not.

Besides being tricky, the idea of the possessive is somewhat misleading, because it has the sense of ownership, as in "the cheerleader's sneakers." But the possessive can indicate other kinds of relationships as well. Consider the example of a student, Elijah, who was having trouble with the difference between *their* (possessive pronoun) and *there* (place). After working on the problem for quite a while, he wrote the following sentence:

The football players had *there* games in the main stadium.

When questioned about this, Elijah said that the games did not "belong" to the football players; they didn't "own" them; and so the proper word was *there*. OK, if the football games don't belong to the players, to whom do they belong? "The coach!" he replied. Clearly, this student had thought the problem through, but he came to the wrong conclusion. His mistake, however, shows that possessives can have meanings other than ownership. We say "my hat" as well as "my hometown" or "my school," but we don't own the town or the school, do we?

So, think of the possessive as a sign of the *relationship* between two words, not just of ownership. Here are some examples of possessives that describe or limit the meaning of the nouns without showing actual ownership:

their president	girls' basketball
our native language	teenagers' ideas
her country	the judge's authority
his favorite musician	child's play
a dollar's worth	at death's door
a moment's notice	the mind's eye
a bachelor's degree	politicians' critics
tomorrow's weather	a mother's love

It is understandable why writers sometimes have problems with the apostrophe. Besides the fact that the apostrophe is only seen and not heard, there seems to be a trend to leave it off entirely, especially on public signs. For example, you will find many signs in public places like the following:

Visitors Parking
Farmers Market

Notice that neither example has a possessive sense. *Visitors Parking* means parking *for* visitors, not parking *of* visitors. And a *Farmers Market* is not a market *of* farmers, or even a market *for* farmers who bring their goods to it for sale; instead, a *Farmers Market* is a market for people to buy goods *from* farmers.

Let us look at another way to think about the apostrophe. Read the following phrases:

an *awkward* girl	a *child's* toy
a *hot* day	the *hero's* welcome
a *huge* headache	the *band's* drummer

Can you see any difference in how the words *awkward* and *child's* work in the first phrases? Both words give us some information about the nouns *girl* and *toy*, which distinguishes those nouns from every other *girl* and *toy*. However, *awkward* is an adjective, while *child's* is a noun. But here, both words act as adjectives. The same is true of all the other italic words; all of them are acting as adjectives. In a way, when you add *'s* or *s'* to a noun, you turn it into an adjective—a word that modifies or describes a noun. However, we cannot depend on this rule to work all the time. For example, read the following phrases:

tape player **not** the *tape's* player
baseball bat **not** the *baseball's* bat
Tuesday morning **not** *Tuesday's* morning

Notice that these examples—and others that you might think of—do not have the sense of possession. They show some other relationship between two words.

Now, consider some examples that can work both ways:

rebel army	*rebel's* army
library book	*library's* book

In these cases, the use of an apostrophe (or not) depends on the meaning of the sentence:

That's a *library* book on your desk, isn't it?

The *library's* book was missing some pages; however, my copy has them.

The second sentence is comparing two different copies of the book, and the apostrophe *s* distinguishes between them.

You might be asking at this point: "Why not just drop the apostrophe? It seems to be more trouble than it's worth. Besides, would anyone really not understand what I wrote if I forgot it?" Well, consider the following example:

The book *of Kareem Abdul-Jabbar* was left on the bus.

In this sentence, the book may be *about* Kareem Abdul-Jabbar—it may be a biography. Now let's add *'s*:

> The book *of Kareem Abdul-Jabbar's* was left on the bus.

Now the sentence means that the book *belongs to* Kareem Abdul-Jabbar—he owns it.

Consider another example:

> The picture *of the rock star* had faded.

This sentence means that the picture is *of* the rock star. Add *'s*:

> The picture *of the rock star's* had faded.

Now the sentence means that the picture *belongs to* the rock star.

In these two examples, leaving off the *'s* does make a difference. However, it is also true that leaving it off may not affect the meaning of some sentences very much. A useful guideline to the question about apostrophes may be that—because of cases like these—it is best to use the apostrophe where it is required. Another, larger reason to use it is one that you have come across before: When reading edited English, the audience expects a writer to follow the conventions that characterize written language. Thus, even though the apostrophe may someday disappear, most writers and readers still prefer it.

◇ *Reread and Review*

Reading and Editing Assignments   ∎

1. Read through your draft or journal entry, and circle the places where you have used *'s* or *s'*. Look also for any nouns that are functioning as adjectives, and decide whether you need to add *'s* or *s'* to them. Did you use *its* or *it's* anywhere? If so, decide whether each one is a possessive (*its*) or a contraction (*it's*).

Exchange your draft with a classmate, and check each other's work.

2. If you made any corrections in your use of apostrophes, you might want to add some notes to your grammar log, under the "Reasons" column.

3. Look for public signs or advertising that omit the apostrophe. Also, look for signs or ads that use the apostrophe when it is not needed. Share your examples in class, and record them on the right-hand side of your journal.

4. As we said above, someday it may be acceptable not to use the apostrophe. What do you think? Can you think of any examples other than the ones in the text where leaving out *'s* or *s'* might make a real difference? What examples can you think of where it would *not* make a difference to omit the apostrophe? Share your ideas in class, and record them on the right-hand side of your journal.

Recognizing Tenses

The Past Tense

Tense is the term we use to indicate time relationships in grammar. For example, to show that something happened in the past, we usually add *-ed* to the verb: I play*ed* hockey yesterday.

Like the pronunciation of the final *-s* on verbs and nouns, the final *-ed* of the past tense often does not get pronounced in speech. Two very common instances are *used to* and *supposed to*:

I can't get *used to* losing you.
You were *supposed to* love me forever.

In these examples, the final *d* of the verb bumps up against the *t* of the preposition, and so the sound of the past-tense marker, *-ed*, gets lost.

Read the following sentences out loud:

I *walk* downtown every day.
I *walked* downtown yesterday.
I have *walked* downtown all week.
I would have *walked* downtown, but it rained.

Chances are, you did not make a distinction between the sound of *walk* and *walked*. Can you see how pronunciation might influence written language in this instance?

Actually, the final *-ed* (again, like the final *-s*) has three different pronunciations, depending on which letters the verb ends with. Read the following groups of verbs out loud, from top to bottom:

Group 1	*Group 2*	*Group 3*
pad padded	buzz buzzed	pass passed
pat patted	call called	pack packed

The words in group 1 end with an *-ed* sound; those in group 2 end with a *d* sound; and the words in group 3 end with a strong *t* sound.

Auxiliary Verbs

We also indicate time relationships by adding "helping verbs" (called **auxiliaries**) to the main verb. Thus, verbs sometimes are combined with other verbs, such as *be, have, will, shall*, and *might*. Auxiliaries and the verb forms of *to be* and *to have* indicate more complex time relationships.

Sometimes writers are confused by auxiliaries, and they omit the *-ed* from a verb because the auxiliary seems to function as the past-tense marker:

Incorrect	*Correct*
In many cases, the child **is** heavily **influence** by what he or she has seen on TV.	In many cases, the child **is** heavily **influenced** by what he or she has seen on TV.
At the moment the can of chewing tobacco **was place** in my hands I became nervous.	At the moment the can of chewing tobacco **was placed** in my hands I became nervous.

Greg Sobczak, student

Let us look briefly at just a few auxiliaries to fine-tune our sense of time. For example, when the auxiliaries *has* or *have* are added to a main verb, the result is the *present-perfect tense*. It shows that an action was started in the past, but was not completed:

> But instead of explaining that to you, she **has tried** to give in on the point of your entertaining in your bedroom.   (Miss Manners)

> The number of Americans living in mobile homes **has** also **grown** dramatically.   (Lynes)

> For thousands of years human beings **have communicated** with one another first in the language of dress. . . . By the time we meet and converse we **have** already **spoken** to each other in an older and more universal tongue. (Lurie)

When the auxiliary *had* is added to a main verb, we get the *past-perfect tense*. It shows that an action was started in the past and was completed in the past:

> I **had found** that, in spite of the economic boom, something was amiss. (Rosengarten)

> King, who carried the blues to Europe, Africa, and the Far East, **had broken** the ice one more time.   (Lee)

> The past, I thought, **had served** its full uses and could bury its own dead; bridges were for burning; "good-bye" meant exactly what it said. One

never looked back *except to judge how far one* **had come**. . . . The assign-ment would shape my life far more than I then suspected; over the years it would teach me to "play cowboy"—to become, strangely, more "Texas" than I **had been**.   (King)

In December, the month before Kennedy's inauguration, civil rights ac-tivists **had won** a victory in the Supreme Court when the justices ordered integration of bus stations and terminals. . . . Eisenhower **had been** reluctant to use federal force after Little Rock.   (Williams)

◇ *Reread and Review*

Reading and Editing Assignments ▪

1. Read again through your draft or journal entry, and circle the places where you have used *-ed*. Also look for places where you might have left off this past-tense marker, and add it.

Exchange your draft with a classmate, and check each other's work.

2. If you made any corrections in verb tenses, you might want to add some notes to your grammar log, under the "Reasons" column.

Spelling

The ability to spell words correctly depends on a combination of visual memory and aural memory (having to do with hearing). Some people have highly devel-oped visual and aural memories, and so they seldom have problems with spell-ing. Everyone, however, has some words that she or he just cannot remember how to spell. Such "spelling demons" give most people trouble. Here's a very short list of words that most people think twice about:

Incorrect	*Correct*
ocassion, occassion	occasion
equivelent	equivalent
existance*	existence*
alot	a lot
anser	answer
artical	article
embarras, embarass	embarrass
gaurd	guard
rythm	rhythm
seperate	separate
Wendesday	Wednesday

*And all other words that end in *-ance* or *-ence*.

In addition, words like the following are frequently misspelled because they sound alike or look alike:

its/it's
led/lead
read/red
their/they're/there
where/were

Finally, of course, we each have personal spelling demons—words that we almost always misspell. Any large dictionary can help us check spellings, but all the definitions and other information make the job time-consuming and more difficult than it has to be. A book that's easier to use is Webster's *33,000 Word Book*, which just lists words alphabetically, without definitions. There are other such books, too—designed to help writers and office workers avoid spelling errors. Many word processors today have spelling checkers built right in, so that they "beep" or otherwise signal the writer as soon as a spelling error is typed.

The fact that there are special books and computer programs to help writers spell correctly tells us that spelling problems are very common and that correct spelling is valued highly. All writers, then, need to identify their spelling problems and work to avoid them. The following essay, by Donald E. P. Smith, outlines one good way that you can do that.

SPELLING IS NONSENSE

For some unaccountable reason, the executive, the parent, the man in the street—sometimes even college professors—judge a man's intelligence by his ability to spell. Such a practice is grossly unjust. The relationship between spelling ability and brightness is so small as to be negligible. And when conditions for learning words are optimum, even this small relationship disappears. . . .

One's intelligence indicates one's ability to deal with ideas, with meanings, in short, with things sensible. Now, no matter how sensible a man is, he won't be able to determine the spelling of *enough* unless he is told. True, some spelling words follow rules; the thinking man is able to spell *sleigh* by applying the crutch, "*i* before *e*, except after *c*, or pronounced as *a* as in *neighbor* and *weigh*." But then what should he do with *either, neither, height, deity, leisure, heir, weird*, and *sieve*, not to mention *heighho*!

[In order to learn how to spell, we must turn to memorization.] We must develop an association between the sound of a word and its picture. Such an association is difficult for some people to establish. Tension may result in obliterating traces [of an association], or attention to a word may be inadequate so that the spelling is not seen clearly or the sound not heard correctly to begin with.

One way to remedy this problem is to increase attention by increasing the strength of stimulation. Greater input = greater number of associations. The procedure is as follows:

1. Limit your words to be learned to two kinds:

a. those which you understand. In general, the more meaning a word has, the easier it is to learn.

b. those which appear to be your personal demons. Most people who consider themselves poor spellers consistently err on only 50 or 100 words. Find those words in your old theme papers.

2. Write the word in large script.

A discharge from blood vessels caused by injury:
[written out in large script: hemorrhage]

3. Trace the word with your index finger three times *saying the word* (not the letters) aloud as you trace. Begin tracing and saying simultaneously and finish both operations simultaneously. (Do this now with the word *hemorrhage*.)

4. Next, close your eyes and try to visualize the word in your "mind's eye." (Do this now. Some people are unable to visualize. If you are one of those, skip this step.)

5. Next, trace the word on the desk, saying it aloud as you trace it. (Do this now. If you are unable to see part of the word or to trace it, repeat steps 3 and 4.)

6. Now, write the word normally. (Do this now.)

7. Compare the word you have just written with that in large script. Find any errors?

8. If there is an error, repeat the whole procedure, paying particular attention to the trouble spot.

Now learning will be relatively complete, and retention will be high. You have provided multiple sensory input: vision, hearing, touch, muscular sensations (kinesthesis), all in the context of meaning.

Now try these:

A physician who specializes in vision:
[written out in large script: ophthalmologist]

Sleeping sickness:
[written out in large script: encephalitis]

A specialist in behavior:
[written out in large script: psychologist]

Chapter 9 described how you can set aside part of your grammar log to help you focus on your own "spelling demons." If you have not set up a spelling log, or have not added to it lately, this is a good time to do so. Look again at the lists of words in this section, and record the ones that give you special trouble. Also look over any papers that have been returned with spelling errors marked, and decide whether those words belong in your spelling log. From time to time, have a friend or classmate read your spelling log to you, and test whether you have learned the correct spellings of the words you listed.

◇ *Reread and Review*

Writing and Editing Assignment   ■

Check your draft or journal entry to see whether you have used any of the words in your spelling log, and whether you spelled them correctly.

Exchange your draft with a classmate, and check each other's work.

If you made any corrections in spellings, you might want to add some notes to your spelling log.

Writing Assignment   ■

Stop for a moment, and quickly skim this chapter. What did you learn that you didn't know before about subject-verb agreement, pronoun-antecedent agreement, the final letters of nouns and verbs, and spelling? On the left-hand side of your journal, write a short description of the things you learned.

part **five**

Applied Writing

Strategies for Writing
The Essay Examination

Introduction

Throughout this book and course, you have examined reading and writing in
detail. Step by step, you have analyzed the characteristics of effective writing,
and you have practiced those characteristics in your own writing. Your journal
and your grammar log have helped you record your ideas and problems as a
writer, and you have worked hard to improve your writing.

Along the way, you probably viewed your successes or frustrations in relation to a grade. Even if you had taken this course only to improve your writing—if it had not been required—it would be difficult *not* to think of success in
terms of a grade. After all, a student's work in any course is graded, one way or
another. And very often, the grade is what motivates you to work. You "need at
least a C," or you "want to get an A," and so you work to earn it.

When it comes to grades, a writing course is a little bit different. For one
thing, a writer's ideas can seldom be marked "right" or "wrong," as a math
problem might be. Your writing instructor must estimate whether your ideas are
effective or not; supported or not; interesting or not; persuasive or not. Yes,
misspellings and grammatical errors can be counted, but that is only one part of
an essay—and most teachers react to errors as things that get in the way of your
ideas, and they respond to them accordingly. Furthermore, once you get a math
problem wrong, the only thing that you can do is make it right. In a writing
course, you get a number of opportunities to examine your own writing and to
improve it as you go along.

However important grades are to a student writer, at some point a particular idea or assignment becomes even more important. The student suddenly wants to write *better*—not just because of a grade on that paper, but because the ideas and the challenge of presenting them effectively seem important. At that point the student wants to *apply* what has been learned throughout the course. She or he wants to connect with readers in the best way possible.

Very likely, you've had that experience, too. Some assignment or idea sparked your interest more than you expected when you set out to write "another paper." You began by working for a grade, but then you saw ways that you could use what you've learned about writing to affect your audience. That's the "hidden" purpose of a writing course: to help you apply what you've learned.

The chapters that follow are designed to help you apply the writing process to any situation—not just to papers in this course. First we'll look at five important strategies for writing, five ways that you can organize material to help an audience understand it. Then we'll look closely at a specific writing situation that every student knows well: the essay examination. The things you practiced and learned in this course about writing can be applied directly to essay exams—in any of your courses.

The need to write effectively will be with you throughout the rest of college, in the workplace, and in your personal life. In every writing situation, you can apply what you've learned about readers, about your purpose, and about drafting and revising to achieve your purpose with that audience. Although you won't be "graded" as you have been in this course, your other teachers, your employers, and anyone to whom you write (even family and friends) will think of the person behind the writing. They will respond to your writing just as you do to other people's writing. They will be your *readers,* waiting to learn what's on your mind.

chapter 13 ∎

Strategies for Writing

Once you know what your main purpose for writing is—whether to express, to inform, or to persuade—you can begin to plan how you will achieve that purpose. In other words, you can develop a **strategy** for writing—a way to shape the parts of your essay or the whole essay.

This chapter will show you how to use five important strategies in your writing:

— Definition
— Comparison
— Classification
— Cause and effect
— Process analysis

Writing with a Strategy in Mind

The kind of strategy you choose depends on at least three things: your purpose, your topic, and your audience. For example, if you wanted to train a newly promoted employee to handle your job as manager of a fast-food restaurant, your topic might be a list of your duties (such as supervising employees, satisfying customers, and ordering supplies). Notice that here you have a specific topic and a specific purpose in mind: You need to prepare a trainee to do your job as well as you do. But you can't assume that the trainee knows anything about your job. In this case, it might be a good strategy to *define* each of your duties in detail, so that the trainee will know exactly what to do.

Consider another example: Suppose you wanted to persuade your neighbors that a home for retarded working adults would be an asset to your community. If you know that your audience isn't open to this idea, you will need a strategy that will be effective in convincing them. In this case, you might describe how the home will operate and how the residents will take care of themselves. In other words, you might *analyze the process* of the home's daily operations.

Few writers begin by deciding to use a particular strategy for its own sake. For example, a newspaper columnist who faces a deadline for writing a 700-word article doesn't say, "Let's see—I haven't written a cause-and-effect essay in months; I'll write one now." Instead, the columnist begins with a subject, a purpose, and an audience and then looks for an *angle*—a way into the subject that will help organize the ideas in an effective way for that audience.

A writer uses a particular strategy because it will be effective in developing the topic and in achieving the purpose for the intended audience. With that in mind, let's examine what the strategies are, and how you can use them in your own writing.

Definition

In using the strategy of **definition,** a writer proceeds by explaining what a word or a concept means—or what several of them mean. In some cases, you may only need to define a term briefly, especially if it is crucial to your readers' understanding of your essay. When the term or concept is basic to your entire essay, you can't risk that your readers might define or understand it in some way that is different from how you mean it.

In other cases, you may use the strategy of definition to discuss a concept in detail and at length. Your whole essay might be organized around the definition. For example, for a paper in a course in industrial relations, you might want to go beyond the textbook definition of what a *laborer* is, because the definition does not fully explore what it means to be a laborer. In that case, you could expand the definition in a personal and vivid way by describing your own experience as a laborer. One student organized an entire essay by comparing the textbook definition of *laborer* with his own first-hand experience with working on a tobacco farm.

Write Before Reading

Many definitions found in a dictionary are not adequate for a thorough understanding of a concept. Before you read the following passage, take a moment to look up the word *slang* in your dictionary. On the right-hand side of your journal, restate the definition in your own words. Then compare it with the definitions in the following passage.

facetious:
humorous or
playful

The definition of slang is vague. The 1957 edition of the Standard College Dictionary defines slang in part as "Language, words, or phrases of a vigorous, colorful, facetious, or taboo nature, invented for specific occasions or uses, or derived from the unconventional use of the standard vocabulary." A good deal of modern poetry can be described by the same terms. The Standard College Dictionary adds a second definition: "The special vocabulary of a certain class, group, or profession: college slang." "The special vocabulary of certain professions" can obviously include the jargon that accompanies most politicians, sociologists, and educators. The lack of preciseness in the dictionary definition does not indicate a weakness in either the dictionary or slang. Rather, the definition suggests the breadth of slang, a breadth not always acknowledged or understood. A comprehensive definition of slang is further made difficult by the fact that often what used to be slang no longer is. Many people think they know instinctively when they encounter slang, and their response is usually negative. These same people may be surprised, however, to discover what slang has been. Nice started out as a slang word, and it now occupies a front position in a long and respected list of nice but meaningless words. A number of other words, as H. L. Mencken points out in his famous discussion of slang, started out as slang and end up filling vacuums in our existing vocabulary. Among others, Mencken mentions rodeo, racketeer, and hold up.

Anne Nichols, "Slang"

Write After Reading ■

This writer argues that a dictionary definition is not broad enough to cover the richness of slang terms, and that slang is more common than many people think. She moves beyond the dictionary definition to make some points about language and about how society shapes it.

On the left-hand side of your journal, opposite your definition of *slang,* explain why the dictionary definition is or is not adequate.

How to Use Definition in Your Writing

The strategy of definition does not limit you to defining only one word in an essay. Complicated ideas like "unilateral disarmament" or "an affair of the heart" may lead you to define a number of terms and to explain how they are related. If you use definition to develop an entire essay, look for ways to make your definitions special and personal. There are several ways to do this.

For example, you might develop your essay by citing several different meanings of a term or phrase. Many words mean different things to different people, depending on our backgrounds, beliefs, and experiences. "Southern," for example, is likely to be defined differently by a person from England than by someone from Michigan; and a native of Mississippi will probably offer a third definition. To get an idea of how people define things differently, ask your classmates what they mean by "reading for fun" or a "good movie."

This leads to another approach in using definition: You can illustrate a term by giving examples. Some concepts (like "fun" reading or a "good" movie) are very abstract, and an example will help your readers understand what you mean. An example can also take the form of a brief comparison. For instance, how would you define "small town hospitality" to someone who had never lived in a small town? You might start by comparing the town to a local neighborhood in a city; that would be the start of a working definition for readers who don't know small-town life.

Suppose you want to define a technical term from some specialized field that you have studied in another class. One good approach would be to trace its historical development: What did the term mean originally, and how did its meaning change over time? What events or developments caused the changes in meaning? To take an example, some psychologists today consider the period of adolescence to extend all the way to age twenty-nine. Surely the concept of adolescence has changed! Unless you explain this to readers, they are likely to define the term as "teenagers" only.

Another useful way to define a term is to show how it differs from some similar term. For example, what is the difference between information and propaganda? Between opinion and prejudice? Between knowledge and intelligence? By explaining how such words differ, you will tell readers exactly what you mean.

Reading and Writing Assignments

1. On the right-hand side of your journal, summarize what the strategy of definition is, and list some ways that you can apply it in your writing.

2. Look for some examples of definition in the passages included in this book. Share these examples with your classmates, and record what you learn on the right-hand side of your journal.

3. On the left-hand side of your journal, write a short passage that uses the strategy of definition to explain what you mean by some word, idea, or abstract concept. Assume that your classmates are your audience, and consider whether your definition should be brief or extended; decide whether or not you should offer examples or comparisons to help readers understand.

Comparison

Using a strategy of **comparison,** a writer looks at two similar things and explains how they are alike or different. We make comparisons all the time: "When he works hard, James, our star forward, is as good a player as Michael Jordan is"; "I like Rhonda more than I like Denise, because Denise is always so touchy."

Comparison is a useful strategy for a discussion of personal preferences. In the following example, a student compares two musicians in order to explain why she prefers one over the other:

> Lionel Richie and Michael Jackson are two popular entertainers. Whenever there is a Lionel Richie or Michael Jackson concert, you immediately picture large audiences filled with many screaming teenagers and even adults, flashing lights, and great dancing. Even though Michael Jackson and Lionel Richie share many qualities as entertainers, I am a much bigger fan of Lionel Richie because I feel he is more outgoing on stage than Michael Jackson is, who often seems to be singing to himself. Lionel Richie, on the other hand, often holds hands with women from the audience, and will look directly into their eyes to create a romantic mood. He also talks more on stage than Michael Jackson does. Lionel Richie, because he is so warm, puts on a better show.
>
> Sharon Washington, student

This writer has some definite reasons for preferring Lionel Richie to Michael Jackson. In comparing them, she focuses on what she thinks is the most important point: how they each interact with an audience.

In the next example, the writer compares the concepts of *parenthood* and *parentage*. Notice that he uses the strategy of definition in order to compare the two concepts:

> It is apparently very necessary to distinguish between parenthood and parentage. Parenthood is an art; parentage is the consequence of a mere biological act. The biological ability to produce conception and to give birth to a child has nothing whatever to do with the ability to care for that child as it requires to be cared for. That ability, like every other, must be learned. It is highly desirable that parentage be not undertaken until the art of parenthood has been learned. Is this a counsel of perfection? As things stand now, perhaps it is, but it need not always be so. Parentage is often irresponsible. Parenthood is responsible. Parentage at best is irresponsibly responsible for the birth of a child. Parenthood is responsible for the development of a human being—not simply a child, but a human being. I do not think it is an overstatement to say that parenthood is the most important occupation in the world. There is no occupation for which the individual should be better prepared than this, for

what can be more important to the individual, his family, his community, his society, his nation, and the world of humanity than the making of a good human being? And the making of a good human being is largely the work of good parents. And it is work—hard work—not to be irresponsibly undertaken or perfunctorily performed. Yet parenthood, perhaps like politics, is the only profession for which preparation is considered unnecessary.

Ashley Montagu, The American Way of Life

Analogy: A Special Kind of Comparison

An **analogy** is a type of comparison in which some difficult concept is compared with something more easily understood; the easier concept helps readers to grasp the difficult one. For example, a student who was learning about impressionist art compared looking at a painting by Monet to looking at a scene under water. Even if readers had never seen a Monet and did not know what impressionist art is, they would be able to imagine it through this analogy.

The following writer uses an analogy to compare the past to a coastline. In fact, he says the past *is* a coastline:

> The past is a distant, receding coastline, and we are all in the same boat. Along the stern rail there is a line of telescopes; each brings the shore into focus at a given distance. If the boat is becalmed, one of the telescopes will be in continual use; it will seem to tell the whole, the unchanging truth. But this is an illusion; and as the boat sets off again, we return to our normal activity: scurrying from one telescope to another, seeing the sharpness fade in one, waiting for the blur to clear in another. And when the blur does clear, we imagine that we have made it do so all by ourselves.
>
> Julian Barnes, Flaubert's Parrot

Barnes could have simply said, "Our interpretation of history changes as we change our perspective and the means by which we study history." Instead, he wants us to compare the study of history to something that we can imagine ourselves doing. By using the analogy of telescopes and a coastline, he helps us understand that our view of history depends on our perspective.

The next example makes an extended comparison by means of analogy. It's worth reading more than once:

> It is raining DNA outside. On the bank of the Oxford canal at the bottom of my garden is a large willow tree, and it is pumping downy seeds into the air. There is no consistent air movement, and the seeds are drifting outwards in all directions from the tree. Up and down the canal, as far as my binoculars can reach, the water is white with floating cottony flecks, and we can be sure that

they have carpeted the ground to much the same radius in other directions too. The cotton wool is mostly made of cellulose, and it dwarfs the tiny capsule that contains the DNA, the genetic information. The DNA content must be a small proportion of the total, so why did I say that it was raining DNA rather than cellulose? The answer is that it is the DNA that matters. The cellulose fluff, although more bulky, is just a parachute, to be discarded. The whole performance, cotton wool, catkins, tree and all, is in aid of one thing and one thing only, the spreading of DNA around the countryside. Not just any DNA, but DNA whose coded characters spell out specific instructions for building willow trees that will shed a new generation of downy seeds. Those fluffy specks are, literally, spreading instructions for making themselves. They are there because their ancestors succeeded in doing the same. It is raining instructions out there; it's raining programs; it's raining tree-growing fluff, spreading algorithms. That is not a metaphor, it is the plain truth. It couldn't be any plainer if it were raining floppy discs.

Richard Dawkins, *The Blind Watchmaker*

algorithms: repeated mathematical formulas

By using such an opening, and describing DNA in such an odd way, the writer makes his point very well about the function of DNA. Note that he says, "That is not a metaphor, it is the plain truth." What is your response to that?

In our final example of analogy, the writer compares the experience of visiting a singles bar to shopping at a sale:

Walking into the typical singles bar on a Wednesday or Friday night is like walking into an overstocked dress department for an after Christmas sale. All the lovely wares on display give you a rush of excitement. But after the first flash of anticipation you become discouraged and dismayed. How will you ever find what you are looking for in this mess of merchandise? There is so much, everything begins to look the same. You leave the store without any merchandise, blaming yourself rather than the shop owner. It was all there for the taking and you couldn't take. With this sense of failure as your only acquisition you leave the bar for the evening, with the idea that you will come back another day.

Suzanne Gordon, *Lonely in America*

You may find an occasional analogy helpful in your own writing. As the above examples show, an analogy is a way to explain something technical or abstract by comparing it with everyday objects or experiences. Analogy is also useful for expressing truths about human experience. For example, although a singles bar is not really like a department store, by focusing on the department store as the main image, the writer can tell us more about the singles bar.

How to Use Comparison in Your Writing

One way to use comparison is to describe something as it changes over time—the "before-and-after" method. For example, suppose your neighborhood has changed a good deal since you were young. Perhaps it is improving, or maybe job opportunities have become scarce and people have less money to spend on keeping their property in repair. You could write an essay comparing your neighborhood as it used to be with how it is now. The same approach can be used with anything you know well: changes in yourself before and after a particular event, changes in your family, or friends, or school.

You may compare TV shows, movies, musicians, writers, or anything else that interests you. But if the two things are very similar or very different, it may be hard to make comparisons between them.

There are two basic ways to write comparison papers: the whole-by-whole method and the point-by-point method. In using the *whole-by-whole method,* a writer first discusses one thing (half the comparison) and then the other. The paragraph comparing Michael Jackson and Lionel Richie is based on this approach. In contrast, the passage that compared parenthood and parentage used the *point-by-point method;* it moved back and forth between the two ideas. Depending on the two things you are comparing, one method may be more useful than the other. In general, however, the whole-by-whole method is easier to apply.

Reading and Writing Assignments ■

1. On the right-hand side of your journal, summarize what the strategy of comparison is, and explain why an analogy is a special form of comparison.

2. Look for some examples of comparison and analogy in the passages included in this book. Share these examples with your classmates, and record what you learn on the right-hand side of your journal.

3. Look elsewhere for some examples of analogy. (Poetry, fiction, and advertisements are good sources of analogies.) When you have collected some examples, use the left-hand side of your journal to write an analogy of your own. For example, use an analogy to explain something technical that you have learned in school or on the job.

4. On the left-hand side of your journal, write a short passage that uses the strategy of comparison to explain why you prefer one thing over another. Use either the whole-by-whole method or the point-by-point method.

Classification

In using a strategy of **classification,** a writer examines three or more things and sorts them into categories based on similarities. At first, this may seem like comparison, because you have to examine how things are alike or different before you can sort them into categories. Notice that classification also involves some definition, since the categories depend on how you define things. (If you are sorting things into "large" and "small," for example, you first have to define what you mean by each category.)

Although classification does require some comparison and definition, the basic question a writer asks in order to classify is: "What do *X, Y,* and *Z* have in common?" When we classify people, for example, we might divide them into "bookworms" and "party animals." To do so, however, we first have to define what characteristics each type of person has; then, the people who share those characteristics can be sorted into one group or the other.

In the following passage, a writer classifies people using a very unusual category:

> It's very easy to classify people and decide whether I'll get along with them or not based on the way they respond to my cat. Some people immediately get down on the floor and begin to make silly noises—"cluck-cluck" and "Pwetty wittle pussy cat." My cat Zera is insulted. Others try to pretend that there isn't a cat in the house, even after Zera leaps on their shoelaces. She knows when she is being ignored. Some are really afraid of cats; unfortunately, Zera knows that, too. Still others will simply stretch out a hand in greeting— Zera's and my favorite type.
>
> Teresa Mackie, student

In the next example, the writer classifies the ways in which people age:

> Man ages in three ways: biologically, psychologically, and socially. One can view an individual as having three ages in accord with the three main processes of aging. His biological age can be defined by the years of remaining life or the extent to which he had "used up" his biological potential for length of life. His psychological age can be defined by the level of his adaptive capacities. His ability to adapt to his environment depends upon his accuracy and speed of perception, memory and learning and reasoning, to mention a few. Man's social age can be defined by the differentiated social roles he leads in society. These ages are mutually dependent upon one another and yet one knows from commonplace experiences that individuals may vary somewhat in their relative youth and age in their major dimensions of existence.
>
> James E. Birren, "Psychological Aspects of Aging: Intellectual Functioning"

How to Use Classification in Your Writing

Setting up a classification strategy in a paper can be tricky. Writers sometimes think it is enough simply to say that the paper will discuss "three things," which they then name. But that approach is weak, because readers are left to wonder *why* those "three things" are important or interesting. Why should they want to read about them?

Consider this statement:

> I have three major problems in my freshman year: not enough privacy, not enough time, and not enough money.

This statement does set up a classification; we know that the paper will cover three things that the writer lacks (privacy, time, and money). But the statement doesn't really lead anywhere. (Why not name four problems? Or five?) It sets up a classification, but that's all it does. A better lead-in might be:

> The three major problems I have as a freshman—too little privacy, time, and money—show that I am learning to handle my independence.

Now we have a good idea of why the writer wants to tell us about these problems, and we have a good idea of where the paper is going. This is a better classification statement because it gives a structure for the paper, and it tells us why we might be interested in these categories of problems. In setting up a classification, try to make a statement that answers the question, "*Why* are the categories I'm talking about important?"

Keep in mind, too, that the categories of a classification system can often be subdivided into subcategories. "Ethnic Food," for example, is the beginning of a classification; its categories might be "Italian," "French," "Mexican," and "American" cooking. But each of these categories includes many subcategories, depending on the writer's definitions and purposes. "American Cooking" might be classified by regions ("Southern," "Yankee," "West Coast," and so on). Or it might be classified by types ("Main Courses," "Soups," "Desserts"); or by nutritional information ("Proteins," "Carbohydrates," "Fats"); or by *any* classification system the writer sets up.

The point is that you should define your system clearly, and be sure that its categories fit that system. If your paper is going to be about the "Varieties of Barbecue," don't mislead your readers by setting up a classification that is too broad, such as "Foods of the World." Nearly everything can be subdivided in some way, and so you want to find the system that focuses on the categories you intend to discuss.

The most useful classification system is one that divides your subject into only a few categories. A good way to discover a system is to use the technique of listing (see Chapter 2). As you list all the possible categories under your main heading, you will be able to see which ones actually have things in common and fit under that heading. By listing categories, you may discover that your real topic is different from the one you set out to explore.

Reading and Writing Assignments ■

1. On the right-hand side of your journal, summarize what the strategy of classification is, and list some ways that you can apply it in your own writing.

2. Look for some examples of classification in the passages included in this book. Share these examples with your classmates, and record what you learn on the right-hand side of your journal.

3. On the left-hand side of your journal, write a short passage that uses the strategy of classification to show what several things have in common and how they are related.

Cause and Effect

In using a strategy of **cause and effect,** a writer traces how and why one thing led to another, trying to show which causes produced which effects. Thus, a cause-and-effect strategy shows the relationship between one thing and another.

Although it is sometimes easy to say *what* happened, it is often more difficult to say *how* and *why* it happened. In a history course, for example, you might study the events of the Vietnam War—its important dates, people, battles, treaties, and so on. Such factual information comes under the heading of *what* happened (effects). But to determine the *causes* of those events and how they affected people in Vietnam and throughout the world is much more difficult. To take a more personal example of cause and effect, you may know what you want to major in and what you want to do when you finish school, but can you trace the reasons *why* you have those goals?

The following passage takes a cause-and-effect strategy to examine anorexia (an aversion to food resulting from some personality disorder). As you read, try to keep track of the various causes and effects that the writer identifies:

The typical anorexic girl comes from a two-parent family of middle- or upper-middle-class status. Her mother has read all the correct books on how to be nurturing and loving without smothering the child's initiative. Her father, an ambitious, upwardly mobile, and driving individual, often participates actively in establishing the household's norms. . . .

Bruch: Hilde Bruch, an expert in anorexia
narcissistic: self-involved

How is it that a good girl raised by well-meaning and concerned parents becomes so dangerously ill? In Bruch's view . . . the girl always lived for others, judged herself by their standards, and let them define her identity. Raised to strive for perfection and to seek approval from narcissistic parents, she now is able to set for herself a daily, relentless, physically torturing challenge, one over which she alone has control. The immediate cause of her desperate choice may be a lower than expected grade at school or it may be the onset of bodily maturation, the uncontrollable fattiness of developing breasts and rounding hips, or it may be a disgusting sexual encounter, but it is the underlying psychological need to gain a sense of self that is the essence.

The anorexic girl feels hopelessly inadequate and ineffective in dealing with others—parents, friends, teachers, psychiatrists. And yet she has become master of herself. Regardless of what others see and prefer, she sees her emaciated appearance as normal and likes it very much.

Rudolph M. Bell, *Holy Anorexia*

Notice that the writer is trying to draw a general profile of the anorexic girl by first describing the sort of family background that contributes to or helps to cause the disorder. Then, the writer moves on to the effects that such a background may have on the girl's attitude toward others. Finally, we see the main psychological effect of anorexia—the girl believes that she has managed to gain some control over her life by denying herself food.

How to Use Cause and Effect in Your Writing

As a writing strategy, cause and effect may be used to support just one important point in an essay, or it may be used to organize and develop the entire essay (as in the passage about anorexia).

If you choose to write an entire essay based on cause and effect, the technique of listing is again very useful (see Chapter 2). After you choose a topic, list all the causes and effects you can think of, and then develop your ideas through some freewriting. This approach will help you discover which causes and effects are really important, and which are really related.

Cause and effect is a good strategy if you want to describe something that happened to you or something that you observed. You can also use it to explore beliefs that you have held for a long time—try to determine what those beliefs are based on. For example, if you belong to a political party (or to a campus organization), you might examine what caused you to join in the first place. Perhaps it has happened that you no longer believe in something that once seemed true— or are no longer interested in something that once fascinated you. You can use cause and effect to trace why your beliefs or feelings changed. You might write a humorous paper to show how some mistaken idea you held about a cause and effect led to a belief or superstition. (For example, does a black cat's crossing your path *result in* bad luck? Or is it just a coincidence?)

A cause-and-effect strategy can be used in many ways. Here are some examples:

— *Single cause, single effect:* I forgot to turn the iron off, and I burned myself when I reached for it.
— *Single cause, several effects:* Now that I have a good job, I don't have to worry about paying the rent; I can afford the beach house this summer; and I can join a gym.
— *Single cause sets off a sequence of events:* Because I got a bad grade on that exam, I drove home too fast, which caused a traffic officer to stop me and give me a ticket, which caused my folks to yell at me, which caused me to take it out on my little sister, who then cried.
— *Several causes, one effect:* I'm in a bad mood today because I got up late, missed the bus, forgot my umbrella, and had to walk in the rain.

Reading and Writing Assignments   ■

1. On the right-hand side of your journal, summarize what the strategy of cause and effect is, and list some ways that you can apply it in your own writing.

2. Look for some examples of cause and effect in the passages included in this book. Share these examples with your classmates, and record what you learn on the right-hand side of your journal.

3. On the left-hand side of your journal, write a short passage that uses the strategy of cause and effect to describe something that happened or to explain why you no longer hold a particular belief.

Process Analysis

Basically, an analysis of a process is a description of how something is done. An *analysis* divides something whole into its parts, and then it investigates each of those parts. As human beings, we constantly analyze things, seeking to understand "what makes them tick." By taking things apart—whether an object, an idea, an event, a person, or a process—we hope to learn why they are as they are. Although we can attempt to analyze anything, our purpose in this section is to analyze a *process*—the step-by-step stages of an ongoing activity.

(The writing process itself, for example, can be analyzed step-by-step—from planning, to drafting, to revising, to editing.)

As a strategy for writing, a **process analysis** presents an orderly, chronologically arranged description of how the steps in a process take place. Any kind of process can be the subject of analysis: how a painting is made (creative); how a lawnmower works (mechanical); how a president is elected (political); how slang develops (social); how inflation occurs (economic); how Hawaii became a state (historical). In all these examples, some kind of process occurs, step by step. A process analysis takes the whole thing apart by examining each of its steps, in order.

The following writer, who teaches people how to draw, uses the strategy of process analysis to give instructions for drawing hair:

> Students often ask me to show them "how to draw hair." I think that what most beginning students mean by that is, "Show me a way to draw hair that is quick, easy, and looks terrific." . . . The way to draw hair is exactly like the way to draw anything: you must perceive the hair as it is, in all of its complexity, and draw what you see. This doesn't mean that you will draw every hair, but it does mean that you must take the time to describe in your drawing at least part of the hair—to show the exact movement of the strands, the exact texture of at least some section of the hair. Look for the dark areas where the hair separates and use those areas as negative spaces. Look for the major directional movements, the exact turn of a strand or wave.
>
> Betty Edwards, *Drawing on the Right Side of the Brain*

The writer wants to teach two lessons here. The first is a lesson in the correct attitude toward drawing. She wants to persuade a would-be artist that "the way to draw hair is exactly like the way to draw anything: you must perceive the hair as it is, in all of its complexity, and draw what you see." Second, the writer does want to inform—a reader could follow her directions and begin to draw hair.

A freshman wrote our next example, analyzing what kind of equipment a camper needs:

> To be properly prepared, you must know the basic items to take with you, such as warm clothes and good boots. A few years ago, I went on a trip to the mountains and forgot to pack my jacket. The temperature dropped from 70 to 40 degrees. By the time the weekend was over, I figured out a good motto: "It is better to pack something and not need it than to not pack it and need it." At all times of the year, a poncho or raincoat with a warm lining should be packed. It should be placed in the top of your pack so it will be easy to get to if you run into some rain while hiking. Bring good hiking boots so that

you won't get blisters. Nothing ruins a camping trip more than having to sit by the campfire soaking your feet while your friends explore the woods.

John Hoyle, student

Notice that this writer, like the previous one, directly addresses the reader. He does this because he intends for the audience to follow his directions. (Do you think this paragraph is more effective or less effective than a simple list would be?) Notice that this textbook also addresses you, the reader, directly; as the author, I hope that you will follow some of my suggestions.

How to Use Process Analysis in Your Writing

One difficulty of process analysis is dividing the process into logical stages and making sure each stage is described accurately. If one link in the chain is weak, if one step is left out or described poorly, the entire explanation can confuse the reader.

Another difficulty is deciding what to leave *out* of your description of a process. You just can't get everything into a paper when the steps of a process are very complex (with dozens, or hundreds, of stages); it would be impossible to analyze each step. First outline the steps in the process, and then decide which steps are essential for your purpose.

Process analysis, like other strategies, can be used to support a single important point in a paper, or it can be the basis for the entire paper. It's an extremely useful strategy for informative writing—if your purpose is to explain how to do something. But process analysis and the other strategies are not tied to any one purpose. You, the writer, decide which approach will be most effective given your audience and purpose.

Reading and Writing Assignments

1. On the right-hand side of your journal, summarize what the strategy of process analysis is, and list some ways that you can apply it in your own writing.

2. Look for some examples of process analysis in the passages included in this book. Share these examples with your classmates, and record what you learn on the right-hand side of your journal.

3. On the left-hand side of your journal, write a short passage that uses the strategy of process analysis to explain how to do something.

Writing Assignment ■

Take a moment to review what you learned in this chapter. What did you learn about writing strategies? Do you understand how to use each one? On the right-hand side of your journal, summarize what you learned about the five strategies discussed in this chapter.

chapter 14 ∎

The Essay Examination

Your days of taking essay examinations are likely to end once you leave college. Occasionally, government agencies or private companies may require job applicants to take an essay exam. But even if you never do have to take another essay exam after graduation day, the skills you learn in preparing for and taking such exams in college will help you with any writing you do in the future.

An **essay examination** forces you to confront a subject. Within a specified period of time, you must reflect on what you know and demonstrate it by writing a well-organized essay. This tests your ability to think and write clearly as much as it tests your knowledge. In many cases, you will have only a general idea of the questions to be asked; you will not be able to use any notes or source materials in the exam, and you will not get a chance to revise your essay after you have handed it in.

Despite the common student folklore that says all-nighters are a necessary part of college life, research shows that studying all night for an essay exam seldom makes up for not having studied during the term. All-nighters may be somewhat useful in memorizing facts for an objective test (multiple-choice or true/false), because cramming can improve short-term memory (assuming you can stay awake to use it). But it also is usually true that students who cram for an exam quickly forget what they have learned. That's why we call it "short-term memory"—facts learned in this manner can only be retained for a little while.

When it comes to essay exams, cramming cannot provide the reflection, organization, good judgment, and creativity that you will need. If you know that an essay exam is coming up, either at midterm or at the end of the course, your best strategy is to keep up with assigned reading, review your class notes often, and pay special attention to the material that your teacher has emphasized.

Preparing the Material

While it never hurts to have a good memory, in an essay exam nothing replaces a thorough understanding of the required material. When you know your subject matter, you can shift facts and ideas around in your mind and organize them in different ways—which, in turn, enables you to answer a variety of questions. Someone who has simply memorized information tends to view that information from one narrow perspective; but someone who *understands* a topic is able to look at it from a variety of perspectives. The student who understands a topic is not thrown off balance by an unexpected question, or by one that is phrased in an unusual way.

Don't get caught at the end of the term staring helplessly at a bulging notebook filled with various handouts and old quizzes. Instead, take time during the course—say, once every week or two—to outline and summarize your class notes and any handouts. If you wait until the end of the term, you may find that your notes have gaps, or that you are behind in your reading. Even if you have kept up, you will have to make some choices. Since you can't prepare *all* the material that was covered, decide how much you can reasonably prepare. Develop a strategy well before exam time.

As you go through your notes, you may want to use different-colored pens to jot down observations and comments and to underline key details and summary statements. You may find it helpful to reorganize some of your notes. This might allow you to compare material more easily, or to see causes and effects more clearly.

Most disciplines have a specialized vocabulary and a set of definitions, and your teacher will undoubtedly point many of these out. Knowing basic terms and their meanings will make it easier for you to understand lectures and required readings, and to talk and write about the subject with greater authority.

Making lists of details—important names, places, events, and dates—is often helpful. It is one thing to discuss a topic in general terms, but solid details and examples will show that you really grasp the material. Any argument that you make in an essay will be much stronger when you provide factual support for your ideas. Readers will look for evidence that your point of view is accurate, reasonable, and believable.

Exam Anxiety

It's not unusual to be nervous when you have to write something in a short period of time. But if you practice taking essay exams, you should be able to lessen the negative effects of test anxiety. It will certainly be helpful for you to study old tests, if you are allowed to see them. (Do not assume, of course, that your teacher will ask the same questions; be prepared to answer a variety of questions.) Practicing with old essay exams should make you more comfortable with the testing situation.

If the exam will be given in a place other than your regular classroom, it's a good idea to visit the location and get familiar with it. And, as trite as it sounds, you would be foolish not to get a good night's sleep before the exam. Get up early, eat a decent breakfast, and—if you think it will help—wear your lucky sneakers, scarf, or T-shirt. Go early to the test site, and pick out a good seat. Remember to bring extra pens; pencils, paper, erasers—and maybe even a candy bar or a piece of fruit.

Writing the Exam

Once the exam starts, stay calm. Take deep breaths if you have to; try to relax your body. It is too late to panic, and, besides, panic may cause you to forget what you so carefully studied. You might want to make some quick notes to yourself *before* reading the exam questions, simply to recall vital information. (*Do not write anything* until the teacher signals that the exam has begun.)

Now it is time to read the exam questions. Read the entire exam, all the way through, and read carefully. Make sure that you fully understand the test's directions before you begin writing. Ask your teacher to clarify any questions that you don't understand. Check whether your teacher has weighted the questions: Is each one supposed to take the same amount of time? Is each question worth the same number of points? Or are some parts of the exam more important than others?

Make mental (or written) notes about the questions, picking out the ones you can answer most easily. Jot down any key words, crucial facts, important concepts, or inspired thoughts that come to mind at this point. Save for last any questions that you think will be difficult. You may find that the easier questions help you to recall information that you need for the more difficult questions. The mind is like a computer file, and it often happens that one question will remind you of facts and ideas that you had forgotten.

Answer the questions in clear, direct language. Give simple, straightforward explanations, and provide supporting details and examples. Don't "pad" your answers—teachers find this annoying, and they can tell when you're making things up. Illegible handwriting designed to obscure a fuzzy answer rarely fools a teacher, either. If you know that your handwriting is hard to read, show a sample of it to your teacher at least a day before the exam; your teacher may want to make some special arrangement if your handwriting is especially bad. Be sure to leave some space after each answer so that you can add material later if you want to. This will save you the trouble of drawing arrows and asterisks all over your exam as you attempt to add sentences.

If you decide to answer questions out of order, be sure to mark their numbers clearly, so that your teacher cannot possibly miss them. (Again, it is best to ask beforehand whether you will be allowed to answer questions out of order.)

Look for key words and phrases in each essay question, and try to include them in your opening sentences. For example, if you are asked to discuss the causes of inflation in the United States in the 1970s, you might begin by writing: "Inflation in the 1970s was caused by three related factors. These were. . . ." Or, if you are asked to state your view about the mandatory seatbelt law and to give examples of legislation concerning it, you might begin with: "Several states have already struck down mandatory seatbelt laws and, in doing so, have seriously underestimated. . . ."

If you use your first paragraph to summarize what you plan to cover in the essay, you will supply a helpful guide to your reader *and* make it less likely that you will wander off track. Organize your answer logically by briefly mentioning your main points early on; then, provide clear introductory sentences as you begin to discuss each new point.

If time is running out, and you know you can't finish answering a given question, write a short outline to show how you intended to answer it. Most teachers will give *some* credit for doing this (but don't expect full credit). Don't spend too much time on any one question; six partly completed answers may earn you more credit than three complete ones. But teachers have different practices when it comes to grading, and you should ask what your teacher prefers.

Try to leave time for editing, proofreading, and checking that you have answered each question fully. A few minutes of fine-tuning can make a fair essay good, or a good essay very good. In checking your answers, also look again at the questions. Be sure that you have actually done what the question asked you to do. Most teachers phrase their questions carefully, and they expect you to follow instructions carefully, too. Here is a list of key words often found in essay exam questions. Study their definitions:

Compare—List or describe similarities, resemblances, parallels; examine what two things have in common.

Contrast—Examine how things differ, how they are *not* alike.

Criticize—In an essay question, *criticize* usually does not mean "take a negative view of"; instead, it means "make a thoughtful, informed judgment about," "analyze."

Define—Explain something, based on known facts, accepted opinions, or informed theories.

Describe—Characterize; recount; picture in words.

Diagram—Make a graph, drawing, or chart; label its parts. The word *diagram* in an essay question may require you to furnish a brief explanation of your drawing.

Discuss—Examine in detail the pros and cons of something; compare and contrast.

Evaluate—Analyze, weigh, make an appraisal of something; examine its advantages and limitations; compare and contrast.

Explain—State how or why; discuss causes and effects; interpret; compare and contrast.

Illustrate—Define; explain; provide examples of something.

Interpret—Comment on something; analyze or explain it; make a judgment about it.

Justify—Prove something; provide evidence or show grounds for it; demonstrate the necessity of something.

List or enumerate—Arrange your answer in a numbered or itemized series.

Outline—Create an organized description of a subject's main points; systematically arrange the main points.

Prove—Confirm or verify something; demonstrate its truth, accuracy, or validity.

Relate—Show the connections, similarities, or relationships between things.

Review—Discuss; comment on; summarize.

Summarize—Make a brief description or outline of something; explain it without including too many details.

State—Explain; tell; report.

Trace—Describe the progress or historical development of something; talk about its causes and effects; outline its origins.

Writing Assignment ■

Following are some essay questions about topics you have covered in this book. Choose one of the questions, and prepare an answer for it as suggested in this chapter. First, review the chapter indicated in the question; then, outline how you would answer the question on an essay exam. In your outline, list any key terms, details, or examples that you would use in answering the question.

1. Chapter 2 says that reading is an active process, that readers "actively put words, sentences, and paragraphs together." Explain why "reading is hard work."

2. Diagram the writing process described in Chapter 2, and explain why "it is a dance, not a march."

3. Justify the value of keeping a journal (Chapter 1) or a grammar log (Chapter 9).

appendix 1 ■

Revision Worksheets

The following worksheets will guide you in revising drafts at different stages of the writing process. Some worksheets are designed to help you with early drafts—your first one or two, say—and others will help you with later drafts.

You don't have to use every single worksheet; in fact, since each covers different aspects of writing, you should decide which ones will be most useful for each draft. Your instructor can suggest which worksheets will work best for you. The worksheets have been modified by teachers and students over the years. You also should feel free to adapt them to fit your own needs.

There are two groups of worksheets here. Worksheets 1 through 6 will help you read your own drafts, while Worksheets 7 through 15 are designed to help you read your classmates' drafts. Since you are likely to use some worksheets more than once, you may want to write your answers in your journal (for Worksheets 1 through 6) or on a separate sheet of paper (for Worksheets 7 through 15).

In answering the questions, think of these worksheets as a framework for revising. If you are not sure where to start revising, the questions will prompt you and nudge you along. Remember as you use the worksheets that you are now reading your own writing for the purpose of revising it. This requires you to put some distance between yourself and the words you have drafted. When you wrote them, you were thinking like a writer; to revise, however, you must think like a reader. You must view your draft as you would view someone else's writing.

Do not respond to the questions with simple yes-and-no answers. Write thoughtful, complete answers, and try to make useful suggestions for revising the draft. Forget that the draft is your own. By reconsidering each idea and how it is expressed, you can help yourself to revise effectively.

worksheet 1 ■

Evaluating your first draft

Name of Writer _____

1. What does your draft really say? (Don't describe what you want it to say; instead, describe what is actually written on the page. A good way to do this is to list the main points that you find.)

2. What might your draft say, or what should your draft say? (Perhaps what you want it to say is still inside your head. Describe what you *want* it to say.)

Continue on next page.

3. What parts of your draft are most successful? Why? (List specific parts that you are satisfied with.)

4. What parts of your draft do you especially want to improve? Why? (Again, list specific parts.)

5. What do you need to do next? (Jot down some notes about how you might revise the draft to get it closer to what you want it to say. Ask your teacher or a classmate to read your draft at this point.)

worksheet **2**   ■

Focused questions for an early draft

Name of Writer ————————————————

1. What is your main point or main idea? Where have you best stated this? (Copy it out.)

   a. Revise the main idea to make it clearer.

   b. If you have not stated a main idea, write a brief summary of your draft.

   c. Turn your summary into a main idea that others can understand.

Continue on next page.

2. List the main examples and details that you have used in your draft.

a. In the above list, put a check mark near each item that is essential to make your point. Put a question mark near each item that might not be needed.

b. Can you think of any more examples or details that you should add? List them, and indicate where you would put them in your draft.

3. How has your idea of the audience changed since you began drafting? Write out a description of your readers. How much do they know about your subject?

Your sense of audience and your tone

Name of Writer ————————————————

1. Write out a description of your audience, and state why you want to reach this audience. (What is your purpose?)

a. What are your main assumptions about the audience? What do you think they know about your subject? How do you think they feel about it? (Point to places in the draft where your assumptions are revealed.)

b. What do you want your audience to think about you? (Point to places in the draft that reveal this.)

Continue on next page.

2. Look over your choice of words and the way you express yourself.

a. How have you revealed your attitude toward your audience?

b. How have you revealed your attitude toward your subject?

3. What is the main emotion in your voice? Are you angry, sad, resigned? Are you serious or humorous? Point to places in the draft that indicate your main emotion.

worksheet **4** ■

Evaluating a late draft

Name of Writer _____

1. Study the major divisions of your essay. (These may or may not be the same as paragraph divisions.)

a. Make notes about what you think are good transitions from one part to another.

b. Make notes about where you can improve transitions from one part to another.

2. Study the paragraphing of your essay, and notice how you move from one paragraph to another.

a. Make notes about what you think are good transitions from one paragraph to another.

b. Make notes about where you can improve transitions from one paragraph to another.

Continue on next page.

3. Study your introduction and conclusion. Are they interesting? Effective? Satisfying? Do they need work?

a. Make notes about how you might revise the introduction.

b. Make notes about how you might revise the conclusion.

Paragraphs and sentences

Name of Writer ⎯⎯⎯⎯⎯⎯⎯⎯⎯⎯⎯⎯⎯⎯⎯⎯⎯⎯

1.   Quickly look over the paragraphs in your essay. Are any of them very, very long? (Indicate where.) Have you written too many paragraphs with only two or three sentences in them? (Indicate where.)

a.   Should any of your long paragraphs be broken into two or more shorter ones? Make notes about how you might revise long paragraphs.

b.   Should any of your short paragraphs be combined into a single paragraph? Make notes about how you might combine paragraphs.

c.   Should any of your short paragraphs be expanded? Make notes about how you might expand short paragraphs.

2.   Next to each paragraph, in the margin, write a summary sentence saying what that paragraph is about. Then, reread these summary sentences.

a.   Does each paragraph say what you want it to say? Make notes about any paragraphs that should be revised.

Continue on next page.

b. Based on your summary sentences, is each paragraph closely related to the essay's main idea? Make notes about any paragraphs that could be cut.

c. Based on your summary sentences, would the paragraphs be more effective if they were rearranged? Make notes about how you might revise the order of your paragraphs.

d. Based on your summary sentences, is it easy to follow the transitions from one paragraph to another? Make notes about how you might revise your transitions.

3. Are the sentences in each paragraph arranged in a logical order? Have you provided clear connecting signals between them? Make notes about how you might revise the order or transitions of sentences within paragraphs.

4. Quickly look over your sentences to see whether they vary in length and type. Do you see any places where you have written a series of short, choppy sentences? (Indicate where.) If your sentences are all the same, can you expand or combine any of them? (Indicate where.) Make notes about how you might revise your sentences.

worksheet **6** ■

Editing your final draft

Name of Writer _____

1. Read your draft out loud, and mark any places where you stumble over words or have to stop to reread a sentence. These may be places that need editing. Make notes about how you might revise the parts that were difficult to read out loud.

2. Read your draft out loud a second time, and ignore the punctuation that is on the page. As you read, put a slash mark (/) where you think sentences ought to end. Then compare your slash marks with the actual punctuation you used. Review Chapter 11 to see if you need to revise any punctuation. Make notes about any punctuation questions that you have.

Continue on next page.

3. Review Chapter 12 to see whether your subjects and verbs agree, and whether your pronouns and antecedents agree. Check nouns and verbs to see whether the final *-s* and final *-ed* are used correctly. Make notes about any questions that you have.

4. Review your grammar log and your spelling log to see whether any of your personal troublespots show up in your paper. Make notes about any questions you have.

See your instructor at this point.

How to Read Your Partner's Draft

Your job in a writing workshop is to read and to respond to a classmate's draft in order to help her or him produce the best possible piece of work.

You will be asked to comment on different features of the drafts you read. However, you will not be asked to rewrite any portions of another student's essay. Instead, point to places where you have questions or need more information. Again, do not respond to questions on the worksheets with yes-and-no answers. Such answers will not be much help.

If you are unsure about the answer to a question, ask the writer for help. For example, you will be asked to sum up the main idea, but if you can't find one or figure it out, ask the writer.

A writer needs (and likes!) to be told what is right with his or her paper. Remember to let your partner know what you like about the paper.

Your teacher may pair you with a classmate, or may put you into small groups. Either way, the following guidelines apply.

Guidelines for the Reader

1. Set aside enough time to respond to your partner's draft. Plan on at least 20 to 30 minutes per paper.

2. Ask the writer to read aloud to you (or to your group). Mark your copy of the draft if you have one, or jot down notes to yourself so that you will remember what questions you have. Don't be nervous about silences. You do not have to respond immediately; give yourself some time to think. Keep in mind that both the writer and you might feel a little awkward at first. That's normal.

3. Ask the writer what questions he or she has about the draft. Where does the writer want help?

4. Respond orally first, before using a worksheet. What are *your* questions for the writer?

5. If you work in groups, try to pick up on comments from other members and expand on them. Encourage everyone to contribute, and give each person enough time to do so.

After the writer has answered your questions, move to the worksheets.

Guidelines for the Writer

1. Take notes about your readers' responses. Don't rely on memory. Ask questions about any responses that you don't fully understand.

2.   Expect to feel tense. Reading your own work aloud to one person, or to a small group, may feel strange at first.

3.   See the instructor for another opinion if you have questions about any suggested changes. After all, it is *your* paper.

4.   If you find that you are spending more time talking about your actual subject than about the paper, perhaps you need to do more writing, and more talking to *yourself*.

Writer and reader: Using writing strategies

Name of Writer _____

Name of Reader _____

1. Look over "Strategies for Writing" (Chapter 13) and the various passages by professional writers and students included in this book. In small groups, discuss how these writers use the strategies of definition, comparison, classification, cause and effect, and process analysis. Jot down some notes to prepare for the discussion.

a. Exchange your draft with a classmate, and look for places where he or she may have used one or another of the writing strategies in Chapter 13. How might your partner use a strategy more effectively? If your partner has not used a strategy, indicate where one might be used. Jot down your suggestions.

Continue on next page.

b. Then, look over your own draft to analyze your use of the writing strategies. Ask yourself how you might use a strategy more effectively. If you have not used a strategy, indicate where you might do so. Jot down some notes for revising.

worksheet **8** ■

Writer and reader: Introductions and conclusions

Name of Writer _____

Name of Reader _____

1. In Chapter 8, review the section "Reading Introductions and Conclusions," and look over the various passages included in this book. In small groups, discuss what you learn about writing introductions and conclusions. Jot down some notes to prepare for the discussion.

2. Exchange your draft with a classmate, and read only the first two sentences of the paper. How do they strike you?

_____ Very interesting; I want to read more.

_____ Not very interesting, but I'm curious.

_____ Not very interesting; I want to stop.

_____ Confusing; I don't know what to expect.

Read the rest of the first paragraph. What does the writer promise to do in the paper?

_____ The paragraph doesn't say.

_____ I can't figure it out.

_____ The writer tells me that (finish the sentence).

Continue on next page.

Did the introduction draw you in and help you anticipate what is to come? If not, what could the writer do to make the introduction more interesting and more helpful?

3. Now quickly skim the rest of the paper, and read the conclusion. Does the conclusion let you know that you've reached the end? How might the writer revise the conclusion to make it more effective?

4. Then, look over your own draft to analyze the introduction and the conclusion. Ask yourself the same questions: Is your introduction interesting? Confusing? Does it draw the reader in? Does it help the reader anticipate what is to come? Do you feel that the conclusion lets you know you've reached the end? Jot down some notes for revising.

worksheet **9**   ■
_____

Evaluating a classmate's first draft

Name of Writer ———————————————————

Name of Reader ———————————————————

1. What does the draft say? Describe the draft in a way that shows you understand what is actually written on the page. A good way to do this is to list the
main points that you find.

2. What general questions about the draft do you have for the writer? Are
there parts about which you want to know more?

Continue on next page.

a. What parts do you think could be left out?

b. What parts do you really like?

c. What parts confuse you?

3. What do you think the writer should do next? Make some suggestions about how the writer might revise to make the draft more effective for you, the reader.

Focused questions for an early draft

Name of Writer ⸺⸺⸺⸺⸺⸺⸺⸺

Name of Reader ⸺⸺⸺⸺⸺⸺⸺

1. What do you think is the main point or main idea? Indicate where the writer has best expressed this. (Copy it out.)

a. What questions do you have about the main idea?

b. What suggestions do you have for the writer to clarify or strengthen the main idea?

Continue on next page.

2. List the main examples and details that you found in the draft. Put a check mark near each item that helps you to understand the writer's point. Put a question mark near each item that might not be needed.

3. What examples or details might the writer add to the draft? Jot down notes, and indicate where the examples might be added.

4. Who do you think is the audience for this paper? Write a description of the intended readers.

5. Write a short comment indicating your reaction to the paper. What do you think has been done well? What do you think needs improvement?

worksheet **11**   ▪

Your classmate's sense of audience and tone

Name of Writer ————————————————————

Name of Reader ————————————————————

1.   Write out a description of the audience.

a.   What are the writer's main assumptions about the audience? Point to places in the draft where these assumptions are revealed.

b.   What suggestions do you have for the writer to get you more interested in the subject?

Continue on next page.

2. What impressions do you get of the writer? Point to specific places in the draft that give you these impressions.

3. Look over the choice of words and the way the writer expresses herself or himself.

a. How has the writer revealed his or her attitude toward the audience?

b. How has the writer revealed her or his attitude toward the subject?

4. What is the main emotion in the writer's voice? Is she or he angry, sad, resigned? Is the writer serious or humorous? Point to places in the draft that indicate the writer's main emotion.

Evaluating a classmate's late draft

Name of Writer _____

Name of Reader _____

1. Study the major divisions of the essay. (These may or may not be the same as paragraph divisions.)

a. Make notes about what you think are good transitions from one part to another.

b. Make notes about where the writer can improve transitions from one part to another.

2. Study the paragraphing of the essay, and notice the movement from paragraph to paragraph.

a. Make notes about what you think are good transitions from one paragraph to another.

b. Make notes about where the writer can improve transitions from one paragraph to another.

Continue on next page.

301

3. Study the introduction and conclusion of the essay. Are they interesting? Effective? Satisfying? Do they need work?

a. Make notes about how the writer might revise the introduction.

b. Make notes about how the writer might revise the conclusion.

worksheet **13** ■

Paragraphs and sentences

Name of Writer _____

Name of Reader _____

1. Quickly look over the paragraphs in the essay. Do any of them seem too long? (Indicate where.) Do too many paragraphs have only two or three sentences? (Indicate where.)

a. Should any of the long paragraphs be broken into two or more shorter ones? Make suggestions about how the writer might revise long paragraphs.

b. Should any of the short paragraphs be combined into a single paragraph? Make suggestions about how the writer might combine paragraphs.

c. Should any of the short paragraphs be expanded? Make suggestions about how the writer might expand paragraphs.

Continue on next page.

2. Next to each paragraph, in the margin, write a summary sentence saying what that paragraph is about. Check to see that your summary sentences match what the writer intended.

a. Is each paragraph closely related to the essay's main idea? Could any paragraphs be cut?

b. Could the order of the paragraphs be rearranged more effectively? Indicate where.

c. Is it easy to follow the transitions from one paragraph to another? Make suggestions about how the writer could improve transitions.

3. Are the sentences in each paragraph arranged in a logical order? Did the writer provide clear connecting signals?

4. Look over the sentences and see if they vary in length and type. If they are all the same, can you suggest how the writer might change or combine some? Do any paragraphs have a series of short, choppy sentences? Indicate where.

Final evaluation of a classmate's draft

Name of Writer ———————————————

Name of Reader ———————————————

1. Can you guess what the writer's purpose is? Write it out. (If you can't guess, ask the writer to describe it.)

2. Write out the main idea of the paper (it's usually in the first paragraph). If you can't find the main idea, write out what you *think* it is; then ask the writer if you're right.

3. Has the writer used enough examples and details to support the main points in the paper? If not, which parts of the essay need more examples and details?

Continue on next page.

4. Can you guess who the writer's audience is? Describe the audience. (If you can't guess, ask the writer to describe the audience.)

5. The following parts of the paper really need work:

6. The following parts of the paper are pretty good:

7. The following parts of the paper would be improved by some library work:

8. Final remarks:

worksheet **15**

Editing your classmate's final draft

Name of Writer ———————————————

Name of Reader ———————————————

1. Read the draft out loud, and mark any places where you stumble over words or have to stop to reread a sentence. These may be places that need editing. What suggestions can you make to your classmate?

2. Read the draft out loud a second time, and ignore the punctuation that is on the page. As you read, put a slash mark (/) where you think sentences ought to end. Compare the slash marks with the writer's actual punctuation. Do you have any suggestions for your classmate?

3. Examine each sentence for misspellings and grammar errors, and point them out to your classmate. Put your initials next to anything that you change.

A Case Study of a Paper in Progress

What follows is a history of an essay from first idea to final draft. The student, Mehegan O'Connor, is responding to Assignment 1, "The Language of Clothes," on page 181 (see Chapter 8, "Writing to Persuade"). Notice how Mehegan's ideas change as she writes and gets feedback from her teacher and her classmates. Although her final draft may leave you with some questions, it is a good illustration of what happens when a writer reads, writes, rereads, writes, talks, and writes again.

After Mehegan read the passage by Alison Lurie, she began the writing process with a journal entry and a class discussion. Then she drafted her paper.

First Journal Entry (Unedited)

Clothing and style not only gives friends, family, and strangers around you, some notion of your personality, but it also may and often does turn these people "on" or "off." People however related or not related to you, come to their own conclustion about the kind of person you may or may not be by what you wear, what you look like, and how you act. The conclusions can end up being false because of ones possible narrow mindedness, prejudice, or even naive"ness".

Luries theory makes sense to me. I know how I think about clothes—a guy in preppy cloths is not my type. So he speaks to me by wearing a Ralph Lauren shirt.

Notes on Group Discussion

We first read our journal entries and found that we said pretty much the same thing. So we decided to look at each others clothes in our group and make up stories based on dress. Some people thought it was fun, and others got mad I think. They said they were not like what we said because of their cloths. Richard said that isnt it interesting we think we shouldnt judge a book by its cover but we do anyway. Ms. Kelly came over and asked us if we could remember changing our minds about someone after we got to know them. We all had examples.

First Draft of Essay (Unedited)

Archaic means ancient or nolonger current. So archaic words are words that we dont use anymore, like forsooth. Another word we dont use anymore is icebox my grandmother uses it no matter how often we tell her its a refrigerator. I can see how in the language of cloths people can wear archaic things and then their out of style.

Being in or out is an important idea to young people in college. Though its not always easy to be in when you have to spend alot of money on clothes.

In Alison Luries Language of Cloths she says that cloths have a language of their own and can communicate things to us unconciously. Archaic clothes communicates several things to me. Sometimes, the person may not be able to afford the newest thing. Or dosent care about fashion. A person may be to busy developing her own style. I see alot of people wearing old clothes on purpose to make a statement. I have a baseball shirt that I wear that belonged to my older brother and I think its pretty cool so do my frieds. When I was little my mother says I refused to wear Oshkosh jeans. I guess I still dont like wearing jeans that much now when everyone wears them so tight. I want to be comfortable so I wear levies. To some people that is archaic because I dont wear Guess jeans.

I have many differnt attitudes about clothing and style because there are many different circumstances. Yet I can come to one conclusion and that is that people are judged or thought about before one has even met them just by what they look like. Sometimes this is the wrong thing to do especially if conclusions made are negative and demeaning. But today in America, it seems to be our nature and I'm sure it is the same other places. I come to a question though, why should it be like this—shouldn't the individual inside be the most important.

Toward a Revised Draft

After writing her first draft, Mehegan reread Lurie's passage and made the following notes in the margins of her draft:

I should try to use the following quote and connect to my idea about archaic clothes—

By the time we meet and converse we have already spoken to each other in an older and more universal tongue.

I should use more examples of archaic clothes and develope that idea more.

Mehegan's teacher looked over her draft and suggested that she use Worksheet 2, which she filled in as follows:

Focused questions for an early draft ■

1. What is your main point or main idea? Where have you best stated this? (Copy it out.)

how people react to archaic clothes unfairly

main idea: "Being in or out is an important idea to young people in college. Though its not always easy to be in when you have to spend alot of money on clothes."

a. Revise the main idea to make it clearer.

Being in or out is an important idea to young people in college. Though its not always easy to be in when you have to spend alot of money on clothes. Sometimes students get stereotyped because they wear last years clothes instead of the latest thing.

b. If you have not stated a main idea, write a brief summary of your draft.

c. Turn your summary into a main idea that others can understand.

2. List the main examples and details that you have used in your draft.

Oshkosh jeans
baseball shirt

a. In the above list, put a check mark near each item that is essential to make your point. Put a question mark near each item that might not be needed.

√ Oshkosh jeans
? baseball shirt (a good example, but it does not illustrate my main idea)

b. Can you think of any more examples or details that you should add? List them, and indicate where you would put them in your draft.

fashions like bicycle pants, leather coats, hairstyles, sneaker laces, surfer shorts—use these instead of the baseball shirt???

c. How has your idea of the audience changed since you began drafting? Write out a description of your readers. How much do they know about your subject?

I think my audience is people like myself who pay too much attention to fashion and who is wearing what. They know alot about fashion.

First Revised Draft (Unedited)

Archaic means ancient or nolonger current. So archaic words are words that we dont use anymore, like forsooth. (Another word we dont use anymore is icebox my grandmother uses it no matter how often we tell her its a refrigerator.) I can see how in the language of cloths people can wear archaic things and then their out of style. Being in or out is an important idea to young people in college. Though its not always easy to be in when you have to spend alot of money on clothes. Sometimes students get stereotyped because they wear last years clothes instead of the latest thing.

In Alison Luries *The Language of Clothes* she says that cloths have a language of their own and can communicate things to us unconciously. "By the time we meet and converse we have already spoken to each other in an older and more universal tongue." Archaic clothes communicates several things to me. Sometimes, the person may not be able to afford the newest thing. Or dosent care about fashion. A person may be to busy developing her own style. I see alot of people wearing old clothes on purpose to make a statement. I have a baseball shirt that I wear that belonged to my older brother and I think its pretty cool so do my frieds. When I was little my mother says I refused to wear Oshkosh jeans. I guess I still dont like wearing jeans that much now when everyone wears them so tight. I want to be comfortable so I wear levies. To some people that is archaic because I dont wear Guess jeans.

Clothing and style not only gives friends, family, and strangers around you, some notion of your personality, but it also may and often does turn these people "on" or "off." People however related or not related to you, come to their own conclusion about the kind of person you may or may not be by what you wear, what you look like, and how you act. The conclusions can end up being false because of ones possible narrow mindedness, prejudice, or even naive"ness".

People do communicate in the language of dress and style. I often come to my own beliefs about strangers I'll probably never meet and I sometimes make up stories about them. This is why "people watching", especially in New York City, is a fun thing to pass the time with when just sitting around. There are also some fun things we can discover or make-up people we look closely at or even through.

People today, especially students rely so much on what they look like and how they present themselves. Some try to look older, some younger; some try to be skinny and some don't care; some try to look sophisticated and some wild etc. We often classify people into groups just by what they are wearing and the style they present. For example, a big look right now is wearing tight black bicycle pants or leotards cut off below the knee with sneakers.

You dont even have to exercise. So if a girl wears a pair of sweat pants even if she is exercizing people dont pay attention to her. Guys use to wear loud colored "surfer" shorts all the time but not so much now. If you see a guy in surfer shorts you think he's not quite with it. Girls in my dorm want leather coats now instead of jackets and girls who have leather jackets feel they cant even wear them because coats are so popular.

This trying to make what you are out of what you wear is something that should come natural and should come from within your own self. You should be your own individual instead of tying to fit in to a group who all dress the same. Sure it's great to look nice or be in hang out clothes or be in dirty grungy closth or dress up real fancy, but all of that should come from your own personality.

I have many differnt attitudes about clothing and style because there are many different circumstances. Yet I can come to one conclusion and that is that people are judged or thought about before one has even met them just by what they look like. Sometimes this is the wrong thing to do especially if conclusions made are negative and demeaning. But today in America, it seems to be our nature and I'm sure it is the same other places. We put too much emphasis on the latest thing and people can be hurt because of it. I come to a question though, why should it be like this—shouldn't the individual inside be the most important.

Toward a Second Revision

After reading her paper to a small group of students in class, Mehegan made the following notes about what they said before she revised her draft a second time.

Maybe I could interview a few people to make it more interesting. I need to compare what L. says and own argument. Quotes:

Long before I am near enough to talk to you on the street, in a meeting, or at a party, you announce your sex, age and class to me through what you are wearing—and very possibly give important information (or misinformation) as to your occupation, origin, personality, opinions, tastes, sexual desires and current mood.

Moreover, as with speech, each individual has his own stock of words and employs personal variations of tone and meaning. . . .

The vocabulary of dress includes not only items of clothing, but also hair styles, accessories, jewelry, make-up and body decoration.

To choose clothes, either in a store or at home, is to define and describe ourselves. Occasionally, of course, practical considerations enter into these choices: considerations of comfort, durability, availability and price.

I repeat myself and have to cut things out.
I need a better introduction.

Second Revised Draft (Unedited)

The other day in class, a guy came in wearing a "Relax" t-shirt. Everyone use to wear these big t-shirts a few years ago when the band Frankie Goes to Hollywood was in. As soon as I saw him, I thought to myself, dosent he know that those t-shirts aren't cool anymore? I realized I didn't like him as much as before.

This is an example of what Alison Lurie says in *The Language of Clothes* she says that cloths have a language of their own and can communicate things to us unconciously. "By the time we meet and converse we have already spoken to each other in an older and more universal tongue." She also says:

> Long before I am near enough to talk to you on the street, in a meeting, or at a party, you announce your sex, age and class to me through what you are wearing—and very possibly give important information (or misinformation) as to your occupation, origin, personality, opinions, tastes, sexual desires and current mood.

I had labeled this guy as wearing archaic clothes. Archaic means ancient or no longer current but for people in college archaic can mean last years or last weeks style. I can see how in the language of clothes people can wear archaic things and then their out of style. Being in or out is an important idea to young people in college. Though its not always easy to be in when you have to spend alot of money on clothes. Sometimes students get stereotyped because they wear last years clothes instead of the latest thing. I think it's time that we stop worrying about clothes so much, or get better at understanding the language of cloths. Though Lurie says, "To choose clothes, either in a store or at home, is to define and describe ourselves," perhaps that is not so true. Perhaps we need to think about misunderstanding the language of clothes.

Archaic clothes communicates several things to me, and I realize that what they communicate may not be what the wearer intended. In fact, I may be putting my own interpretation on clothes. Sometimes, the person may not be able to afford the newest thing. Or dosent care about fashion. A person may be to busy developing her own style. I see alot of people wearing old clothes on purpose to make a statement. For example, I have a baseball shirt that I wear that belonged to my older brother and I think its pretty cool so do my frieds. When I was little my mother says I refused to wear Oshkosh jeans. I guess I still dont like wearing jeans that much now when everyone wears them so tight. I want to be comfortable so I wear levies. To some people that is archaic because I dont wear Guess jeans. Do people look at me in class and decide not to get to know me because I dont wear Guess jeans? I decided to find out what interpretation other people have of me.

I borrowed my girlfriends Guess jeans and took a picture of myself in them and then took a picture of myself in levies. I then asked friends and people in my Psych class which I looked better in and why. (I got the idea for this experiment in Psych.) A few people liked me better in Guess jeans but couldn't say exactly why. But one guy said I looked more sexy in the Guess jeans. When I pointed out that both jeans fit me about the same, he shrugged. People who didnt wear Guess jeans thought I looked better in my levis. When I asked why they said they didn't like Guess jeans or light colored jeans because they were *too* fashionable.

People today, especially students rely so much on what they look like and how they present themselves. For example, a big look right now is wearing tight black bicycle pants or leotards cut off below the knee with sneakers. You dont even have to exercise. So if a girl wears a pair of sweat pants even if she is exercizing people dont pay attention to her. This is a mistranslation. Guys use to wear loud colored "surfer" shorts all the time but not so much now. If you see a guy in surfer shorts you think he's not quite with it. Girls in my dorm want leather coats now instead of jackets and girls who have leather jackets feel they cant even wear them because coats are so popular. The girls are too aware of the message their clothes sends.

This trying to make what you are out of what you wear is something that should come naturally and should come from within your own self. You should be your own individual instead of trying to fit in to a group who all dress the same.

I have many differnt attitudes about clothing and style because there are many different circumstances. Yet I can come to one conclusion and that is that people are judged or thought about before one has even met them just by what they look like. Sometimes this is the wrong thing to do especially if conclusions made are negative and demeaning. But today in America, it seems to be our nature and I'm sure it is the same other places. We put too much emphasis on the latest thing and people can be hurt because of it. I come to a question though, why should it be like this—shouldn't the individual inside be the most important.

Toward a Third Revision

Mehegan then exchanged papers with another student, Tom. They both used Worksheet 14. Here are Tom's comments about Mehegan's draft.

Final evaluation of a classmate's draft ■

1. Can you guess what the writer's purpose is? Write it out. (If you can't guess, ask the writer to describe it.)

something about archaic clothes and misinterpretation. It's not clear, though.

2. Write out the main idea of the paper (it's usually in the first paragraph). If you can't find the main idea, write out what you *think* it is; then ask the writer if you're right.

> "Sometimes students get stereotyped because they wear last years clothes instead of the latest thing. I think it's time that we stop worrying about clothes so much, or get better at understanding the language of cloths. Though Lurie says, "To choose clothes, either in a store or at home, is to define and describe ourselves," perhaps that is not so true. Perhaps we need to think about misunderstanding the language of clothes."

3. Has the writer used enough examples and details to support the main points in the paper? If not, which parts of the essay need more examples and details?

I think you have used enough examples, but you need to explain them more.

4. Can you guess who the writer's audience is? Describe the audience. (If you can't guess, ask the writer to describe the audience.)

people who misunderstand clothes

5. The following parts of the paper really need work:

focus of paper and conclusion

6. The following parts of the paper are pretty good:

the introduction and the idea

7. The following parts of the paper would be improved by some library work:

I don't think you need to go to the library

8. Final remarks:

you have a good idea, and you should focus on it more

Mehegan then had a conference with her teacher. Part of their talk follows:

> *Teacher:* What do you like most about this paper?
> *Mehegan:* I think I have an interesting idea to contrast with Lurie's idea about clothes. But I can't get it right. Tom was right.
> *Teacher:* Does this mean that you aren't interested in archaic clothes any more?
> *Mehegan:* I guess so.
> *Teacher:* It's hard to cut out stuff from a paper that you've spent time on, isn't it?
> *Mehegan:* Yes. Do you think I should drop the archaic clothes?

Teacher: Can you use those parts to support your idea about misinterpreting the language of clothes?

Mehegan: I could make some changes . . . but why can't I write what I mean?

Teacher: Just try to tell me now what you mean.

Mehegan: Well . . . I was thinking about language and reading—you know, from the early part of the book—and I wanted to make a connection between cues and clothes.

Teacher: What connection do you see?

Mehegan: Like a reader makes interpretations, and it isn't just the text, but the reader and text . . . that's how clothes work.

Teacher: Sounds like you just said what you wanted to write. Write down what you just said! And think about Tom's suggestions about developing your ideas more when you revise. Remember, you don't have to fit in everything into one essay.

Third Revised Draft (Unedited)

Reading the Language of Clothes

The other day in class, a student came in wearing a Hawian shirt with flowers all over it, like someone out of a 50s movie. I couldnt figure out if he was nerdy or trying to be cool. As I looked at him some more, I noticed that he wore acid-washed jeans and white sneakers and his hair was longish but cut well. I decided he was wearing the shirt on purpose. But what if I had decided he was just nerdy and I had been wrong? I would not have received the message he wanted to communicate, but would have misinterpreted his clothes entirly. This probably happens more than we would like to think.

This is an example of what Alison Lurie says in *The Language of Clothes* that clothes have a language of their own and can communicate things to us unconciously. "By the time we meet and converse we have already spoken to each other in an older and more universal tongue." She also says:

> Long before I am near enough to talk to you on the street, in a meeting, or at a party, you announce your sex, age and class to me through what you are wearing—and very possibly give important information (or misinformation) as to your occupation, origin, personality, opinions, tastes, sexual desires and current mood.

Perhaps I was the victim of "misinformation." Being in or out is an important idea to young people in college. Though its not always easy to be in when you have to spend alot of money on clothes. Sometimes students get stereotyped because they wear odd clothes (cowboy shirts would be considered odd at my school) or last years clothes instead of the latest thing. I think it's time that we stop worrying about clothes so much, or get better at understanding the language of cloths. Though Lurie says, "To choose clothes, either in a store or at home, is to define and describe ourselves," perhaps that is not so true. Perhaps we need to think about misunderstanding or reading the language of clothes. Clothes can say more about the people who see them that about the people who wear them.

Clothes communicates several things to me, and I realize that what they communicate may not be what the wearer intended. In fact, I may be putting my own interpretation on clothes. Sometimes, the person may not be able to afford the newest thing. Or dosent care about fashion even if she does care about what people think. A person may be to busy developing her own style. I see alot of people wearing old clothes on purpose to make a statement. For example, I have a baseball shirt that I wear that belonged to my older brother and I think its pretty cool so do my frieds. But maybe if I wore it to school, students that I didnt know would laugh. Another example is that I want to be comfortable so I wear levies. To some people that is not cool because I dont wear Guess jeans. Do people look at me in class and decide not to get to know me because I dont wear Guess jeans? I decided to find out what interpretation other people have of me.

I borrowed my girlfriends Guess jeans and took a picture of myself in them and then took a picture of myself in levies. I then asked friends and people in my Psych class which I looked better in and why. (I got the idea for this experiement in Psych.) A few people liked me better in Guess jeans but couldn't say exactly why. But one guy said I looked more sexy in the Guess jeans. When I pointed out that both jeans fit me about the same, he shrugged. People who didnt wear Guess jeans thought I looked better in my levis. When I asked why they said they didn't like Guess jeans or light colored jeans because they were *too* fashionable.

People today, especially students rely so much on what they look like and how they present themselves. For example, a big look right now is wearing tight black bicycle pants or leotards cut off below the knee with sneakers. You dont even have to exercise. But the message she wants to send is that she is in good shape and does aerobics. So if a girl wears a pair of sweat pants even if she is exercizing people dont take her seriously? This is a mistranslation.

Girls in my dorm want leather coats now instead of jackets and girls who have leather jackets feel they cant even wear them because coats are so popular. These girls are too aware of the message their cloths sends.

I can come to one conclusion and that is that people are judged or thought about before one has even met them just by what they look like. Sometimes this is the wrong thing to do especially if conclusions made are negative and demeaning. We put too much emphasis on the latest thing and people can be hurt because of it. I come to a question though, why should it be like this—shouldn't the individual inside be the most important.

The Final, Edited Paper

Once Mehegan was satisfied with what her third revised draft said, she used Worksheet 6 and her grammar log to edit the paper. She also asked Tom to fill out Worksheet 15 to help her locate grammar, punctuation, and spelling errors. Finally, she took another close look at her wording choices, and she carefully prepared her final paper. As you read it, look back at Mehegan's first journal entry and her various drafts—her ideas have come a long way!

Reading the Language of Clothes

The other day in class, a student came in wearing a Hawaiian shirt with purple flowers all over it, like someone out of a 50s movie. I couldn't figure out if he was joking or not. However, as I continued to look him over, I noticed that he wore acid-washed jeans and white sneakers. His hair was long but cut well. I concluded that he was wearing the shirt on purpose. But what if I had decided the wrong way, and thought he was just a nerd? Would he have become just one more person to cross off my list of potential friends? I would not have received the message he wanted to communicate, and I would have misinterpreted his clothes entirely. This probably happens more than we would like to think.

Alison Lurie argues in *The Language of Clothes* that clothes have a language of their own and can communicate things to us unconsciously. She says:

> Long before I am near enough to talk to you on the street, in a meeting, or at a party, you announce your sex, age and class to me through what you are wearing—and very possibly give important information (or misinformation) as to your occupation, origin, personality, opinions, tastes, sexual desires and current mood.

Sometimes people can get stereotyped because they wear odd clothes (cowboy shirts would be considered odd at my school, for example) or last year's clothes instead of the latest thing. Though Lurie says, "To choose clothes, either in a store or at home, is to define and describe ourselves," perhaps that is not so true. Perhaps we need to think more about "reading" clothes. In other words, the same article of clothing can mean different things to different people, depending on who they are. Clothes can say more about the people who see them than about the people who wear them.

Clothes communicate several things to me, and I realize that what they communicate may not be what the wearer wanted to communicate. For example, a person might not be able to afford the newest thing. Another person might not care about fashion, even if she does care about what people think. A person may be too busy developing his or her own style. I see a lot of people wearing vintage clothes on purpose to make a statement. For example, I sometimes wear a baseball shirt that belonged to my older brother. I think it's pretty cool, and so do my close friends. But if I wore this shirt to school, maybe students that I didn't know would laugh at me. They would interpret it wrongly because of *their* idea of fashion.

Another example is the jeans that I wear. I want to be comfortable, and so I wear Levis. To some people, only Guess jeans are worth "reading." Do people look at me on campus and decide not to get to know me because I don't wear Guess jeans? I decided to find out what interpretation other people make of my Levis.

I borrowed my girlfriend's Guess jeans and took a picture of myself in them, and I also took a picture of myself in Levis. I then asked people in my Psychology class which jeans I looked better in, and why. (I got the idea for this experiment in Psychology class.) A few people liked me better in Guess jeans, but they couldn't say exactly why. But one guy said that I looked sexier in the Guess jeans. When I pointed out that both jeans fit me about the same, he shrugged. I noticed that people who didn't wear Guess jeans thought I looked better in my Levis. When I asked why, they said they didn't like Guess jeans or light-colored jeans because they were *too* fashionable. I learned that one pair of jeans could be read a number of different ways.

Young people today rely so much on what they look like and how they present themselves. For example, a big look right now is wearing sneakers with tight black bicycle pants or leotards cut off below the knee. These pants say, "I am in shape and I exercise." But women who never exercise wear them. The message they want to send is sometimes not the truth. If a woman wears sweat pants to exercise, does that mean that people don't take her seriously enough? This is an example of a misreading on their part.

For another example, some girls in my dorm want leather coats now, even though they already have nice leather jackets. They feel that they can't even wear their leather jackets anymore because they are "out." These girls are too aware of the message their clothes send. They want to be read in a certain way.

The obvious question is, "Shouldn't the individual inside be the most important thing?" This is the most important thing once people get to know each other. But most people, because they read each other's clothes the wrong way, miss out on a lot of good friendships.

*appendix*3 ■

Glossary

When you study a new subject, such as philosophy or economics or psychology, you learn a whole new set of terms—and, what is more, you expect to. You may groan over having to learn the meaning of *existentialism* (a philosophy that emphasizes individual freedom of choice in a universe perceived as meaningless), or *deficit spending* (borrowing money), or *schizophrenia* (a mental illness that is characterized by severe withdrawal from reality); but you accept the need to learn a new vocabulary because it will allow you to discuss important concepts.

Besides technical terms, you sometimes learn new uses for more common words. In philosophy, for example, you might learn that the word *subject* means "the essential nature of something as distinguished from its attributes"; in psychology, you might hear the word *affect* used as a noun to refer to a person's emotional state.

Perhaps you have never thought that there might be a specialized vocabulary in writing classes, other than such grammatical terms as *gerund* or *predicate*. However, composition teachers often use everyday words in particular ways. Thus, this glossary includes both grammatical terms and special uses of words used in composition courses. To learn more about these glossary terms, check the text discussion (page numbers are given in parentheses).

active voice (208)   A term which describes verb constructions that clearly show who is doing the action, as in the sentence "I did it." See *passive voice*.

adjective (212)   A word or group of words that adds details to nouns and pronouns. An adjective can be tested by its position in a sentence, as follows:

The _____ NOUN is very _____ .

Only an adjective will fit into both slots. Notice that adjectives usually come *before* a noun or pronoun.

An adjective can be made from verbs by adding *-ed* (called the past participle) and *-ing* (called the present participle). An adjective may be one word, or it may be a string of words.

adverb (213)   A word, phrase, or clause that adds details to a verb. (Many grammarians say that adverbs may modify adjectives, other adverbs, and sometimes an entire sentence.) Adverbs provide information about time, place, frequency, cause, and manner.

An adverb—more accurately, an *adverbial*—can be a string of words with a subject and a verb that is introduced by a one-word adverb.

analogy (258)   A type of comparison in which some difficult concept is compared with something more easily understood; the easier concept helps readers to grasp the difficult one. For example, a student who was learning about impressionist art compared looking at a painting by Monet to looking at a scene under water. Even if readers had never seen a Monet and did not know what impressionist art is, they would be able to imagine it through this analogy.

apostrophe mark (240)   The apostrophe mark (') has several uses in English.

(1) It takes the place of one or two letters when we make a contraction by joining two words. A word like *don't* is *do not* run together, and the apostrophe mark takes the place of the second *o*; *there's* is a contraction for *there is*; and *I'll* is a contraction for *I will*.

(2) It indicates the plural of a letter or a number: "I got three *C's* on my lab reports"; "His *I's* look like *7's*."

(3) When it appears with the letter *s*, the apostrophe indicates that a noun has a possessive quality, as in the singular *girl's* and the plural *girls'*. Note where the mark goes in relation to the *s*: singular = *'s*; plural = *s'*.

audience (27)   The reader whom you intend to reach; a sense of audience can often shape your writing. To say that your audience is "someone who would like to know more about this subject," or "someone who doesn't know anything about it," isn't very helpful, because you have to make revisions based on your idea of your reader. The better defined your audience is, the better focused your paper is likely to be.

auxiliary verb (246)   Sometimes called *helping verbs*, auxiliary verbs combine with other verbs to indicate time, voice, mood, and so on. English has a very limited number of auxiliaries:

> have, has, had, having
> be, is, are, am, was, were, been, being
> can, could, will, would, shall, should
> may, might, must, ought to
> do, does, did

The following are sometimes auxiliaries:

> have to, has to, had to
> get, gets, got
> keep, keeps, kept

Auxiliaries are sometimes in a negative form:

> dare not, need not

brainstorming (14)   A technique for discovering ideas. Sometimes, listening to other people will give you ideas for writing. When a group of people with a common problem to solve gets together and calls out their ideas—no matter how far-fetched or unrelated they seem—they are brainstorming.

broken sentence (227)   A sentence fragment which reflects thought that has been interrupted in some illogical way. Broken sentences are not found in formal writing. See *minor sentence* and *sentence fragment*.

case (238)   Left over from older forms of our language, case refers to the relationship between a pronoun and the verb. Is *X* doing the action (*subject case*), or having the action done to it (*object case*)? Case also shows the relationship that we call possession (*possessive case*). We don't have to worry about subject and object case when using nouns. Only pronouns still have cases, as follows:

Subject Case	Object Case	Possessive Case
I	me	my/mine
who	whom	whose
he	him	his
she	her	her

cause and effect (263)   A strategy for writing in which a writer traces *how* and *why* one thing led to another, trying to show which causes produced which effects. Thus, a cause-and-effect strategy shows the relationship between one thing and another. See Chapter 13.

classification (261)   A strategy for writing in which a writer examines three or more things and sorts them into categories based on similarities. See Chapter 13.

clause (210)   A part of a sentence that contains a subject and a predicate. Therefore, all sentences are clauses, because they also have a subject and a predicate. However, not all clauses are sentences.

A clause may function as a noun, an adjective, or an adverb in a sentence. If so, the clause will contain signal words (such as *who*, *which*, and *that*) to tell you that the clause it is not functioning as a sentence.

A clause that has a subject and a predicate but no signal words is called the *main clause* (or *independent clause*). But if a clause has a signal word plus a subject and a predicate, it is a *dependent clause* (or *subordinate clause*).

collective noun (236)   A noun that looks singular but may have a plural meaning, such as *people*, *committee*, *group*, *class*, *team*, and so on. A collective noun usually needs a singular verb, but sometimes it needs a plural verb.

comma splice (comma fault) (225)   A mispunctuated sentence in which two main clauses are joined by a comma only:

Freda played tennis all last summer, this year she has taken up raquetball.

This can be fixed by adding a *conjunction* after the comma, or by replacing the comma with a semicolon (;).

comparison (257)   A strategy for writing in which a writer looks at two similar things and explains how they are alike or different. See Chapter 13.

complex sentence (221)   A sentence that has one or more main clauses and one or more dependent clauses.

compound-complex sentence (222)   A sentence that has two or more main clauses and one or more dependent clauses.

compound sentence (220)   A sentence that has two main clauses, each with a subject and a predicate. A compound sentence is two or more simple sentences joined together, as in this example: "The cowhand rounded up most of the stubborn steers, but he lost three of them."

conclusion (173)   The final part of an essay, in which you let readers know you have finished saying all that you want to say.

conjunction (124, 126–127, 223)   A word that connects words, phrases, and clauses within a sentence, or that connects two sentences. The text covers many different kinds of conjunctions. See the pages noted for important discussions. Following are some examples of major types of conjunctions.

> **coordinating conjunctions**: and, or, but, for
>
> **correlative conjunctions**: both/and, either/or, neither/nor, not only/but also
>
> **conjunctive adverbs**:
>
>> *of result*—so, yet, therefore, consequently, as a result, thus, then, likewise, also
>> *of concession*—however, nevertheless, yet, at any rate, also
>> *of apposition*—namely, for example, that is
>> *of addition*—moreover, furthermore, also, in addition
>> *of time*—in the meantime, meanwhile
>> *of contrast*—instead, on the contrary, on the other hand
>
> **adverbial prepositional phrases**: in the meantime, on the contrary, on the other hand
>
> **subordinators**: after, although, because, before, if, since, when, while, etc.; and as if, as long as, as soon as, even though, in order that, provided that, etc.
>
> **relatives**: who, whose, whom, which, that, where, when, why

contraction (240)   See *apostrophe mark*.

coordinate conjunction (124)   See *conjunction*.

definition (254)   A strategy for writing in which a writer proceeds by explaining what a word or a concept means. See Chapter 13.

demonstrative pronoun (99)   A type of pronoun that can refer back to particular words or to whole phrases in a sentence. Examples include *this*, *that*, *these*, *those*.

dependent (subordinate) clause (210)   A clause that has a subject and a predicate plus a signal word which tells you that the clause is *dependent* on the rest of the sentence for its meaning. See *clause* and *main clause*.

double-entry journal (4)   A journal in which a writer writes on side-by-side pages. It is both a personal journal and a place to record notes about your reading and writing.

editing (45)   The process of fine-tuning the grammar, spelling, and punctuation of a paper without really changing its basic ideas or structure. As shown in Figure 1 (page 46), we do both editing and revising during all stages of the writing process. See *revision*.

essay (76) An essay is a brief prose discussion of a particular topic; the writer takes a single idea as far as it can go in a few pages. An academic essay in a freshman writing class can be anywhere from 250 to 5,000 words long. An essay may examine a topic thoroughly or may investigate it only in a tentative, exploratory way.

One might define the essay by describing its overall structure: Most essays have an introduction, discussion, and conclusion. One can further describe the essay in a more formal, detailed way: An essay might have an introduction with a main idea (or thesis statement); a brief statement of supporting data, facts, or arguments; a transition to the main discussion, with examples; and a transition to the conclusion.

Another way to define the essay is to list its varieties. The most familiar kinds include a letter; a narrative of a personal experience; a description; a critique of a film, book, or restaurant; a continuing column in a newspaper; an editorial or an article in a magazine; a critical discussion in an academic journal; a sermon; a lecture. (It is important to note that many of the varieties of essays do not follow—or require—the structure described above.)

essay examination (269) A way to test knowledge through the medium of writing. An essay examination forces you to confront a subject, reflect on what you know about it, and demonstrate your knowledge by writing a well-organized essay within a specified time period. This tests your ability to think and write clearly as much as it tests your knowledge of a subject.

explanatory writing (117) See *informative writing*.

expressive writing (79) A type of writing in which the writer's purpose is to freely express his or her personal recollections, ideas, and observations. Examples include letters, diaries, journals, autobiographies, and prayers. A narrative or description is also usually expressive, since a storyteller or observer puts it in his or her own words. See Chapter 6.

focus (50) A clear center of interest in an essay. Once the topic has been narrowed down, the essay has a focus for both the writer and the reader.

form (27) The *type* of writing you decide to do—whether an essay, a report, a letter, a poem, and so on.

freewriting (13) A technique for discovering ideas. Freewriting is writing without worrying about correctness or subject matter. When you are freewriting, don't stop and stare off into space—just keep going, even if you simply repeat yourself, and even if you write over and over, "I can't think of anything to write; I can't think. . . ."

generic (36) A word that includes all members of a group, regardless of their characteristics. The pronouns *he*, *him*, and *his* are used generically when they are intended to include both men and women. Many people argue that generic pronouns and words like *mankind* and *businessman* are sexist, because they ignore the role of women in society.

gerund (207) A noun that is formed from a verb plus *-ing*, as in the sentence "*Laughing* is good for you."

grammar log (195) A written record of any errors you often make in your writing. See Chapter 9.

independent clause (210) See *main clause* and *clause*.

infinitive (205) The form of the verb that contains no time—no past, present, or future. It is formed with *to* plus the verb, as in *to swim*.

infinitive phrase (210) A phrase that is formed from a verb but functions as a noun, as in "*To swim well* is my goal."

informative (explanatory) writing (117) A type of writing in which the writer's main purpose is to convey information. See Chapter 7.

introduction (169) Sometimes called a *lead* or *lead-in*, an introduction gets readers into the essay. It may include the main idea, or background information, or an anecdote.

lead, lead-in (169) See *introduction*.

local (specific) detail (64, 69–70) In any kind of essay, details and examples help to clarify your general ideas, to explain the nature or character of something, and to support your opinions. *Local detail*—that is, the particulars of the thing, place, person, or idea that you are writing about—creates a mental picture that readers can visualize.

logic (178) Logic is sound and adequate critical thinking: getting from A to B without any wrong turns.

main (independent) clause (210) A clause that has a subject and a predicate and can stand alone as a sentence. A main clause may have one or more dependent clauses attached to it. See *clause* and *dependent clause*.

main idea (50) Also called a *thesis*, a main idea tells the reader *why* you are writing about the subject. It states your purpose for writing.

A main idea must go beyond stating the obvious so that readers won't say, "So what?" For example, in one of C. S. Lewis's stories for children, "The Voyage of the Dawn Treader," the narrator says:

Indeed most of [their] remarks were the sort it would not be easy to disagree with: "What I always say is, when a chap's hungry, he likes some victuals," or "Getting dark now; always does at night," or even "Ah, you've come over the water. Powerful wet stuff, ain't it?"

minor sentence (227)   A phrase or clause that has become separated from the main clause, either deliberately or through mispunctuation. Minor sentences are found in many contemporary essays and novels. Writers of advertisements use them to create short, snappy, dramatic sentences. See *broken sentence* and *sentence fragment*.

modifier (212)   A word or group of words that adds details to a noun or a verb. Sometimes called *qualifiers* or *limiters*, modifiers answer questions like Where? Which? When? Why? How? How much? Under what conditions? Basically, *adjectives* modify nouns and pronouns, while *adverbs* modify verbs.

nonrestrictive clause (230)   A clause that is set off by commas because it simply modifies the main clause. See *restrictive clause*.

noun (207)   A noun is traditionally defined as a word or group of words that *names* things. It often can be found by other words that signal it (like *a*, *an*, *the*, and so on) or by parts of words that signal it (like *-ion*, *-ment*, *-ance*, *-al*, *-y*, *-ure*, *-er*, *-ness*, *-hood*, and so on).

Nouns can be made plural and they can function as a possessive or as the subject or object in a sentence. When a noun is made by adding *-ing* to a verb, it is called a *gerund*; some regular nouns also end in *-ing*, such as *clothing*.

noun clause (211)   A group of words with a subject and a predicate that functions as a single noun. Such clauses can function as subjects or objects in a sentence, and they usually begin with *that*, as in "I see *that the bird outgrew its cage*."

object (204)   The part of a sentence that follows the verb and receives the action of the verb. Most words and phrases that follow the verb are called the object of the sentence.

organization (55)   See *unity*.

paragraph (59)   A way to signal small beginnings and endings. Paragraphs organize your material into logical, manageable units. There is no formula to determine how long a paragraph should be. A paragraph may be one word long or may even cover several pages, depending on the effect a writer wants to create. Think of paragraphing as part of the revision process—not as part of drafting.

participial phrase (210) See *verbal*.

parts of speech (204) Since the middle of the nineteenth century, conventional grammar books have referred to word classes as the "parts of speech." The traditional classes of words are *noun, pronoun, adjective, verb, adverb, preposition, conjunction*, and *interjection*. (An interjection is some sort of short remark or noise, like Oh! or Hee-hee!)

You probably learned this classification system and are used to thinking about words as parts of speech. However, it is more accurate to classify words (1) by their *form*—what they look like, and what changes they go through; and (2) by their *function*—how they work in a sentence.

Many words do not change at all in form, but their function changes:

He *dishes* (verb) up wonderful Cajun *dishes* (noun).

Some words change in form, but not in function:

I *walk* downtown every day.
I *walked* downtown.
A *scarf was draped* over the arm of the chair.
Scarves were draped over the arm of the chair.

Sometimes, the best way to classify a word is both by how it looks and by how it functions.

passive voice (208) A verb construction that reverses the order of subject plus predicate so that the predicate comes first.

The passive version of the sentence "I did it" is "It was done by me." The order is predicate plus subject. Notice that the passive voice of the verb changes the subject from *I* to *by me*.

The passive voice weakens writing when it adds unnecessary padding to sentences. Many readers object to the passive voice because it seems that the writer hides behind it or uses it to avoid responsibility. See *active voice*.

persuasive writing (161) A type of writing in which the writer's purpose is to urge readers to take some direct action (to vote in a certain way, for example) or simply to stop and think about an issue (such as air pollution or drug abuse). Some common types of persuasive writing are advertisements, political speeches, sermons, and editorials. See Chapter 8.

phrase (210) A group of two or more words that forms a unit and expresses a meaning. Common types are *prepositional phrases* ("*toward* the teacher"); *infinitive phrases* ("*to dance* divinely"); and *verbal*, or *participial*, *phrases* ("*running* to work"). A phrase is never a sentence, ever though it may contain a word formed from a verb.

possessive pronoun (99)   See *pronoun*.

predicate (204)   The predicate means the same thing as the main verb in a sentence—and more. In the sentence "The young but determined student passed all of her exams" the verb is *passed*. Grammarians would include some additional words in identifying the predicate: "all of her exams" are words that add information to the verb, and so they are therefore seen as part of the predicate "chunk."

preposition (210)   A word that links a noun or a pronoun to the rest of the sentence (*pre* = "before"; *position* = "place"). A preposition must be followed by a noun phrase (otherwise it is *not* functioning as a preposition).
  Here are the most common single-word prepositions:

> about, above, across, after, against, along, among, around, at, before, behind, below, beneath, beside, between, beyond, but (except), by, concerning, down, during, for, from, in, into, near, of, off, on, onto, out, over, past, regarding, since, through, throughout, till, to, toward, under, underneath, until, up, with, within, without

Some prepositions are phrases; common examples are

> along with, up to, but for, off of, out of, according to, because of, in accordance with, in connection with, in front of, in lieu of, in place of, in spite of, instead of, in regard to, on account of, on top of

prepositional phrase (210)   A phrase that includes a preposition and whatever follows it: *toward the teacher*.

pronoun (98, 206)   A word that stands for a noun or a noun phrase; the noun or noun phrase that the pronoun replaces is called the *antecedent*. Pronouns change *case* (page 238), and they substitute for nouns and noun phrases. Pronouns are a small, closed group, all of which are listed below.

personal pronouns:

I	we
you	you
he, she, it	they

pronouns by case:

subjective:	I	we	you	he	she	it	they
possessive:	my	our	your	his	her	its	their
	(mine)	(ours)	(yours)	(his)	(hers)		(theirs)
objective:	me	us	you	him	her	it	them

reflexive pronouns:

myself	ourselves
yourself	yourselves
himself, herself, itself	themselves

reciprocal pronouns:

each other (refers to two nouns)
one another (refers to three or more nouns)

demonstrative pronouns:

this	these	(near)
that	those	(distant)

relative pronouns:

who (possessive = whose; objective = whom)
which
that

indefinite relative pronouns:

whoever, whosoever, whomever, whatever

interrogative pronouns:

who (whose, whom), which, what

indefinite pronouns:

quantifiers: all, some, many, much, any, enough
specifiers: each, every, either, neither
    (sometimes: one, none)
some, every, any, no + body, thing, one

pronoun-antecedent agreement (236) A singular noun needs a singular pronoun, and a plural noun needs a plural pronoun; they must agree in number.

process analysis (266) A strategy for writing in which a writer describes the step-by-step stages of an ongoing activity. Basically, an analysis of a process is a description of how something is done. An *analysis* divides something whole into its parts, and then it investigates each of those parts. See Chapter 13.

purpose (74) A writer's intention or reason for writing in the first place. A writing assignment from a teacher may contain a built-in purpose; but writers often have to decide on a purpose for themselves, and it often changes as they explore ideas through the writing process.

This textbook emphasizes three important purposes:

— to *express* yourself in an imaginative or personal way (see Chapter 6)
— to *inform* someone or to explain something (see Chapter 7)
— to *persuade* someone to agree with you (see Chapter 8)

restrictive (defining) clause (230)   A clause that is not set off by commas because it defines the main clause. See *nonrestrictive clause.*

revision (45)   The process of rewriting a whole paper, of doing what we might call a complete overhaul. Editing focuses on matters like word choice, grammar, and spelling, while revision is the opportunity to rethink the content of a paper. See Figure 1 on page 46.

rhetoric (161)   The art of arranging language in order to change the way people think or feel, or to persuade them to go out and do something.

run-on sentence (225)   A mispunctuated sentence in which the two clauses run into each other without any punctuation at all. A run-on sentence is not one that "runs on" for too long; it is a sentence that is mispunctuated.

sentence (203)   Grammarians have offered the following definitions, of which the last seems most useful:

— A sentence begins with a capital letter and ends with a period.
— A sentence is a group of words that expresses a complete thought or idea.
— A sentence includes a subject, a verb, and sometimes an object.

sentence fragment (227)   A sentence fragment is not really a "sentence," because it is missing either the subject or the verb. A main cause of sentence fragments is that writers make sentences with things that look like verbs but don't completely function like verbs. See *broken sentence* and *minor sentence.*

simple sentence (219)   A sentence that contains a single main clause. See *compound sentence.*

strategy (253)   A way to shape the parts of an essay or the whole essay. Once you know what your main purpose for writing is—whether to express, to inform, or to persuade—you can begin to plan how you will achieve that purpose. Chapter 13 describes the chief strategies for shaping an essay: *definition, comparison, classification, cause and effect,* and *process analysis.*

subject (27)   The general idea or notion that a writer starts out with; the topic of a paper.

subject of a sentence (204, 206)   The part of a sentence that is the doer of the action implied by the verb (see *object*). The subject means the same thing as the main noun in a sentence—and more. The subject of the sentence "The young but determined student passed all of her exams" is *student*. But grammarians would also include some additional material in identifying the subject: "The young but determined" are words that describe the student, and so they are therefore seen as part of the subject "chunk."

subject-verb agreement (233)   A basic principle of English sentences is that subjects and verbs must *agree*, or share in, the same number. Singular subjects take singular verbs; plural subjects take plural verbs. Here are a few examples (the subject is underlined; the verb is in boldface):

Singular
>   After all, America **faces** an even bigger challenge in this sphere than Western Europe **does**. Because our divorce rate **is** enormously high, our family structure **is** much weaker than that typical of many Western European nations. . . .   (Hewlett)

Plural
>   The fact that languages (and *not* a single language, with many dialects) **are** at issue here must be emphasized from the outset. . . . The structural details of Indian languages **reflect** profound appreciation for the physical world and its natural order.   (Leap)

subordinate clause (210)   See *dependent clause* and *clause*.

subordinate conjunction (124)   See *conjunction*.

tense (245)   The term that indicates time relationships in grammar. For example, to show that something happened in the past, we usually add *-ed* to the verb: "I play*ed* hockey yesterday." But some verbs show tense another way: *break*, *broke*, *broken*.

thesis (50)   See *main idea*.

topic sentence (61)   The sentence that indicates the subject or main idea of the paragraph or provides a transition from one idea to another. A topic sentence is a very common signal for readers; it is a kind of glue that holds paragraphs together. The topic sentence points clearly to the subject matter of the rest of the paragraph. One can anticipate what will come next. However, just as some successful essays do not have a main idea, some paragraphs do not have topic sentences.

transition (54, 122)   A word or words that supply a connection between separate, unrelated ideas in a sentence or paragraph. With no transition from one part to the next, ideas may simply be *next to* each other, but they are not *connected to* each other.

unity (55)   Unity (or organization) is probably the hardest quality of a piece of writing to define. Readers who recognize unity in an essay will say things like "the writing flows" or "feels complete" or even that it "satisfies."

verb (207–208)   A word that shows action or a state of being. It has a special form, (*to* + *verb*) called the *infinitive*, which can never function as a verb, but only as a noun, an adjective, or an adverb. A verb can found by parts of words that signal it: *-ify*, *-en*, *-ate*, and *-ize* are the most common signals at the end of a verb.

The majority of verbs have *-s* and *-ing* forms. And most verbs take *-ed* to form the past tense; others are irregular (*break, broke, broken*).

Sometimes, what looks like a verb is not functioning as a verb. If it also appears to be a subject or an object, or if it appears to be modifying something in the sentence, then it is a *verbal*. In that case, it cannot be the verb of the sentence, and the phrase or clause cannot be punctuated as a sentence.

verbal (participial) phrase (210)   A verbal or participial phrase ("*running to work*") may look like a verb, but it does not act like a verb. Phrases are never sentences, even though they may contain a word that is formed from a verb.

writing process (19)   All the steps a writer goes through to arrive at a final paper (see Figure 1, page 20). These steps include *planning* (finding a topic, narrowing it down, and coming up with examples to support or illustrate it); *drafting*; *revising*; and *editing*. At any step in this process, the writer may find it helpful to leap ahead or backward.

When a writer begins to put sentences or even just ideas on paper, we can say that a rough draft is under way. The various drafts of an essay are a writer's acknowledgment that she or he has not finished making decisions about the paper to be. The writing process continues until the writer sees no reason to revise the paper further.

bibliography ∎

Bardwick, Judith M. "Dependency, Passivity, and Aggression." *Psychology of Women: A Study of Bio-Cultural Conflicts*. New York: Harper, 1971. 115–134.

Barnes, Julian. *Flaubert's Parrot*. New York: Knopf, 1985. 101.

Bell, Rudolph M. *Holy Anorexia*. Chicago: U of Chicago P, 1985. 17–19.

Better Hearing Institute. Advertisement in *Time* (Oct. 26, 1987): F3.

Birren, James E. "Psychological Aspects of Aging: Intellectual Functioning." Ed. Cary S. Kart and Barbara Manard. *Aging in America: Readings in Social Gerontology*. Van Nuys, CA: Alfred, 1976. 184–191.

Bolinger, Dwight. *Aspects of Language*. 2nd ed. New York: Harcourt, 1975. 25.

Boorstin, Daniel J. *The Discoverers*. New York: Random, 1983. xv, 472.

Boyer, Carl B. *The Rainbow: From Myth to Mathematics*. New York: Yoseloff, 1959. 17.

Bradley, Marian Zimmer. As quoted in Lois Rosenthal, "From the Mists Comes Marion Zimmer Bradley." *Writer's Digest* (June 1988): 40–42.

Brooks, Geraldine. "Australians Have a Devil of a Time Tracking (Extinct) Tasmanian Tiger." *The Wall Street Journal* (22 Apr. 1987).

Brunvand, Jan Harold. "Customs and Festivals." *The Study of American Folkore*. 2nd ed. New York: Norton, 1978. 244–258.

Burke, James. *The Day the Universe Changed*. Boston: Little, Brown, 1985. 11.

Chandler, Raymond. *The Big Sleep*. 1939. New York: Vintage, 1976. 1.

Chaucer, Geoffrey. *Troilus and Cresyde. The Works of Geoffrey Chaucer*. 2nd ed. Ed. F.N. Robinson. Boston: Houghton Mifflin, 1957. 401. (Book II.22–25)

Clark, Rev. Jonas. *Opening of the War of the Revolution*. Lexington, MA: Lexington Historical Society, 1901. 5–6.

Cost, Bruce. *Ginger East and West*. Berkeley and Los Angeles: Aris, 1984. 30.

Dawkins, Richard. *The Blind Watchmaker*. New York: Norton, 1986. 111.

D'Eloia, Sarah. "The Uses—and Limits—of Grammar." *Journal of Basic Writing* 1 (Spring–Summer 1977): 1–48.

Edwards, Betty. *Drawing on the Right Side of the Brain*. Rev. ed. Los Angeles: Tarcher, 1989. 162.

Erdoes, Richard, and Alfonso Ortiz, ed. *American Indian Myths and Legends*. New York: Pantheon, 1984. xiii.

Feldman, Robert S. *Understanding Psychology*. New York: McGraw, 1987. 170, 172.

Fields, Mamie Garvin, and Karen Fields. *Lemon Swamp and Other Places: A Carolina Memoir*. New York: Macmillan, 1983. xv.

Flint, Roland. "The Aging Mother at the Grandmother's Death Said" *and* from "Rosalind's Poem for Beate and the Houseplants." *Say It*. Washington, D.C., and San Francisco: Dryad, 1979. 13, 58.

Francis, Doris. *Will You Still Need Me, Will You Still Feed Me, When I'm 84?* Bloomington, IN: Indiana UP, 1984. 47, 157.

French, Allen. *The Day of Concord and Lexington*. Boston: Little, Brown, 1925. 129, 130–131.

Garrow, David. *Bearing the Cross*. New York: Morrow, 1986. 11–12, 221.

Gordon, Susan. *Lonely in America*. New York: Simon, 1975. 230.

Hall, Donald. "Four Kinds of Reading." *New York Times* (26 Jan. 1969).

Hammett, Dashiell. *The Maltese Falcon*. 1929. New York: Vintage, 1972. 1.

Harris, Trudier. *From Mammies to Militants*. Philadelphia: Temple UP, 1982. 3–4.

Havighurst, Robert J. "Personality and Patterns of Aging." *Aging in America: Readings in Social Gerontology*. Ed. Cary S. Kart and Barbara Manard. Van Nuys, CA: Alfred, 1976. 192–199.

Hellman, Lillian. *Pentimento*. Boston: Little, Brown, 1973. 3.

Herr, Michael. *Dispatches*. 1968. New York: Avon, 1980. 182.

Hewlett, Sylvia Ann. *A Lesser Life*. New York: Morrow, 1986. 23, 133.

Hoagland, Edward. "The Ridge-Slope Fox and the Knife-Thrower." *The Tugman's Passage*. New York: Random, 1976. 85–113.

Hoberman, Barry. "Wenceslas of Bohemia." *Harvard Magazine* (Nov–Dec 1978): 37. And sample writing/history assignments (with some deletions). By permission of the author.

Holmes, Betty C. "The Effect of Prior Knowledge on the Question Answering of Good and Poor Readers." *Journal of Reading Behavior* 15.4 (1983): 1–18.

Hughes, Robert. *The Fatal Shore*. New York: Knopf, 1987. 1.

Jaffrey, Madhur. *Madhur Jaffrey's Indian Cooking*. New York: Barron's, 1982. 144.

James, Bill. "1962: A Warm Cup of Coffee." *The Bill James Historical Baseball Abstract*. New York: Villard, 1988. 238–239.

Kachru, Braj B. "American English and Other Englishes." *Language in the USA*. Ed. Charles A. Ferguson and Shirley Brice Heath. Cambridge, MA: Cambridge UP, 1981. 21–43.

Karnow, Stanley. *Vietnam: A History*. New York: Viking, 1983. 319.

Katz, William Loren. *The Black West*. Garden City, NY: Anchor/Doubleday, rev. ed., 1973. 4.

Kilbridge, Joseph. "Flamingo." By permission of the author.

King, Larry. "Playing Cowboy." *Of Outlaws, Con Men, Whores, Politicians, and Other Artists*. Harmondsworth, England: Penguin, 1980. 54–73.

Kuralt, Charles. *On the Road*. New York: Putnam's, 1985. 17, 246.

Leap, William L. "American Indian Languages." *Language in the USA*. Ed. Charles A. Ferguson and Shirley Brice Heath. Cambridge, MA: Cambridge UP, 1981. 116–144.

Lee, Andrea. *Russian Journal*. New York: Random, 1979. 172.

Lemoniak, Michael D. "The Heat Is On." *Time* (19 Oct. 1987): 58–67.

Lewis, Bernard. *The Muslim Discovery of Europe*. New York: Norton, 1982. 242–243.

Lewis, C. S. *The Voyage of the Dawn Treader*. 1952. New York: Macmillan, 1970. 121.

Lobsenz, Norman M. "Sex and the Senior Citizen." Ed. Cary S. Kart and Barbara Manard. *Aging in America: Readings in Social Gerontology*. Van Nuys, CA: Alfred, 1976. 200–212.

Lorde, Audre. *The Cancer Journals*. Argyle, NY: Spinsters, Ink, 1980. 58–59.

Lurie, Alison. *The Language of Clothes*. New York: Random, 1981. 3–6, 180.

Lynes, Russell. "The Movers." *The Domesticated Americans*. Harper, 1957, 1963. 6.

Márquez, Gabriel García. Interview. *Writers at Work: The "Paris Review" Interviews*. 6th Series. George Plimpton, ed. New York: Viking, 1984. 319–320.

Martin, Judith. *Durham Sun* (30 Oct. 1985).

Marx, Groucho. *The Groucho Letters*. New York: Simon, 1987. 56.

McCarthy, Mary. *Memories of a Catholic Girlhood*. 1946. New York: Berkeley, 1963. 9–12.

McGee, Harold. *On Food and Cooking*. New York: Scribner's, 1984. 22, 520.

Mehta, Ved. *Vedi*. New York: Norton, 1981. 3.

Microsoft Word Manual. 1987. 11.

Montagu, Ashley. *The American Way of Life*. New York: Putnam's, 1967. 95.

Nichols, Anne. "Slang." *Tradition and Dissent: A Rhetorical Reader*. Ed. Florence B. Greenberg and Anne Heffley. Indianapolis, IN: Bobbs-Merrill, 1967.

O'Hanlon, Redmond. *Into the Heart of Borneo*. New York: Random, 1984. 3, 119.

Petroski, Henry. *To Engineer Is Human*. New York: St. Martin's, 1985. 22.

Raup, David M. *The Nemesis Affair*. New York: Norton, 1986. 212.

Rorty, Amélie Oksenberg. "The Historicity of Psychological Attitudes: Love Is Not Love Which Alters Not When It Alteration Finds." *Mind in Action: Essays in the Philosophy of Mind*. Boston: Beacon, 1988. 123–126.

Rose, Mike. *Lives on the Boundary*. New York: Macmillan, 1989. 51.

Rosengarten, Theodore. *Tombee: Portrait of a Cotton Planter*. New York: Morrow, 1986. 10.

Rybczynski, Witold. *Home*. New York: Viking, 1986. 20.

Sendak, Maurice. *Where the Wild Things Are*. New York: Harper, 1963.

Shakespeare, William. *The Complete Works of Shakespeare*. Eds. Irving Ribner and George Lyman Kittredge. New York: Wiley, 1971. 1718.

Shaw, Irwin. "The Eighty-Yard Run." *Short Stories: Five Decades*. New York: Delacorte, 1978. 1.

Smith, Donald E. P. "Spelling Is Nonsense." *Learning to Learn*. Harcourt, 1961. 75–76.

Smitherman, Geneva. "White English in Blackface, or Who Do I Be?" *The Black Scholar* (May–June 1973): 32–39.

Spencer, Elizabeth. *The Salt Line*. Harmondsworth, England: Penguin, 1984. 1.

Steinem, Gloria. "Ruth's Song (Because She Could Not Sing It)." *Outrageous Acts and Everyday Rebellions*. New York: Holt, 1983. 129–146.

Sterne, Lawrence. *Tristram Shandy*. New York: Signet, 1962. 90.

Stone, Albert. *Autobiographical Occasions and Original Acts*. Philadelphia: U of Pennsylvania P, 1982. xiii.

Theroux, Paul. *Kingdom by the Sea*. Boston: Houghton Mifflin, 1983. 2–3. And *Sunrise with Seamonsters: Travels and Discoveries, 1964–1984*. Boston: Houghton Mifflin, 1985. 131.

Thurber, James, and E. B. White. *Is Sex Necessary?* 1929. 2nd ed. New York: Harper, 1984. 64.

Trillin, Calvin. *Alice, Let's Eat*. 1978. New York: Vintage, 1979. 8.

Truman, Margaret. *Women of Courage*. New York: Morrow, 1976. 41.

Turow, Scott. *Presumed Innocent*. New York: Warner, 1987. 84.

Tuttle, Donald R. "Composition." *The Case for Basic Education: A Program of Aims for Public Schools*. Ed. James D. Koerner. Council for Basic Education. Boston: Little, Brown, 1959. 83.

de Varon, Tina. "Growing Up." *Twelve to Sixteen: Early Adolescence*. Ed. Jerome Kagan and Robert Coles. New York: Norton, 1971. 337–348.

Vygotsky, Lev. "The Role of Play in Development." *Mind in Society: The Development of Higher Psychological Processes*. Ed. Michael Cole et al. Cambridge, MA: Harvard UP, 1978. 92–104.

Walker, Alice. *Meridian*. 1976. New York: Simon, 1986. 52.

Watson, James. *The Double Helix*. New York: Signet, 1968. ix, 128.

Weitzman, Lenore J., et al. "Sex-Role Socialization in Picture Books for Preschool Children." *American Journal of Sociology* 77.6 (May 1972): 1125–1150.

Wells, Tim. *444 Days*. New York: Harcourt, 1985. ix, 213–215.

West, Candace. *Routine Complications: Troubles with Talk Between Doctors and Patients*. Bloomington, IN: Indiana UP, 1984. 41, 71.

West, James Edward, and William Hillcourt. *The Scout Field Book*. New York: Boy Scouts of America, 1948. 281–282.

Whatley, Elizabeth. "Language Among Black Americans." *Language in the USA*. Ed. Charles A. Ferguson and Shirley Brice Heath. Cambridge, MA: Cambridge UP, 1981. 92–107.

Wilford, John Noble. *The Mapmakers*. New York: Knopf, 1981. 250–251.

Williams, Juan. *Eyes on the Prize*. New York: Viking, 1987. xi, 147.

Woititz, Janet Geringer. *Adult Children of Alcoholics*. Pompano Beach, FL: Health Communications, 1983. 44, 74.

X, Malcolm. *Autobiography of Malcolm X as Told to Alex Haley*. 1964. New York: Ballantine, 1987. 172–173.

Robert S. Feldman, excerpt from *Understanding Psychology*, pp. 170, 172. Copyright © 1987 by McGraw-Hill Publishing Company. Reprinted by permission.

Roland Flint, "The Aging Mother at the Grandmother's Death Said" and excerpt from "Rosalind's Poem for Beate and the Houseplants." Copyright by Roland Flint and reprinted from *Say It*, published by Dryad Press.

David Garrow, excerpts from *Bearing the Cross*, pp. 11–12, 221. Copyright © 1986 by William Morrow and Co. Reprinted by permission.

Charles Kuralt, excerpts from *On the Road with Charles Kuralt* by Charles Kuralt, pp. 17, 246. Reprinted by permission of The Putnam Publishing Group. Copyright © 1985 by Charles Kuralt.

William L. Leap, excerpt from "American Indian Languages" in *Language in the USA*, edited by Charles A. Ferguson and Shirley Brice Heath, p. 116. Copyright © 1981 by Cambridge University Press. Reprinted by permission of Cambridge University Press.

Audre Lorde, excerpt from *The Cancer Journals*, pp. 58–59. Copyright © Audre Lorde 1980, Spinsters/Aunt Lute Book Co., PO Box 410687, San Francisco, CA 94141, $5.50.

Alison Lurie, excerpts from *The Language of Clothes*, pp. 3–6, 180. Copyright © 1981 by Random House, Inc. Reprinted by permission.

Gabriel García Márquez, excerpt from "Interview with Gabriel García Márquez," *Writers at Work, Sixth Series*, ed. George Plimpton, pp. 319–320. Copyright © 1984 by The Paris Review, Inc. All rights reserved. Reprinted by permission of Viking Penguin, Inc.

Judith Martin, excerpt from "Miss Manners," *Durham Sun*, October 30, 1985. Reprinted by permission of United Media.

Amélie Oksenberg Rorty, excerpt from "The Historicity of Psychological Attitudes: Love Is Not Love Which Alters Not When It Alteration Finds," from *Mind in Action: Essays in the Philosophy of Mind* by Amélie Oksenberg Rorty. Copyright © 1988 by Amélie Oksenberg Rorty. Reprinted by permission of Beacon Press.

Maurice Sendak, excerpt from *Where the Wild Things Are*. Copyright © 1963 by Maurice Sendak. Reprinted by permission of Harper & Row, Publishers, Inc.

Irwin Shaw, excerpt from "The Eighty-Yard Run," *Short Stories: Five Decades*, p. 1. Copyright © 1978 by Delacorte Press. Reprinted by permission.

Donald E. P. Smith, excerpt from "Spelling Is Nonsense," pp. 75–76. From *Learning to Learn* by Donald E. P. Smith, copyright © 1961 by Harcourt Brace Jovanovich, Inc. Reprinted by permission of the publisher.

Paul Theroux, excerpt from *Kingdom by the Sea* by Paul Theroux, pp. 2–3. Copyright © 1983 by Cape Cod Scriveners Co. Reprinted by permission of Houghton Mifflin Company. And excerpt from *Sunrise with Seamonsters: Travels and Seamonsters: Travels and Discoveries* by Paul Theroux, p. 131. Copyright © 1985 by Cape Cod Scriveners Company. Reprinted by permission of Houghton Mifflin Company.

Tina de Varon, excerpt from "Growing Up," *Twelve to Sixteen: Early Adolescence*, edited by Jerome Kagan and Robert Coles, pp. 347–348. Copyright © 1971 by W. W. Norton & Company, Inc. Reprinted by permission of the publisher.

Alice Walker, excerpt from *Meridian*, p. 52. Copyright © 1976 by Simon & Schuster. Reprinted by permission.

Tim Wells, excerpt from *444 Days*, pp. ix, 213–215. Copyright © 1985 by Tim Wells. Reprinted by permission of Harcourt Brace Jovanovich, Inc.

James Edward West and William Hillcourt, excerpt from *The Scout Field Book*, 1948, pp. 281–282. Reprinted by permission of the Boy Scouts of America.

Elizabeth Whatley, excerpt from "Language Among Black Americans" in *Language in the USA*, edited by Charles A. Ferguson and Shirley Brice Heath, p. 93. Copyright © 1981 by Cambridge University Press. Reprinted by permission of Cambridge University Press.

Janet Geringer Woititz, excerpts from *Adult Children of Alcoholics*, pp. 44, 74. Reprinted with the permission of the publishers, Health Communications, Inc., from *Adult Children of Alcoholics*, by Janet G. Woititz, Ed.D., copyright date 1983.

index ∎